Free Trade
and
Economic Restructuring
in Latin America

Free Trade and Economic Restructuring in Latin America

A NACLA Reader

Edited by Fred Rosen and Deidre McFadyen

Monthly Review Press
New York

NACLA was founded in 1966 to investigate the underlying dynamics of U.S.-Latin American relations, and to encourage a more humane and democratic U.S. inter-American policy. *NACLA Report on the Americas* is its bi-monthly magazine on Latin America and the Caribbean.

Library of Congress Cataloging-in-Publication Data
Free Trade and Economic Restructuring in Latin America : A NACLA
    Reader/edited by Fred Rosen and Deidre McFadyen.
        p. cm.
    Includes bibliographical references (p.   -   ).
    ISBN 0-85345-952-5 (cloth : alk. paper). — ISBN 0-85345-953-3
(pbk. : alk. paper)
    1. Free trade—Latin America. 2. Latin America—Commercial
policy. 3. Structural adjustment (Economic policy)—Latin America.
4. Labor—Latin America. 5. Latin America—Social conditions—1982-
I. Rosen, Fred, 1942-   . II. McFadyen, Deidre.
HF1770.5.Z7F74 1995
382'.71'098—dc20   95-12119
                                                                                          CIP

Monthly Review Press
122 West 27th Street
New York, NY 10001

Manufactured in the United States of America

10 9 8 7 6 5 4 3 2 1

Contents

Foreword

Rubén Zamora

Our struggles and hopes in Latin America, with all their contradictions and complexities, have been framed by two global processes over the past fifteen years: the end of the welfare state and the fall of existing socialism. These are processes which have certainly marked the end of the twentieth century and will likely have a decisive influence on the first decades of the next. The dominant ideology in the capitalist world during the postwar period was characterized by political democracy, anticommunism, and the welfare state. In the third world, though, anticommunism tended to receive more emphasis than political democracy, and the welfare state was presented as a goal to be reached through "development." Although the first two elements are still in force, the welfare state has crumbled under a ferocious attack by the ideologically fundamentalist notions known as neoliberalism: the return to the rule of the market, the cutback of the state and of social policies, and the liberation of entrepreneurial energies.

There is no doubt that Thatcherism and Reaganomics wrought a real "cultural revolution," albeit a capitalist one. That's why it evokes such support. Just as Mao launched his cultural revolution by appealing to what he saw as the fundamental revolutionary energy of the masses, bypassing such mediating agents as the party or the state, neoliberalism seeks to unleash the primordial energy of free enterprise, to liberate it from the bonds imposed by the interventionist state. Just as the cultural revolution had one sole objective, socialism, neoliberalism focuses its ideology and the underpinnings of its policies on the market, the guide and judge of economic activity. And lastly, just as Mao was not held back by the enormous costs his revolution incurred, proponents of neoliberalism are impervious to the damage that their model causes, considering such suffering to be the unavoidable cost of realizing their ideals.

This ideology, helped along by favorable breezes from the international financial institutions, fairly flew through Latin America, and took hold with great strength and coherence. While Japan, Germany, and other developed countries maintained a prudent distance, governments from Mexico to Patagonia embraced Thatcherism and Reaganomics with devotion. Neoliberalism became the economic religion that accompanied the transitions to electoral democracy that were taking place across the continent. Thus we renewed our historical tradition of keeping economics and politics out of sync. After years of inclusive economic-development policies married to exclusionary military authoritarianism, we now have political openings in bed with economic policies that are highly exclusionary.

Meanwhile, the past fifteen years have also been dominated by the crisis and death of existing socialism. From perestroika—that desperate but belated recognition—to the fall of the Berlin Wall and the breakup of the Soviet Union, the world has witnessed one of the most profound changes in history. What was believed to be irreversible—Soviet socialism born of the most powerful revolution of the twentieth century—showed itself to have feet of clay and fell to pieces in less than five years. The world became unipolar.

The failure of real socialism had a double significance for Latin America. First, it reinforced neoliberalism's claim to be the "ultimate truth," definitive proof that only the market and private enterprise can save us. Secondly, for the left it meant not only the disappearance of a possible foreign rearguard to provide political, economic, and military support, but also the loss of the "historic model." No matter how fierce the critiques of the form of socialism adopted in the socialist camp, the determinant factor was its mere existence. Simply being a reality that could be counterposed to that of U.S. capitalism made Soviet socialism a model to be emulated, or at least a frame of reference.

Thus, as the 1990s began, the continent found itself immersed in the transition to democracy, with governments that embraced neoliberalism as a religion and with the model of an alternative society in its death throes.

As has always been the case, the Latin American left represents a multicolored tapestry of positions. At one extreme are Fidel Castro and several Communist parties, who respond to neoliberal bourgeois fundamentalism with a no-less fundamentalist affirmation of existing socialism, and for whom any important change is a concession forced by adverse external conditions, not a conscious internal process of strategic modification. At the other extreme stand the former guerrillas who have discovered modernity and, in their haste to arrive, go straight to the most conservative incarnations of social democracy, without even paying a courtesy call on democratic socialism.

Neoliberalism is a challenge to the entire left, the most important political, ideological, and economic challenge we face today. In the unipolar world of neoliberalism, popular movements are not confronted as mortal enemies, but rather are condemned to irrelevance. The expansion of neoliberalism in Latin America demands an ideological critique, especially its assertion that the kingdoms of the market and democracy are, if not synonymous, then entities so closely linked that democracy can only be put into practice by means of the market.

The left should lay bare the ideological content of neoliberal proposals, but for the critique to have real political meaning, the left must also accept political democracy in practice. Only when the left takes democracy on as its own, which would require a profound critique of its own practice, will its ideological battle with neoliberalism attain credibility and political significance.

The painful evolution of the Latin American left from Allende to the national-security regimes forced it to begin to value political democracy. People began to abandon the old dichotomies—economic democracy versus political democracy, formal (bourgeois) democracy versus real (workers) democracy—which were only smokescreens that concealed a pitiful reality: an undemocratic, authoritarian left, politically cast in the Soviet mold, which raised the banners of political liberties to attack its opponents, but was not prepared to practice them inside its own structures, not to mention if it ever achieved power. Widespread torture, disappearances, and exile, combined with a growing world climate in favor of respect for human rights, produced an important "conversion" among broad sectors of the left who today consider public freedoms to be a conquest of humanity, and who are working to broaden and deepen them.

Today's popular struggles point to practical ways for the left to embrace democracy and to critique neoliberal ideology. In their struggle to broaden participation beyond the act of voting, people aren't rejecting elections, but rather making use of them. Similarly, the broad, autonomous, and pluralist activity of the organizations of civil society have swept aside the old party structures and the social organizations traditionally linked to them.

In this respect, the prospects for alternative forces are highly positive, since neoliberal ideology, especially in its concrete application to third world societies, is based on a paradox: while it claims to be universal and egalitarian, with the market as the impersonal instrument for assigning resources and success, in practice, its capacity for mobilizing people is purely corporative, and the reality of capitalism conforms ever less to the rosy picture neoliberalism paints.

One of the practical political functions of ideology is to create social "dreams" that allow dominated peoples to reconcile themselves with those who dominate them, and to feel that both share the same endeavor. Neoliberal ideology inverts this, since the only ones for whom it makes "dreams" are private entrepreneurs. The neoliberal image of the perfect free market is the dream of a rich man using his freedom to succeed by his "own efforts." For the poor, on the contrary, neoliberalism is a "destroyer of dreams" since it undercuts the basis on which people's dreams of a better life rest—state social services—and it puts people face to face with a life of scarcity, without horizon or hope. To paraphrase Marx, neoliberalism is the opiate of the business class.

What's more, if ideology is supposed to fill the cracks that exploitation produces in the social structure, neoliberalism makes rather poor mortar. The version of capitalism it proposes is precisely the one that is most difficult to put into practice. How can we return to the "golden age" when the free market and free competition were the indisputable actors on the economic stage, now when the level of economic concentration is higher than ever before? The greatest interference with the laws of the market come not from the state but from capital itself.

Where the task of confronting neoliberalism becomes most difficult is at the level of political economy, especially its claim to be the only rational alternative for productive economic development. In part, this is because it is backed by the international economic and financial institutions and the web of supranational agreements, treaties, and accords they have woven. It is also due, however, to the failure of the political economy of existing socialism. This critique will only be meaningful to the degree that the left is able to propose a viable and real alternative. In other words, the critique has to make practical sense and embody an alternative proposal, no mean feat in today's world.

The failure of existing socialism actually offers several advantages: the old and simple certainties that once were mechanically counterposed—the market versus planning, private enterprise versus state companies, and "free competition" versus fixed prices—are no longer viable. Likewise, the assumption that any criticism of the market, private enterprise, or free competition automatically validates the alternative of socialism has been overturned.

The imposition of neoliberal policies obliges us to revise many of our own concepts and policies. Faced with elections and the need to become a national majority, the movements of the left face a quandary. They have shown themselves capable of garnering the support of more than a fourth of the electorate (in Uruguay, Venezuela, Brazil, El Salvador, Nicaragua, and Chile), and they have a clear shot at winning in the future. But they also face the terrifying possibility that their stay in power will be nothing more than an updated version of the governorship of Sancho Panza on the island of Barataria, in which a new Dr. Pedro Recio will appear on the scene (in the form of GATT, the IMF, and World Bank) and, in the name of preserving financial health and stability, will oblige progressive governments to defraud the people by abandoning their promises to divide up the pie more equitably.

Faced with this prospect, it might seem tempting to take refuge in "the purity of revolutionary struggle and of socialism." But to do that would be to condemn ourselves to continue being what the left has been for many years on this continent: a group of marginal actors. And even more seriously, it would mean renouncing the ethical responsibility of changing policies that are condemning more and more Latin Americans to misery and death without hope.

Therein lies the paradox: never before have so many political movements of the progressive left been so close to taking power, but never before has power seemed to be so strongly predetermined by external forces adverse to the interests of the majority. To resolve this paradox is one of the puzzles that neoliberalism presents to those of us who think that the end of history has not arrived and that a humane world awaits us beyond the capitalist empire of the market.

To resign ourselves passively to the dynamics of neoliberalism, perhaps hoping to soften some of its more brutal aspects, would be political suicide, not only for the left, but perhaps for all humanity. All the more now, when even some apostles of neoliberalism in the international financial institutions are waking up to the devastation they have wrought, particularly in the third world, and increasingly their alarmed voices cry out, "please, not so fast, not so far." The desire among certain sectors of the left to humanize neoliberalism in the name of viability or governability seems destined to accelerate the ungovernability that is a congenital condition of the model.

Frontal opposition, on the other hand, while it might have great testimonial value, seems politically inviable. The international balance of forces would drown such an effort much more easily than in decades past. And should the left assume power, such opposition would be exposed as either an expression of populist demagogy or an act of political suicide.

I don't see any other alternative for the left in Latin America but to develop a strategy of resistance. The struggle against neoliberalism will undoubtedly be prolonged and its rhythm will be dictated more by the unfolding of new global issues, and by the level of conflict that neoliberalism itself generates, than by our impatient desire to be agents of liberation. However, if we don't transform our impatience into active hope, the only thing we will do is prolong the life of neoliberalism.

A strategy of resistance does not mean passivity or inaction. On the contrary, if our capacity to modify the macroeconomic variables has been temporarily but substantially reduced, then we ought to seek to modify variables that are not macro. In other words, we should link ourselves as closely as possible to the poor, to their basic needs and their survival strategies. We should do our part so that community efforts are not atomized by the market, so they have meaning and content as new economic agents, prefiguring an alternative.

A strategy of resistance also implies the active search for alliances with sectors of capital who feel their survival is directly threatened by the brusque and indiscriminate opening to the world market. The point is not to resurrect the protectionist model of decades past, but rather to design economic-development policies that actively promote our competitive niches, achieve a reasonable margin of autonomy, and allow us to preserve our comparative advantages as much as possible, while not falling into the fatalism of thinking that our only advantage is the hunger wages we pay our people.

In the same vein, a strategy of resistance to neoliberalism implies an active search for foreign alliances, among third world countries through regional integration, and with those sectors of the first world who maintain a more global vision of humanity's destiny and who are capable of seeing beyond the narrow limits of the market. The fact that the foreign rearguard of third world revolutions has disappeared does not mean that revolutionary change is no longer possible. The revolutions of the twenty-first century will be different, and one of the differences lies in the type and breadth of alliances which must be built with forces in the first world.

Finally, a strategy of resistance implies making greater use of negotiations. We must refrain from embracing the ingenuous illusion that everything is negotiable, since powerful countries do have interests that are not negotiable. Similarly we must escape the defeatism of believing the correlation of forces makes any negotiation a futile gesture from the start. We need to negotiate because we can win certain margins and because we can gain time so that the new problems generated by neoliberal development can mature. Ecological deterioration and its consequences can no longer be resolved within national borders, not even by building a "green curtain" that would purify the North and leave all the pollution in the South. These problems are already having grave consequences and are going to come to a head in the near future. Therein lies an opportunity to push for a more profound change in North-South relations.

The new global economic order will emerge not only from the problems that neoliberal capitalism causes, but also from our efforts and capacity to create alternatives on a global scale. Utopia has not died. The suffering and misery that neoliberalism wreaks among millions of poor people on our continent is a medium, a culture where utopia grows. What counts is that we are present in that medium as active bacteria, carriers of the ancient dream that history can bring better times.

—San Salvador, December 1994
Translated by Mark Fried

1

Introduction

Fred Rosen and Deidre McFadyen

"The word of the day in Latin America," says Mario Vargas Llosa, the great novelist and free-marketeer, "is *liberal*." *Liberal*, to Vargas Llosa's evident delight, has replaced *social* as the region's most fashionable political adjective. In Latin America and the Caribbean, the word refers back to the individualism of Adam Smith and John Locke, and has an unmistakable connection with free markets. When accompanied by the prefix *neo*, it refers to the kinds of economic policies North Americans have become familiar with over the past two decades or so: privatization of public activity, deregulation of private activity, cuts in social spending, the encouragement of market solutions to social problems, and—the cornerstone of U.S. inter-American policy—free trade.

As embodied in accords like the North American Free Trade Agreement (NAFTA), free trade is the globalization of the neoliberal agenda. Beyond the relaxation of trade barriers between nations, these accords attempt to elevate international trade to the status of the motor force of social and political life. NAFTA, as currently written, allows a variety of any one country's historically negotiated rights and regulations to be overridden by the trade agreement among the United States, Mexico, and Canada. However inadequate those rights and regulations may be, their erosion by NAFTA would leave large networks of social—and environmental—protection at risk.

So completely do the free-market/free trade ideas called "neoliberal" dominate the current Latin American debate that opposing ideas are increasingly treated with the bemused condescension usually reserved for astrological charts and flat-earth manifestos: We hope the astrologers will come around, but there's nothing left to argue about. North American "opinion leaders," in particular, have closed the debate on Latin American development. We hear only of the struggles between "modernizers" (all of whom have studied economics and speak flawless English), and the (pick an adjective) ignorant or corrupt or ideological or nationalist or special-interest old guard.

When, for example, the newly-elected centrist Brazilian president, Fernando Henrique Cardoso—an early advocate of state-sponsored development, and co-author of one of the seminal works on Latin American underdevelopment—spoke in early 1993 to an audience of bankers and investors at Manhattan's Americas Society, he was introduced as a well-known dependency theorist who had *outgrown* his old ideas: an astrologer finally come to terms with Copernicus.

The North American Congress on Latin America (NACLA) was founded in 1966 to investigate the underlying dynamics of U.S.-Latin American relations, and to encourage a more humane and democratic U.S. inter-American policy. The bi-monthly *NACLA Report on the Americas*, in which most of these essays appeared over the past two years, is the most widely-read English-language magazine on Latin America and the Caribbean. This *NACLA Reader* is intended both as a complement and an antidote to the mainstream discussion of neoliberal structural adjustment, most of which remains on the level of macroeconomic strategies of actions and indicators of success. The book points out that in all the neoliberal "success" stories, macroeconomic growth has been accompanied by stagnant or declining real wages, an unambiguous growth in poverty, a loss of social benefits, urban and rural decay, a breakdown of community, environmental degradation, and explosive growth of the informal, marginal sector of society. These contradictions force us to extend our consideration of neoliberalism to the political, social, and cultural spheres. It is our hope that by extending the discussion of economic adjustment and trade to that fuller set of social and political relations, this book will make a valuable contribution to the debate.

The essays included here examine the effects of neoliberal structural-adjustment policies in twelve countries of the Americas, ranging geographically from Mexico and Haiti to Argentina and Chile. It also examines the U.S. role in the elaboration and proliferation of those policies, a role so crucial that, taken as a whole, these free-market policies are known in development circles as "the Washington consensus." Part I, "The Underpinnings of Free Trade: Implementation of the Neoliberal Model," consists of articles which attempt to decipher and explain the historical and political genesis of the model, and its implementation in a number of representative countries. Part II, "The Reorganization of Work and Class Relations," focuses on the consequent restructuring of the social relations of production—on a global as well as a local level—and the changing nature of work itself. Part III, "The Broader Social and Cultural Consequences," the most broadly conceived part of the book, extends the examination to the political, social, and cultural structures of daily life.

The basic ideas of neoliberalism are embedded in the development strategies of the International Monetary Fund (IMF), the World Bank, and the Inter-American Development Bank (IADB). They are nowhere better spelled out than in several recent annual reports of the IADB, the institution most directly responsible for overseeing the implementation of these ideas in the hemisphere. The IADB's four "strategic directions" for Latin American reform contain the crux of the neoliberal agenda.

The Bank's first—and key—strategy, "outward orientation and hemispheric integration," calls for a greater openness to international trade and investment. Countries are encouraged to develop export-oriented industries and to attract foreign investment to finance that development. Latin American and Caribbean countries pursuing export-led development strategies have historically exported primary goods (food, fuels, and raw materials), and used their export earnings to purchase manufactured goods from the North. Since primary goods are subject to much more volatile price swings than manufactured goods, and have suffered a century-long price decline relative to manufactured goods, this has put Latin American countries at a trade disadvantage. This disadvantage has been exacerbated since 1980 when the global demand for raw materials began falling precipitously.

More recently, therefore, the lending agencies have encouraged the development of an export-oriented manufacturing sector, usually linked to the production needs of transnational companies. Countries are encouraged to link their development strategies with an increasingly common practice among transnationals: the establishment of low-cost production facilities in underdeveloped countries which supply capital goods (like motors for cars, or chips for computers) to divisions of the same firm in other countries. Because of this practice, a growing percentage of world trade is between affiliates of the same transnational firms. The World Bank, for example, has estimated that about 40 percent of global trade is intra-firm trade between the 350 largest transnationals and their affiliates in other countries.

Whether a country exports mainly primary goods—as in the case of Chile and Costa Rica, for example—or whether a significant percentage of its export earnings come from manufactured goods—as in Brazil, Argentina, and Mexico—the country's resources are diverted from the production of goods for domestic consumption and increasingly allocated to the export sector. To sell exports and attract transnational investment, currencies are devalued, lowering the cost (to foreigners) of the country's output and productive resources (like labor), and raising the price of imports. This, combined with the concurrent cutback in production for domestic consumption, has had the effect of raising the real cost of living—especially for the poor.

The IADB's second strategy, "modernization through private sector development," means privatization and deregulation. The Bank hopes to finance the privatization of state firms through a combination of foreign direct investment, and the return of "flight capital"—the assets that wealthy nationals have sent abroad to earn a higher return. Thus, privatization has meant that a small number of big investors (both foreign and domestic) have been encouraged to buy state companies and make them sleek, efficient, and profitable. Wealth has thus become ever more concentrated—in Mexico, for example, twenty-five holding companies now produce 47 percent of the GNP—and the gap between rich and poor has continued to grow.

The third strategy, "public sector reform," calls for a reduction in the size of government, cutbacks on public expenditures, and the development of a technocratic, "de-ideologized" state. While neoliberals can convincingly point to examples of bloated, corrupt, and autocratic governments in Latin America, the state can be—and has frequently been—a repository of rights, benefits, and social protection for large numbers of the working population. State cutbacks mean that rights that have been won through decades of political dialogue and struggle—the right to organize, for example, or the right to the public maintenance of water and sewage lines—have become increasingly precarious.

The IADB's fourth strategy is "human-resource development." There is an obvious recognition here that the market cannot by itself create the best conditions for its own development—not to mention its hegemony. The productive abilities of the population must be nurtured in the same way that roads and airports must be built. Poverty must be kept under control, lest populations revolt. States that have taken on this responsibility—Costa Rica for example—have relatively productive economies, and are well positioned to insert themselves into the world economy.

Included in this strategy is the understanding that capital accumulation does not take place in a vacuum; that a population's basic needs and expectations must be satisfied for a social order to thrive, or simply to hold together. The political dangers here are explicitly recognized in the IADB's 1991 Report: "A further deterioration of the already highly uneven income distribution in most of the countries in the region could effectively block recovery by creating political and social unrest, reducing private inflows and turning domestic saving outward again." Human-resource development is a real test of—one is tempted to say contradiction in—the model. How does a government develop human resources, take care of the basic needs of the poor, and still privatize, deregulate, and cut back?

The Clinton administration may be indecisive about all other aspects of inter-American policy, but when it comes to letting the market—and those who have market power—take control of hemispheric economies, it has shown the ability to be expeditious. It has acted in the context of its three stated goals for the Americas: free trade, free elections, and the amelioration of poverty. These can probably be taken at face value, as long as we remember that free trade is *primus inter pares*; the other two are only relevant as long as they support the first. U.S. policy toward Mexico, for example, where free trade and free elections have not yet shown themselves to be perfectly compatible, clearly demonstrates the primacy of trade. In the wake of Mexico's political uncertainty over the past two years, Clinton publicly supported former President Carlos Salinas's pronouncements that both political stability and the implementation of free-market economic policy must precede the democratization of the country.

The simultaneous—though uneven—promotion of trade and electoral democracy comes together in a policy that National Security Advisor Anthony Lake has called "enlargement." Lake has called for the replacement of the old policy of the "containment" of communism with a policy of "enlargement... of the world's free community of market democracies," all of whom can take advantage of that "immense entrepreneurial opportunity" that's out there, almost within their grasp. The idea is to make the Americas into one vast land of opportunity where, in the famous words of Al Capone, "all you have to do is reach out and take it."

Free trade may, however, simply be a way to allow U.S.-based transnational companies to do business in countries desperate for their investment dollars, before unions, environmentalists, and land-rights claimants catch up with them. Many mining companies, for example, which have rushed into the suddenly regulation-free Andean countries complained to the *New York Times* "of increasing 'barbed wire' at home: environmental hearings and native-Indian land ownership disputes that either block new projects outright or stretch out approval time for years on end." Environmental degradation, the sell-off of the national wealth, and the development of an economic model driven by cheap-labor export platforms for transnationals are all at issue in the "enlargement" of U.S.-based capital.

The Clinton administration's support for neoliberal reform—the Washington consensus—stems, of course, from an interest in a certain kind of hemispheric prosperity. "Exports," says Richard Feinberg, director of inter-American affairs at the National Security Council, "have become a major engine of our economic growth, and Latin America is one of our most dynamic markets. U.S. exports to Latin America have more than doubled in seven years to nearly $80 billion in 1993." Given the prevalence of intra-firm trade, of course, the "hemispheric prosperity" necessary to sustain those exports need not be all that deep. Moreover, the magnet for investment is precisely the low costs of production made possible by the desperate straits most of the population finds itself in. It should come as no surprise, therefore, that the promotion of free trade seems often to work at cross-purposes with the administration's other professed goals for the Americas: democracy and the alleviation of poverty.

As cracks begin to appear in the hegemony of free-market ideas, debates have tended to focus on the kind of capitalist development the region should pursue. With no viable socialist model to draw upon, the choices range from the unregulated trade and investment strategies of neoliberalism, to a more controlled, socially oriented capitalism. Trade union and leftist critics of NAFTA, for example, have argued for a trade agreement that would take into account not only the *number* of jobs created by the agreement, but the *kinds* of jobs, the *security* of jobs, the *rights* inherent in jobs, and the nature of the relationship between employer and employee. Most, like labor analyst Harley Shaiken, have argued for a "social charter" that would institutionalize worker and union rights as "the foundation of further economic integration in the Western Hemisphere." A "good" agreement, say Mexican political scientists Jorge Castañeda and Carlos Heredia—and much of the opposition in Canada, Mexico, and the United States—would subsidize adjustment costs in all three countries, especially the retraining and employment of displaced workers. In doing so, it would attempt to harmonize standards upward, in part by establishing a common regulatory framework. It would deal fairly and even-handedly with the difficult issue of worker migration. It would encourage long-term national planning and open, democratic dispute resolution. Castañeda and Heredia would have the agreement foster a "European Community-style social-market economy" rather than its present free-market "Anglo-Saxon neoliberalism."

No country—especially since the debt crisis of the 1980s—has been more central to these debates than Castañeda and Heredia's Mexico. In August, 1982, in the midst of global recession, skyrocketing interest rates, and declining commodity prices, the Mexican government of José López Portillo announced that Mexico was unable to service the interest payments on its foreign debt. Mexico's default set in motion the chain of events that produced the Latin American debt crisis, the endless negotiations with first-world lenders and governments, and the ultimate implementation of the free-market economic reforms insisted upon by international financial institutions. Mexico, the first in the hemisphere to acknowledge its debt crisis, was thus among the first to embark on a course of neoliberal adjustment and reform.

Under the presidencies of Miguel de la Madrid (1982-1988) and Carlos Salinas de Gortari (1988-1994), this course of reform was embodied by the country's determined insertion into the global economy—most dramatically by way of NAFTA—and by the growing importance of domestic and transnational capital as driving forces of social and economic relations. First under de la Madrid, and then more forcefully under Salinas, the government deregulated markets, promoted foreign investment, sold state enterprises, abandoned the collective *ejidos*, shrunk the public sector, and pursued policies to maintain Mexico's "comparative advantage"—low wages and a flexible workforce—in the world market. In keeping with this agenda, Salinas and his successor, Ernesto Zedillo, within the loosely authoritarian framework of Mexican politics, have sought to create a more efficient and technocratic form of government. Under these last three presidents, the technocratic factions of the ruling Revolutionary Institutional Party (PRI)—particularly those associated with the Treasury and the Central Bank—saw their influence expand, while the clout of the old-guard *políticos* and the PRI-affiliated labor leadership was sharply diminished.

Since Mexico was one of the pioneers of the Latin American neoliberal project, it should come as no surprise that the project should bear so much of its contradictory fruit in the Mexican political arena first. Neoliberal contradictions—macroeconomic growth and increasing investment opportunity accompanied by declining real wages, fiscal contraction, and explosive growth of the informal, marginal sector of society—are at the center of the Chiapas rebellion, the internal conflicts within the ruling PRI, and the great social crisis caused by the presence of 13 million peasants considered "redundant" by government planners. As inequality heightened, the high-visibility components of neoliberal success were no longer sufficient to prevent a social explosion. And when high-visibility success was suddenly transformed into the high-visibility devaluation and capital-flight crisis which began just after Zedillo's inauguration in December, 1994, the whole model threatened to dissolve.

The current Mexican crisis has sparked a new display of U.S. power in the hemisphere—one long in the making, but brought to a head by the Clinton rescue package: $20 billion in loans and loan guarantees from the U.S. Exchange Equalization Fund, $17.5 billion from the International Monetary Fund (IMF), and increased commitments from the European-based Bank for International Settlements (BIS), for a total pool of credit guarantees of $50 billion. Clinton's Mexican "rescue" is more complex and ambiguous an exercise in U.S. power—and on the surface a good deal less brutal—than the military interventions of the past few decades. It has, however, no less profound an effect on a sister country's sovereignty and is no less motivated by a need to bolster a U.S.-dominated world system.

Clinton has been criticized—from the right as well as the left—for having the interests of wealthy investors in mind with his Mexican intervention, but this criticism is misplaced. Clinton did not intervene to save a few wealthy U.S. citizens, but to salvage the system of global investment and production upon which U.S. wealth and power rest. Mexico was still the bright shining star of the Washington Consensus. Demand from the Mexican market was meant to be the motor force of the U.S. export-led future. Low-wage Mexican industry was meant to act as a high-return stimulant for U.S. investment funds. A massive outflow of those funds would not only dim the luster of the Mexican star, but would severely damage the entire system. It would trigger an outflow of confidence—and capital—from the dozens of "emerging markets" around the world dependent on those same investment funds, and playing the same role *vis-à-vis* U.S. capital.

These investment flows, as we have seen, hold each country's policy-making process hostage to the dictates of transnational capital and to the mass-psychology of the financial marketplace. The salvation now being proposed for Mexico—already effectively adopted in Argentina—is known as a "currency board." This would be as sovereignty-depriving a measure as having the U.S. Marines in charge of your army. A currency board is a scheme to prevent virtually all budget deficits, prevent the printing of pesos not fully backed by dollar reserves, fix the value of the peso to the dollar, and make pesos fully convertible, upon demand, into dollars. It would effectively remove all discretionary power from fiscal and monetary authorities. This is the face of the new dependency: He who holds the dollar calls the tune.

The plight of the region's peasantry must also be seen in the context of Latin America's growing insertion into the global capitalist economy which now penetrates into nearly all aspects of social and economic life. The consumption of food imports—from Cheerios to Kentucky Fried chicken to Kansas corn—is skyrocketing. Agroexports, especially non-traditional products such as mangos, roses, and snow peas, are being actively promoted both by regional governments and foreign-aid organizations. As their economies grow ever more dependent on Northern-dominated markets, countries have given up any pretensions of food self-sufficiency.

Foreign investors, transnational food corporations, and some domestic enterprises have reaped big profits, while the land's direct producers have borne the brunt of the costs. Peasants are being squeezed on all sides—by foreign and domestic capital eager to snap up the best farm land, by protracted political violence and repression, and by the withdrawal of most government-sponsored supports for the poor. With land reform off the agenda, peasants must put up a fierce struggle just to hold on to the land they have. And with rare exceptions, they don't have access to the technology, capital, and credit that they need to compete effectively in the global market.

In this context, the subsistence farmer is considered by many to be a relic of the past, engaging in unproductive work and occupying land that could be put to better use. Yet once pushed off the land, peasants migrate to cities that are ill-prepared to absorb them. Upheaval in the countryside has thus gone hand-in-hand with upheaval in the city. The rural crisis is widely felt as the emptying out of the countryside, while the urban crisis is felt as an inexorable flood in what is already the most urbanized region in the underdeveloped world.

One of the most disturbing social effects of the transformation of most Latin Americans into city dwellers has been the severing of the connection between people and the land. Communal—and even *latifundio*—land is being inexorably transformed into real estate. Land—the institution that organizes and gives coherence to daily life in the countryside—has been turned into just one more commodity. As a result, age-old peasant communities and the way of life they represent are rapidly disappearing.

The rapid cross-border mobility of capital has uprooted workers throughout the region. This has produced an international and increasingly casual workforce loosened from its local and national moorings. And since labor is one of the anchors of social life, casual labor has tended to produce a casual basis of social existence. When labor is "available"—read desperate and willing—we may have reached the ideal point for economic *theory*: individuals, unencumbered by tradition or government regulation, selling their ability to work on perfectly free markets. But we have reached an untenable juncture for social—and in the long run, economic—*practice*, since people live in communities, in social arrangements.

The poet-farmer Wendell Berry says the argument over free trade "is between people who belong to communities that they wish to preserve, and people who belong to no community and who therefore are willing and ready to destroy any community that gets in their way." That's as good a point of departure as any for the trade debates that still lie ahead. But for now, Mario Vargas Llosa is right: liberalism is an idea whose time has come in Latin America. Since you can't beat something with nothing, it will last until a credible alternative arises to take its place.

Part I

THE UNDERPINNINGS
OF FREE TRADE:
THE IMPLEMENTATION
OF THE NEOLIBERAL MODEL

2

Clinton's Trade Policy

Doug Henwood

It's usually said that the 1992 U.S. presidential election was a repudiation of Reaganomics, and it was. But did a new administration in Washington mean a substantially new orientation towards trade and development? Absolutely not. Economic policy was too important a matter to be left to popular opinion. One reason for the absence of fundamental change is Clinton's essential conservatism; after all, he was more-or-less endorsed by the *Economist*, Milton Friedman, and the guru of supply-side economics, Arthur Laffer.[1] For the first time in modern history, the Democratic Party's campaign platform did not mention labor unions, but celebrated business as a "noble endeavor."

Clinton's early steps confirmed impressions of his conservatism. His top aides were drawn from a pool of bankers, lobbyists, and management consultants. He and Congressional Democrats seemed eager to put the United States through an austerity program—gentler than the IMF kind, but an austerity program nonetheless—which the Republicans, the supposed business party, were incapable of implementing. And his appointment of Lawrence Summers, the former chief economist of the World Bank, as undersecretary of the Treasury for international affairs—the U.S. government's top debt and development post—was highly revealing.

Summers became famous when a memo he wrote commenting on a draft of the 1992 *World Development Report* (WDR) was leaked to the press. In a section wittily titled "Nuggets," Summers suggested that the third world, especially Africa, was "vastly under-polluted," and that the bank should be encouraging "more migration of the dirty industry to the LDCs [less-developed countries]." Reasoning like an economist, Summers argued that since the "costs" of pollution are measured in the "foregone earnings from increased morbidity and mortality" it causes, it makes sense to locate our most noxious activities in poor countries.

"I think the economic logic behind dumping a load of toxic waste in the lowest-wage country is impeccable and we should face up to that," he declared. "The problem with the arguments against...these proposals for more pollution in LDCs (intrinsic rights to certain goods, moral reasons, social concerns, lack of adequate markets, etc.)," he accurately concluded, is that they "could be turned around and used more or less effectively against every Bank proposal for liberalization."[2]

The publication of the memo provoked an appropriate storm of outrage, and demands for Summers's resignation, which were ignored. But Summers was only being more honest than his colleagues at the Bank and in the economics profession, for whom money is the measure of all things.

Similarly, resistance to Clinton's choice of Summers was, as economists say, misspecified. One nongovernmental organization distributed a press release denouncing the nomination as a perpetuation of "Reaganomics" by an administration elected in repudiation of that doctrine.[3] But Summers is a Democrat; his World Bank appointment (where he succeeded a genuine Reaganite, Stanley Fischer) was pushed by David Obey, a liberal Wisconsin congressman; and much of his academic work has been devoted to showing that financial markets are not the rational, efficient places that Chicago school economists say they are.[4] Summers is living proof that in U.S. political life, some things transcend party affiliation, among them a deep faith in the more-or-less free flow of capital and goods across borders and a belief that money is the universal metric.

Though Clintonites had paid little attention to foreign affairs prior to the election, hints of a fundamental continuity in U.S. policy could be gleaned from their writings. A case in point is *Mandate for Change,* the manifesto produced by the president's comrades at the Progressive Policy Institute (PPI). The PPI is the think tank for the Democratic Leadership Council, the business-sponsored clique of conservative Democrats that Clinton helped found and which he led from 1990 to 1991.

Only two of *Mandate*'s fourteen chapters are devoted to international affairs, a measure of the inwardness of Clinton's agenda. In one, PPI President Will Marshall recommends that a "democracy doctrine" be the guiding force of the new era. Dismissing both the cynical *realpolitik* of Bush, Nixon, and Kissinger, and the nationalism of Ross Perot,

Marshall promotes instead a new vision of "U.S. global leadership for democracy."

Political democracy, Marshall argues, produces nicer countries. But there are certain inconsistencies in his assumptions. Democratic leaders, he says, are less likely to make war (assuming the United States is a democracy, this will be news to citizens of Vietnam, Nicaragua, and Iraq), less likely to build weapons of mass destruction (meaning, one wonders, that the United States, Britain, France, and Israel are not democracies?), and are more environmentally responsible (news to residents of Bhopal and readers of Summers's memorandum).[5] Such contradictions arise because this concept of democracy—one of "individual rights, market economies, the rule of law, and popular sovereignty," in Marshall's words—is highly selective and inseparable from free-market ideology. In a world where critical investment decisions are made by transnational corporations (TNCs), how far can popular sovereignty really extend?

A remark by the National Security Council's Richard Feinberg illuminates how constricted this definition of "democracy" is: "If a society fundamentally disagrees on fundamental issues—the nature of property and what constitutes a legitimate political system—democracy can't handle it. If people agree on what constitutes good politics and good economics, the preconditions for democracy are in place."[6]

Behind that notion of democracy, which assumes away all life's interesting questions, lies an apology for Pinochet and d'Aubisson. Happily for him, Clinton inherited a largely pacified third world. In many countries, a generation of radical leadership was literally slaughtered—disappearances in Argentina and Chile, death squads in Central America—giving Feinberg-style democracy free reign. And the debt depression snuffed all economic strategies that deviated from orthodoxy.

While easy access to commercial bank loans in the 1970s and early 1980s allowed countries some freedom in designing their economic policies (much of it misused, much of it not), the outbreak of the debt crisis in 1982 changed everything. In the words of Jerome I. Levinson, a former official of the Inter-American Development Bank:

> [To] the U.S. Treasury staff...the debt crisis afforded an unparalleled opportunity to achieve, in the debtor countries, the structural reforms favored by the Reagan Administration. The core of these reforms was a commitment on the part of the debtor countries to reduce the role of

the public sector as a vehicle for economic and social development and rely more on market forces and private enterprise, domestic and foreign.[7]

Levinson's analysis was seconded by Sir William Ryrie, executive vice president of the International Finance Corporation, the World Bank's private-sector arm. "The debt crisis could be seen as a blessing in disguise," he opined in a 1992 speech, though he conceded that the disguise "was a heavy one." It forced the end to "bankrupt" national development strategies like import substitution and protectionism. "Much of the private capital that is once again flowing to Latin America is capital invested abroad during the run-up to the debt crisis," he said. "As much as 40–50 cents of every dollar borrowed during the 1970s and early 1980s… may have been invested abroad. This money is now coming back on a significant scale, especially in Mexico and Argentina."[8]

That millions have suffered to service these debts seems to matter little. Desperate Southern governments had little choice but to yield to Northern bankers and bureaucrats. Import substitution was dropped, state enterprises privatized, and borders made porous to foreign investment.

In the second of two chapters of *Mandate for Change* devoted to international matters, D. Holly Hammonds, now of PPI but formerly of the Reagan and Bush administrations (where she served as a NAFTA negotiator), argued for a more "muscular" trade policy, one that concentrates more on "winning." This, and the young administration's rhetoric and actions, suggest that Clinton will wave an even bigger stick at U.S. trade partners than the Bush Administration did in the interests of opening up markets—though Europe and Japan probably have more to fear from this than Latin America and the rest of the South. But Hammonds does not blame foreigners for all the country's problems. She argues that U.S. trade performance would be improved by a domestic industrial policy, and that too often anti-dumping moves and other aggressive trade gestures are inadequate, belated responses to home-grown failings.[9]

Yet despite these shifts, Hammonds's world is still fairly conventional; sovereign nations with discrete interests engage in trade, from which all parties can gain if rules are transparent and playing fields level. The argument for free trade has hardly changed, except for a pseudoscientific overlay of mathematics, since David Ricardo laid it out in 1817. Ricardo, like generations of model-building economists after him, imagined a two-commodity, two-country world in which Britain was the most efficient producer of cloth (the high-tech product of its day) and Portugal, of wine. Ricardo argued that the welfare of both countries would be maximized if Britain concentrated on making cloth and imported its wine from Portugal, and vice versa. For Britain to try to make wine would be a waste of time and money (and probably an offense to the palate as well), as would Portugal's attempts to make cloth.[10]

There is plenty wrong with Ricardo's argument even on his own terms. In the real world, few commodities are like wine, which is best produced only in certain regions. And Portugal's lack of access to British weaving equipment had nothing to do with geographical accident; it had more to do with how advanced countries jealously guard their technological dominance. Joan Robinson offered this concise critique of the received Ricardian doctrine in its mid-twentieth century variant:

> The economist's case for free trade is deployed by means of a model from which all relevant considerations are eliminated by the assumptions. Each country enjoys full employment. There is no migration of labor and no international investment, however great the differences in the level of profits in different countries may be. At the same time there is perfect mobility and adaptability of factors of production within each country. Perfect competition prevails. Fixed exchange rates are taken for granted. Equality between the values of imports and exports of each country is quickly established, in the face even of large disturbances, by movements of relative prices brought about through the international monetary mechanism. All this has to be taken for granted before the argument begins. Yet prescriptions for policy were drawn from it, with great confidence, to apply to a world which by no means conformed to the assumptions.[11]

Of course, this dogma, Robinson acknowledged, had "solid interests behind it"—the imperial-corporate classes of Britain in the nineteenth century and the United States in the mid-twentieth century. Robinson's critique of orthodox trade, written in 1965, focused on the contradictions between assumptions and reality. But Robinson's critique, pungent as it was, still spoke of *countries*; the true TNC was only a toddler. In an earlier day, Ricardo himself thought cross-border capital flows would never account for much, as this quaint passage shows:

> Experience, however, shows that the fancied or real insecurity of capital, when not under the immediate control of its owner, together with the natural disinclination which every man has to quit the country of his birth

and connections, and intrust himself, with all his habits fixed, to a strange government and new laws, check the emigration of capital. These feelings, which I should be sorry to see weakened, induce most men of property to be satisfied with a low rate of profits in their own country, rather than seek a more advantageous employment for their wealth in foreign nations.[12]

Obviously, today's business cosmopolitans are a long way from Ricardo's sentimental patriots, and today's transnational corporation a long way from Ricardo's national firm. Though capitalism has always been international, until recently it was characterized by the trading of manufactured goods between national corporations, or of raw materials between imperium and colony. The TNC—distinguished by the global organization of production—didn't really emerge until after World War II. U.S. firms, facing relatively mature markets at home, plunged into Europe and, later, the third world.

Though companies first invested abroad to seek oligopolistic advantages over their competitors, often wiping out local producers in the process, any reduction of competition in the early stages of transnationalization has since given way to a more intense, now global, competition. In the 1992 edition of the World Bank's *Global Economic Prospects and the Developing Countries*, the Bank gives a flavor of just how different our world is from Ricardo's. After noting that TNCs had shifted "labor intensive stages of production" to third world sites, the anonymous authors continued (internal references omitted):

> By the early 1980s, intrafirm trade within the largest 350 transnational corporations (TNCs) contributed about 40 percent of global trade. More than a third of U.S. trade is between foreign affiliates and their U.S.-based parents. Similarly, East Asian affiliates of Japanese firms ship a quarter of their exports to parent companies in Japan and buy from them more than a third of their imports. In 1982, 47 percent of Singapore's exports were by U.S.-owned firms. Fifty-two percent of Malaysia's exports to the United States were from U.S. affiliates; and Taiwan['s] five leading electronics exporters are U.S. firms. Similarly, exports of electrical goods by Japanese producers in Korea had much to do with the rise of Korea in world electronics.[13]

Examples can easily be drawn from this hemisphere. A list of the top importers to and exporters from Mexico is dominated by names like Chrysler, General Motors, Volkswagen, Kimberly Clark, Hewlett–Packard, Ericsson, Renault, Xerox, and IBM—not Mexican companies.[14]

And a recent study by the Conference Board of Canada, a business-sponsored research group, declared that "intrafirm trade is an integral part of the Canadian economy, and is one of the main links between the Canadian and U.S. economies."[15]

Classic theories relating wages to labor productivity must also be discarded. According to theory, wages are low in poor countries because output per hour worked is commensurably low. That may have been true in the days before TNCs, but now workers paid pennies an hour can be furnished with advanced machinery and managed with advanced techniques by multinationals or their local subcontractors. To take an extreme example, U.S. shirtmakers are slightly less than twice as productive as their colleagues in Bangladesh, but their wages are seventeen times as high. To equalize payment according to worker productivity, wages in the U.S. textile industry would have to fall to $0.45 an hour. Similarly, studies by Harley Shaiken show U.S.-owned plants in Mexico are 85 percent as productive as U.S. plants, but pay their Mexican workers only 6 percent as much as their Northern counterparts.[16]

In the light of these intrafirm relations, which hardly deserve the name "trade," Ricardo's doctrine of comparative advantage should be pronounced dead. But almost every issue of the *Economist* carries a version of Ricardo's argument, delivered in the magazine's best *ex cathedra* tone.

A new model is badly needed. One of the best is being offered by what used to be known as the United Nations Center on Transnational Corporations (CTC), but which has recently been reorganized and renamed as the Transnational Corporations and Management Division (TCMD) of the UN's Department of Economic and Social Development.[17] In the 1991 and 1992 editions of its *World Investment Report,* the TCMD argued that TNC investment patterns were increasingly driving the evolution of the world economy. Three major clusters have formed, each one dominated by TNCs based in one of the major powers—the United States, Japan, and the European Community (EC), who together make up "the Triad" [see Table 1]. Around each pole of the Triad are gathered a handful of "developing" countries to serve as sweatshops, mines, and plantations.[18] (Of course, the TCMD would never use such blunt language.)

But unlike popular theories of trade blocs, which focus on divisions among the major powers, the TCMD points to the deep ties cemented

TABLE 1

Foreign Direct Investment Clusters of Triad Members, Late 1980s

UNITED STATES:
  Latin America: Argentina, Bolivia, Chile, Colombia, El Salvador,
    Guatemala, Mexico, Panama, Paraguay, Venezuela
  Asia: Bangladesh, Pakistan, Philippines
  Other: Papua New Guinea, Saudi Arabia

EUROPEAN COMMUNITY:
  Latin America: Brazil
  Asia: India, Sri Lanka, Vietnam
  Africa: Ghana, Morocco
  Other: Czechoslovakia, Hungary, Poland, the former
    Soviet Union, the former Yugoslavia

JAPAN:
  Asia: South Korea, Singapore, Taiwan, Thailand
  Other: Fiji

Source: UN Transnational Corporations and Management Division, *World Investment Report 1992* [ST/CTC/130] (New York: United Nations, June 1992): 33.

by TNC investments among the three poles of the Triad. Around three-quarters of investment flows take place among the Triad, and about two-thirds of the remainder are accounted for by just ten developing countries, mainly in East Asia and Latin America. The other one hundred-odd countries of the world—the Caribbean, the smaller countries of Latin America, South Asia, Africa, and much of the Middle East—have little place in this new arrangement.

Trade patterns reflect these investment clusters. Almost 60 percent of U.S. trade is with developed countries, with a handful of large countries like Mexico, Brazil, and South Korea making up most of the balance. Over half of Japan's trade is with the developed world and another third is with Asia, leaving only 15 percent for the rest of the third world. Europe trades largely with itself, the United States, Japan, Eastern Europe, and Africa. Much of this "trade" is the transborder migration that goes on within TNCs.

So, there are two parallel movements occurring—regional integration around the poles of the Triad, and integration among the Triad members themselves—both driven by the investment strategies of TNCs. As the TCMD notes:

> Regional production integration goes beyond trade integration and extends to the liberalization of barriers to cross-border flows of capital, technology, skills, and to some extent, people.... More specifically, the

policies that allow for such movements go much further in integrating national economies and regulatory systems than policies designed to support intraregional trade, since adjusting to a regional production system implies harmonizing...a wide range of fiscal, monetary, and industrial policies among member countries....[19]

Though the initial impetus to integration may come from government policies, once momentum develops, TNCs often take the lead. For example, European integration was led by politicians and bureaucrats in the 1950s, but the movement towards a single market in the 1980s was pushed by TNCs. Asian integration is even more a private affair, since government efforts in the area have been minimal. North American integration, too, has been led by TNCs; much of the work in joining the Mexican and U.S. economies was accomplished in the 1980s before anyone had ever heard of NAFTA. NAFTA's value is that it will tie the hands of future Mexican governments that may be less starry-eyed about their marriage to the United States; in the words of the World Bank study just cited, "An international treaty with a large and rich neighbor is much harder to repudiate than national legislation."[20]

Triad-driven integration is quite hierarchical. Capital flows, for example, are largely a one-way street. In 1991, Mexico accounted for only 0.1 percent of the total foreign direct investment (FDI) in the United States. And though U.S. investment dominates Mexico—66.9 percent of new FDI in Mexico in 1991, and 63.1 percent of the cumulative total—this commanding presence still represents a rather small portion of the cumulative U.S. worldwide FDI—2.6 percent of 1991's total.[21]

The trade picture is similarly one-sided. In 1980, 63.1 percent of Mexico's trade was with the United States; in 1991, it was 72.5 percent. The losers were mainly the EC and other developing countries in the Western Hemisphere. By contrast, Mexico's share of U.S. trade rose from 5.9 percent to 7.0 percent over the same period; U.S. trade is far more diversified than Mexico's.[22] Such numbers suggest dependency more than mutuality.

The recent World Bank study declares that regional integration makes sense only if a Triad member is involved; South–South efforts are "mistake[s] not worth repeating." South–South integration cannot work, the Bank argues, because markets are too small (and, they might have added, direct investment flows too tiny) to cement the agreement; "penalties for breaking an agreement with a small developing country are small relative to breaking an agreement with a large industrial country"; "interest group politics" are more likely to get in the way; and actual experience with regional agreements in Latin America and Africa have been disappointing, even "harmful."[23]

In the current environment, then, regional free trade associations like Mercosur (Brazil, Argentina, Uruguay, and Paraguay), the Andean Pact (Colombia, Bolivia, Peru, and Ecuador), Caricom (twelve Caribbean countries), and the Central American Common Market can only be seen as preparations for eventual integration with NAFTA. But whatever benefits the Mexican government hopes to gain by integrating with the United States will be diluted should more countries join (another way of saying that Mexico's gains from NAFTA could be seen as stolen from its neighbors); for U.S. TNCs, however, their hunting grounds will only grow.

Options facing third world countries were expressed in homey form by David Mulford, Bush's undersecretary of the Treasury for international affairs. "The countries that do not make themselves more attractive will not get investors' attention. This is like a girl trying to get a boyfriend. She has to go out, have her hair done up, wear makeup...."[24] Crudeness aside, Mulford's argument is little different from that offered by Clinton's Labor Secretary Robert Reich—that in a world of mobile capital and fading boundaries, countries must focus on making themselves more attractive to TNCs through improved education, training, and infrastructure investment.[25]

The TCMD discreetly draws upon theories first developed by Stephen Hymer in the 1960s and 1970s. To explain the geography of the evolving TNC-dominated world, Hymer cited the three-level model of corporate management developed by Alfred Chandler and Fritz Redlich. Level III is the lowest level, the day-to-day management of the firm. Level II, which appeared when corporations grew enough that the head office would be separated from the field office, manages the managers of Level III. Level I is top management, which plans the whole corporation's strategic goals.

These structural levels have geographic and demographic counterparts. Level III operatives are posted all over the globe; Level II, in provincial cities; and Level I, because of their need to work closely with financial markets, media, and government, in or near global cities like New York, Tokyo, and London. Employees from third world countries are common in Level III; they can be hired cheaply, and their familiarity with local customs are good for business. Ambitious locals can be promoted to Level II, but they are almost never seen in Level I positions, which are reserved for natives of the metropolitan countries.

Despite this glass ceiling, third world employees of TNCs come to identify with their employers' global interests, a marked difference from attitudes prevailing under old-style national capitalism. And globalized managers and financiers would, Hymer rightly imagined, develop an interest in the global health of the system, not their national piece of it. Against this solidarity, Level III workers are divided and weak. So much for Ricardo's notion that capitalists' patriotism would act as a brake on foreign investment.[26]

As the political leader of the top country of Level I, Clinton is not doing anything to upset either the solidarity among the Triad, or the hierarchy among the Levels. There have been changes of tone and style—some pretty codicils on environmental protection and labor rights draped over NAFTA, the new emphasis on "democracy"—but some forces are larger than personnel and political party. Challenges to those forces are not coming from the White House.

Notes

1. "Lexington: The Emperor of Emptiness," *Economist*, 25 July 1992, 32; interview with Friedman, *Forbes*, 17 August 1992, 42 (an article the magazine thought worthy of a press release); Laffer endorsement reported in Alan McConagha, "Inside the Beltway," *Washington Times*, 18 September 1992, A6.
2. Internal memorandum from Lawrence H. Summers, 12 December 1991, 3. Summers's observations seem to have made their way into the *WDR* in highly euphemized form. In a box titled "Environmental damage—why does it matter," the Bank observed that while "many people believe" that nonhuman organisms have "intrinsic value" aside from their use to humans, such value is not measurable. "Thus," the box concludes, "intrinsic values can be captured only imperfectly and partially under the notion of amenity values." World Bank, *World Development Report 1992* (New York: Oxford University Press for the World Bank, 1992): 45. For more on Summers, see Doug Henwood, "Toxic Banking," *Nation*, 2 March 1992, 257.
3. "Summers Nomination to Treasury Sparks Opposition: Citizen Groups Call for Rejection of Reaganomics in Third World," the Development Group for Alternative Policies (Development GAP), Washington DC, 22 February 1993.
4. See, for example, James M. Poterba and Lawrence H. Summers, "The Persistence of Volatility and Stock Market Fluctuations," *American Economic Review* 76 (1986): 1142–1151, and Lawrence H. Summers, "Does the Stock Market Rationally Reflect Fundamental Values?," *Journal of Finance* 41 (1986): 591–600.
5. Will Marshall, "U.S. Global Leadership for Democracy," in Will Marshall and Martin Schram, eds., *Mandate for Change* (New York: Berkley Books, 1993), 289–320, especially 295–298.
6. George D. Moffett III, "Democracy: Today's Calls for Liberty Echo the Popular Revolts of the Mid-19th Century," *Los Angeles Times*, 23 June 1991, A23.

7. Jerome I. Levinson, "New Proposals for the Debt Crisis," in Robert C. Effros, ed., *Current Legal Issues Affecting Central Banks* 1 (Washington DC: International Monetary Fund, 1992), 94.

8. William Ryrie, "Latin America: A Changing Region," *IFC Investment Review*, Spring 1992: 4–5.

9. D. Holly Hammonds, "Strategic Success in the Global Economy," in Marshall and Schram, *Mandate for Change*, 81–105. Hammonds is not the only ex-Bush official welcome in the Clinton camp. Clinton also retained Rufus Yerxa, Bush's deputy trade representative—himself a living symbol of bipartisanship; before joining the Bush Administration, Yerxa was a Democratic congressional staffer.

10. David Ricardo, *Principles of Political Economy and Taxation*, chap. 7, "On Foreign Trade."

11. Joan Robinson, "The New Mercantilism," in *Contributions to Modern Economics* (Oxford: Basil Blackwell, 1978), 201–202.

12. Ricardo, "The New Mercantilism." Ironically, though born in London, Ricardo was of Dutch origins, and he was educated in Holland.

13. World Bank, *Global Economic Prospects and the Developing Countries* (Washington: World Bank, April 1992), 33.

14. World Bank, *Global Economic Prospects*, 102–112.

15. Stephen Krajewski, *Intrafirm Trade and the New North American Business Dynamic* (Ottawa: The Conference Board of Canada, July 1992).

16. Walter Russell Mead, *The Low-Wage Challenge to Global Growth* (Washington DC: Economic Policy Institute, February 1991), 15.

17. The transformation of the Center came on "orders from the top," in the words of a CTC staff member—the Bush White House. U.S. conservatives regarded the old CTC as a hotbed of Bolshevism, and hoped that the reorganization would domesticate the agency.

18. UN Transnational Corporations and Management Division, *World Investment Report 1992* [ST/CTC/130] (New York: United Nations, June 1992), chap. 1.

19. TCMD, *World Investment Report 1992*: 35.

20. Jaime de Melo and Arvind Panagariya, *The New Regionalism in Trade Policy: An Interpretive Summary of a Conference* (Washington DC: World Bank, 1992), 12.

21. U.S. General Accounting Office, *North American Free Trade Agreement: U.S.–Mexican Trade and Investment Data* (GAO/GGD-92-131, September 1992): 68, 70.

22. Computed from figures in IMF, *Direction of Trade Statistics Yearbook*, various issues. Canada also experienced a more Mexico-like increase; its trade with the United States rose from 63.9 percent of total trade in 1980 to 69.2 percent in 1991.

23. De Melo and Panagariya, *The New Regionalism in Trade Policy*, 14–21.

24. Quoted in John Cavanagh and John Gershman, "'Free Trade Fiasco,'" *Progressive*, February 1992, 32.

25. This is a central argument of Reich's *The Work of Nations* (New York: Alfred A. Knopf, 1991), a book whose epigraph comes from one of Ronald Reagan's heroes, Calvin Coolidge—an example of bipartisanship across the decades.

26. Stephen A. Hymer, *The Multinational Corporation: A Radical Approach* (Cambridge and New York: Cambridge University Press, 1979), 64-65.

3

Mexico: The Wages of Trade

Ricardo Grinspun
and Maxwell Cameron

Until its embrace of free trade and market-oriented reform during the mid-1980s, Mexico was a paragon of nationalism and inward-oriented development. The Mexican state created a framework for capitalist development in which the demands of the working class were coopted and controlled, national capital was protected and encouraged, and foreign capital was extensively regulated. From the mid-1950s through 1970, Mexico's development strategy of import-substituting industrialization resulted in a robust 9 percent average annual growth rate, giving rise to the "Mexican miracle."[1] Sustained growth ensured political stability under the moderately authoritarian rule of the Institutional Revolutionary Party (PRI).

The PRI maintained an equilibrium among competing classes and economic sectors by distributing the rewards of economic expansion among a heterogeneous coalition base.[2] The state restrained societal demands on the political system within limits compatible with the overall growth of the economy. A judicious blend of cooptation, occasional harsh repression, carefully cultivated elite consensus, interlocking pacts and alliances, and a low level of popular mobilization guaranteed the survival of a regime that Mario Vargas Llosa once called "the perfect dictatorship."[3] Recently, the perfect dictatorship has shown signs of imperfection. The first sign was in 1988 when PRI candidate Carlos Salinas was narrowly elected in fraudulent elections. In the August 1994 election, the combined opposition of the left (the Party of the Democratic Revolution [PRD], led by Cuauhtémoc Cárdenas) and the right (the National Action Party [PAN], led by Diego Fernández de Cevallos) garnered the support of almost half the electorate. The internal discipline of the ruling party has eroded, as illustrated by Mexico City Mayor Manuel Camacho's refusal to quash rumors of an independent electoral bid after the *destape* (the party-sanctioned "unveiling") of his rival Luis Donaldo Colosio in November 1993. The assassination of Colosio in March 1994 is widely attributed to a disgruntled faction of the PRI. Finally, prominent leaders of the PRI—and Carlos Salinas's brother Raúl—have been implicated in the September 1994 assassination of PRI Secretary General José Francisco Ruiz Massieu.

Despite these signs of erosion, the PRI won an electoral victory in 1994, thus perpetuating, for the time being, the one-party dominance of the Mexican system. Mexican democracy remains marred by manipulation and fraud, especially in the countryside. The ruling party still monopolizes the mass media, controls the state apparatus, condones the use of torture, arbitrary arrest, and indefinite detention without charges, and practices widespread harassment of political dissidents. The victory of PRI candidate Ernesto Zedillo, however, seems to have vindicated these strategies.

Salinas posed a two-pronged modernization program for his six-year term: deep economic reforms and a more open political system. He insisted, however, that economic change must come before democratization. We will "respond to the call of Mexicans for improved well-being," he said. "It's a matter of the two reforms going at different rhythms, but the priority is economics."[4] That priority was present already in the administration of Salinas's predecessor, Miguel de la Madrid. Under the two administrations, the role of the state has been redefined to create a framework in which large corporations and transnational capital are the engines of growth. The transformation, boasted an undersecretary of financial affairs a few years ago, "took ten years of adjustment, ten years of political corrections, and ten years of political guts."[5] Salinas sought to build a political system compatible with the neoliberal agenda; he tried to create a leaner, more efficient and technocratic form of authoritarian rule. At the same time, he attempted to respond to the political crisis of support and legitimation for the PRI manifested in the 1988 elections, and in the political violence of 1994.

The National Solidarity Program (PRONASOL) became the centerpiece of that political response. While reducing state welfare spending, Salinas increased the discretionary spending power of the president. Under PRONASOL, ostensibly a program of assistance to the Mexican popular sectors, selected communities were given supplies and equipment for locally initiated development projects. By 1991, this new brand of "liberal populism" accounted for 35 percent of non-debt government spending. The program served Salinas's economic agenda by diffusing potential social discontent, centralizing power, and adapting the state's traditional social role to an era of shrinking government.[6]

If PRONASOL was the political response, the North American Free Trade Agreement (NAFTA) became the centerpiece of the economic response. The NAFTA initiative culminated and consolidated the previous decade's deep and accelerated restructuring of the Mexican economy. NAFTA creates strong "conditionality" for Mexican economic and social policies.[7] It restricts Mexican government policies in areas such as regional and sectoral development, export subsidies, redistributive policies, social welfare, research and development, foreign investment, and intellectual property.[8] NAFTA is intended, in part, to make the neoliberal transformation irreversible and create the stable economic framework required for long-term foreign investment.

Salinas aggressively pursued deregulation of markets, promoted foreign capital inflows, sold state enterprises, further liberalized trade, and fought inflation through high real interest rates and fiscal contraction. Privatization, initiated in 1983 by de la Madrid, accelerated under Salinas. Of 1,050 state enterprises in 1983, only 285 were left in 1990.[9] Toward the end of his term, Salinas completed the reprivatization of the banks nationalized in 1982. As he relinquished power to Ernesto Zedillo, his hand-picked successor, in 1994, Mexico no longer had a significant state-enterprise sector.

Mexico, it is argued, must maintain low wages and a flexible workforce if the country is to remain attractive for transnational capital. Recently the government announced plans to change labor laws, with the intent of "rewriting" collective agreements in this direction.[10] Along these lines, the fight against inflation has benefited from price and salary controls agreed to in the Economic Solidarity Pacts (PSEs) with participation of the state-sponsored and controlled, although increasingly feisty Confederation of Mexican Workers. The PSEs, renewed periodically under different names, have restrained real wages— making workers the main victims of anti-inflationary policies and continued foreign-debt service. At the same time Salinas continued the Mexican government's long-standing practice of thwarting the formation of independent trade unions. As a result, 1992 saw a growing number of unauthorized strikes in the country.[11]

When Salinas's predecessor and mentor Miguel de la Madrid took office in 1982, his first priority was to restore investor confidence—deeply disturbed by debt crisis and bank nationalization—and patch up relations between the private sector and the PRI. Along with restrictive fiscal and monetary policies, he adopted a package backed by the International Monetary Fund (IMF) and the U.S. Treasury to control inflation and set a more realistic exchange rate. Faced with the failure of oil-led development and the need for other sources of foreign-exchange earnings, Mexico began to mend fences with the United States, and became less able to withstand pressures from the IMF, the World Bank, and the private commercial banks. These external actors were mainly concerned with guaranteeing continuous service of the foreign debt, both private and public. Trade liberalization was required to boost export-led growth, as well as to reduce inflation by introducing import competition to control prices. A major component of de la Madrid's strategy was to promote the in-bond assembly plants, or *maquiladoras*, along the U.S.-Mexico border and in Mexico City. Mexico also sought a bilateral agreement with the United States on subsidies and countervailing duties in 1985. The following year, it joined the General Agreement on Tariffs and Trade (GATT).

The new economic strategy has not been able to resolve the contradictions of the old inward-oriented and state-led strategy, nor has it promoted democracy in any meaningful way. On the contrary, inequality and human suffering intensified under harsh structural-adjustment measures of the 1980s. Debt servicing required a real transfer to the North of an average 4.8 percent of GDP each year between 1983 and 1988.[12] During the 1980s, labor's share of national income declined and real wages fell by half. Roughly half of the Mexican labor force lives below the official poverty line.[13] Under Salinas, real wages increased without recovering their 1980 levels. Minimum wage increments under the Pact for Stability and Economic Growth (PECE) were kept in line with inflation and productivity gains, but remained at 61 percent of their 1987 purchasing power. The distribution of wealth became more skewed. Whereas at the beginning of the Salinas administration there was one billionaire in Mexico, by 1994 there were twenty-four. Most were close friends and business associates of Salinas and his team. One made his early fortune in the 1940s by cultivating a friendship with Salinas's father who was then the head of the trade ministry. One government official said: "we haven't really sought to stop concen-

THE OLD STRATEGY

The de la Madrid-Salinas reforms can be seen as a response to problems created by the Mexican model of import-substitution industrialization that governed policymaking during the postwar period. Under Luis Echeverría's administration (1970-1976) these problems showed up as growing public deficits, high inflation, inequality in the distribution of income, and balance-of-payments disequilibria. The strategy of ISI, which was widely pursued in Latin America at that time, created a significant manufacturing sector, but one that was inefficient and protected, dependent on imported capital goods and technical assistance, capital-intensive, and heavily subsidized by the public sector. Skewed income distribution meant only the middle and upper classes had significant purchasing power. The small size of the domestic market severely limited industrial growth.

Artificially low prices for food staples impoverished the rural sector, and subsidized urban wages. An overvalued peso cheapened imports of capital goods for manufacturing and consumer goods for affluent groups, and hurt agricultural exports. These policies resulted in rural and urban unemployment, accelerated migration to the cities, a large informal economy, and the persistence of income inequality. While Mexico City and other cities grew, and the urban middle class aspired to European lifestyles, the shantytowns and rural areas remained poor and underdeveloped.

President José López Portillo (1976-1982) ignored the signs of impending crisis. He avoided making the necessary adjustment of the economy after the discovery of huge deposits of petroleum coincided fortuitously with oil price hikes caused by the formation of the OPEC cartel. In 1976 Mexico had been forced to approach the International Monetary Fund (IMF) for a stand-by agreement to stabilize the economy. The oil boom made the international financial markets optimistic about Mexico's future growth. Oil revenue allowed Mexico to overborrow because the international banks did not believe that an oil exporter could become an insolvent debtor. López Portillo paid off the IMF and returned to expansionary policies. As a result, the Mexican foreign debt more than doubled between 1978 and 1983, while the current-account deficit reached a record US $12.5 billion in 1981.[1] However, these were not used productively, creating the basis for the crisis in the early 1980s.

Between 1978 and 1981 Mexico's annual growth rate was over 8 percent. Expansionary policies resulted in inflation and social unrest as the economy overheated and struggles over income distribution intensified. Central bank loans to the private sector caused the money supply to grow and the currency to weaken. An inevitable devaluation of the peso was postponed, and capital flight ensued as investors sought safe havens for their capital. Thus, capital flight and loss of reserves occurred simultaneously.[2] As the international environment became increasingly adverse with the decline in the price of oil and other exports, global recession, high real interest rates, and protectionism in the developed countries, Mexico announced in August 1982 that it was unable to service the interest on its international debt obligations. The next month, López Portillo nationalized the Mexican banks.

The decisive policy shift took place when Miguel de la Madrid took office. Under López Portillo, state-owned enterprises grew, the Ministries of Finance and Treasury (traditional mainstays of financial orthodoxy) were weak, and the alliance between the PRI and the private sector broke down. De la Madrid's government embodied "a strong political resurgence of the technocratic factions associated with the Treasury and the Central Bank, a sharply diminished role for *políticos* connected with the PRI and the labor movement, and the virtual elimination of structuralist and neo-Keynesian economists from top levels of government."[3]

---

tion of wealth. We just wanted to remove the barriers to competition."[14] Yet under liberalization as under protection, the same elite has benefited.

The prospects for shared benefits in the future are dim. Mexican policymakers have consistently claimed that the best way to address inequality is by creating many and more productive jobs through the outward-reorientation of the economy.[15] However, the promise of full employment seems elusive, as unemployment hovers around 20 percent, and underemployment is at least twice as high.[16] The 80 percent growth of the informal economy during the 1980s is the best indicator of the inability of the current economic program to provide enough jobs.[17] Through industrial parks, credit, and administrative facilities, the government encourages marginal businesses and informal entrepreneurs to integrate their activities with large transnational corporations, especially through the *maquiladora* program.[18] This allows large firms to avoid unionization and to pass on to small- and medium-sized businesses the risks associated with fluctuating demand.

High levels of informal employment and disguised unemployment therefore remain despite the aggressive industrialization drive. Unemployment has been exacerbated by Mexico's rapid population growth during the 1980s—more than 3.5 percent of the economically active population annually.[19] Despite job gains in the export-oriented sector, and in particular in the *maquiladora* industry, liberalization of the Mexican market is hurting domestic industries located in the triangle between Mexico City, Monterrey, and Guadalajara. These industries employed 2.5 million workers in the past.[20] Since the *maquiladora* sector has never employed more than half a million people, the net effect has been a loss of jobs in the industrial economy.[21] The number of jobs in the rural sector will also diminish as a result of land-holding (*ejidal*) reform, the dismantling of support for agriculture, and freer trade in basic grains. With the implementation of NAFTA, giant agroexporting firms have begun lobbying for protection in the form of countervailing duties on imports from U.S. producers which they claim—correctly—are subsidized. Small rural producers cannot afford to lobby the government, and since they are not exporters, officials are not interested in their plight. The result has been free trade for small producers and new forms of protection for large agro-exporters.

It is far from certain that real wages will rise significantly even if the new economic strategy is able to create enough jobs. High rates of population growth and unlimited supplies of labor in the countryside create continuous downward pressures on wages. Moreover, the outward orientation creates tremendous urgency to maintain "international competitiveness." This is achieved mainly by regressive competition with other "cheap-labor havens," which results in lowered wages, coerced trade unions, and lax enforcement of labor and environmental regulations. Further, *maquiladora* plants are mobile, and can shift to other countries with relative ease. The resulting competition over scarce capital resources with other low-wage countries is unhealthy, producing more pressure to lower costs of production at the expense of workers and the environment. Moreover, there is little evidence of a shift in the *maquiladora* sector toward high-skill, high-wage jobs.[22]

Finally, it is unclear whether the current economic program will create sustained and broad productivity growth. Mexico must find a way to raise productivity. This requires investment in human capital—education, health and occupational safety, job training, occupational rights—as well as in technology, research and development, and plant, equipment, and materials. The new industrialization strategy does not adequately address these requirements.[23] Foreign capital flowing into the *maquiladora* sector adds new physical plants and equipment, creates jobs, and introduces some technological know-how into the country. However, it seems unlikely that money will be invested in the worker, given the sector's track record in terms of wages, benefits, living conditions, labor turnover, occupational safety, social disruption, and environmental degradation. The pressures on all levels of government for fiscal austerity (that is, to spend less on social programs, health, and education) will only worsen the straits of the Mexican worker. As has happened in Canada, NAFTA is restricting the Mexican government's ability to apply domestic policies that contribute to these objectives.[24]

Privatization was supposed to increase the competitiveness of Mexican exports in the global marketplace. The shift of assets to the private sector, however, has promoted concentration rather than competition. As Mexico scholar Judith Teichman explains: "The purchasers of Mexico's most important parastatals [state-run companies] have been Mexico's most powerful economic groups in association with foreign consortia, in the cases of the biggest purchases, such as TELMEX. In some cases the degree of economic concentration is startling: Jorge Larrea, a principal shareholder in nine of Mexico's industrial conglomerates, including two major banks, now controls over 90 percent of Mexico's copper production through his company, Minera Mexico."[25]

The outcome is an economy controlled by a select few. Where twenty-five holding companies produce 47 percent of the GNP (in the formal economy), free competition is an ideal, not a reality.[26] Also, the privatization process has been marred by accusations of a lack of transparency and irregularities in pricing. It appears that rent-seeking (the quest for windfall gain) has persisted, and in fact become more sophisticated, under economic liberalization. The old strategy, with its reliance on cheap food pricing policies, was biased against the development of the rural sector (see "The Old Strategy," p. 43). Neoliberal reforms have, if anything, worsened conditions. During the 1980s, fiscal support for rural development shrunk from 12 percent of total public expenditure in 1980 to 7.5 percent in 1988.[27] During the same period

A LESSON FROM SOUTHEAST ASIA?

Mexico has the potential for a more equitable and beneficial type of economic growth. Economist René Villareal, for example, has recently argued that "the most viable Mexican industrialization strategy involves (1) an expansion of manufacturing exports and (2) endogenous industrial growth centering on basic goods and inputs. In turn, this external orientation should be supported by (3) a process of selective import-substitution industrialization in which links in the productive chain are created that promote intra-industrial and inter-sectoral articulation, and competitive and efficient production."[1] Such a strategy draws upon the experience of the Southeast Asian "tigers": South Korea, Taiwan, Singapore, and Hong Kong.

Indeed, some lessons can be learned from these tigers since every facet of the new Mexican industrialization strategy differs markedly from their export-led success. South Korea, for example, never adopted indiscriminate economic liberalization, but rather a mix of active export promotion and efficient import substitution. Moreover, industrialization was preceded by a massive redistribution of wealth and income through land reform. These reforms increased employment and reduced poverty in the countryside, slowing emigration to the cities. A more equitable distribution of income created the foundation for an expanding domestic market, so that growth was both outward- and inward-oriented.

Strong state intervention in South Korea played a key role in turning private-sector activities into a coherent industrialization strategy. An efficient state bureaucracy had the institutional capacity and independence to run such a strategy. Foreign and domestic private investment was directed and controlled to avoid the creation of "enclave" economies. Export-processing zones quickly became a source of forward and backward linkages: forward through rising real wages that created demand for other industrial and agricultural goods; backward by encouraging the use of intermediate inputs made by domestic industry.[2] Unfortunately, NAFTA conditionality precludes Mexico from engaging in these types of policies. Mexico must first free itself from such external constraints before it can engage in a different type of developmental policy.

the gap between the production and consumption of basic grains widened.[28] Mexico must now import a larger share of the food it requires to feed its growing population. The promotion of agribusiness—a centerpiece of current policies—only increases dependency on external factors and threatens food security each time another balance-of-payments crisis hits the country.[29] The government has promoted agribusiness ventures in the northern states, with active support or participation of foreign capital, especially giant U.S. food conglomerates. Small farmers are linking themselves to this export-oriented drive, which has economic, social, and environmental perils.

At the economic level, more capital-intensive agribusiness enterprises may require less labor and eliminate jobs. Recent constitutional changes affecting *ejido* holdings will mean that many small-holding peasants will lose their lands, and that the class of landless rural workers will grow, feeding migration to the cities.[30] Trade liberalization in basic grains such as corn and beans, embedded in NAFTA, will further threaten the livelihood of at least 2 million peasants who still grow the traditional staples.[31] Moreover, the chemical-intensive nature of agribusiness will damage the environment. This massive process of commercialization will upset the natural balance of Mexico's delicate ecosystems.[32]

The new policies have attracted foreign capital but, perversely, a large part of it has gone into financial speculation through the Mexican stock market.[33] Increased foreign ownership will probably result in a greater outflow of profits, interest payments, and royalties. Large capital inflows contributed to an appreciation of the peso, a fact that contributed, together with trade liberalization, to a huge increase in imports into Mexico, and the country reaching record levels of current-account deficit.[34] The possibility that Mexico could face another loss of faith by foreign investors, a round of capital flight, and a large devaluation that would discredit the government has been a matter for nervous speculation in Mexico during recent years.[35]

These fears were borne out at the tail end of 1994, just three weeks into Zedillo's presidency. On Tuesday, December 20, the new government signalled its inability to support the value of the peso by allowing it to drop from 3.5 to just over 4 to the dollar. Alarmed investors immediately began removing their capital from the Mexican stock market, touching off a collapse that ran well into 1995.

Salinas's promise that economic liberalization would promote a political opening rings hollow—especially after this most recent economic debacle. NAFTA's reliance on unaccountable panels of "experts" to make economic decisions that elected representatives should make, as well as the shift of power to large transnational capital embedded in the agreement, do not contribute to a more democratic and participatory society. The concentration of wealth and market power in the hands of *grupos económicos* closely linked to foreign capital, on the one hand, and large parts of the population suffering from deprivation and economic insecurity, on the other, do not contribute to democracy either.

Despite the assassination of a presidential candidate, the indigenous uprising in Chiapas, and major electoral challenges from the left and right, the 1994 elections illustrated the PRI's ability to remain in power through electoral means. For some observers, the results can be attributed to fear, intimidation, cooptation, and government control over the media. Others stressed the widespread perception that economic reform would lead to material improvement once the macroeconomic changes "trickled down" and produced gains in the efficiency and productivity of firms and individuals.[36] Most observers agreed that while Mexicans wanted change, they were suspicious of the alternatives. Neither the PAN nor the PRD won the confidence of the electorate, and the violence in Chiapas allowed the PRI to stress the need for stability and continuity in order to achieve welfare and peace.

"At the moment when Mexico was approaching North America," said Carlos Fuentes, just after the uprising in Chiapas, "its leaders were forced to recognize that portions of the country are still part of Central America." As economic integration proceeds, the disparities within Mexico will become increasingly apparent. President Zedillo will need to generate rapid economic growth in order to provide the income and employment opportunities for a rapidly expanding population that will watch the lion's share of the benefits of economic integration go to a tiny privileged elite.

Notes

This chapter is an updated version of an article originally published in NACLA Report on the Americas, *volume 26, number 4, February 1993. It draws on the edited volume by Ricardo Grinspun and Maxwell A. Cameron,* The Political Economy of North American Free Trade *(New York: St. Martin's Press, 1993). Funding for this project was provided by the Government of Ontario, the Centre for Research on Latin America and the Caribbean (CERLAC) at York University, and research grants for Maxwell*

Cameron from the Social Sciences and Humanities Research Council of Canada and Carleton University and for Ricardo Grinspun from York University. The authors are grateful to Kathy Kopinak, Louis Lefeber, Maureen A. Molot, Viviana Patroni, Fred Rosen, Judith Teichman, Carol Wise, and in particular Tom Legler, for helpful comments on an earlier draft of this article. Final responsibility for ideas in this paper rests exclusively with the authors.

1. The figure is taken from Gary Gereffi, "Paths of Industrialization: An Overview," in Gary Gereffi and Donald L. Wyman, eds., *Manufacturing Miracles: Paths of Industrialization in Latin America and East Asia* (Princeton: Princeton University Press, 1990), 10.
2. Thus the term "inclusionary corporatism" is sometimes used to characterize the PRI model of governance.
3. The PRI regime has often been called a "dicta*blanda*," instead of a "dicta*dura*." In Spanish, *dictadura* means dictatorship; *dura* means hard; and *blanda* means soft.
4. Salinas interviewed by Tim Padgett, "Reform at Two Different Rhythms," *Newsweek*, 3 December 1990, 39.
5. Angel Gurría, undersecretary of international financial affairs in the Finance Secretariat (Hacienda), quoted in Claudia Fernández, "Successful Privatization Plan Provides Model," *El Financiero International*, 7 December 1992, 14.
6. Denise Dresser, *Neopopulist Solutions to Neoliberal Problems* (La Jolla: Center for U.S.-Mexican Studies, University of California at San Diego, 1991), 1-2.
7. The term "conditionality" has been widely applied to IMF "policy packages" that dictate domestic policy. We are suggesting that NAFTA creates similar—although permanent, not temporary—constraints on domestic policies on Canada and Mexico. See our "The Political Economy of North American Integration: Diverse Perspectives, Converging Criticisms," chap. 1 in Grinspun and Cameron, eds., *The Political Economy of North American Free Trade* (New York: St. Martin's Press, 1993).
8. This conclusion is warranted by the Canadian experience. NAFTA explicitly prohibits direct export promotion, following GATT. However, U.S. trade law, legitimized by NAFTA but not by GATT, sees many government interventions as "unfair trade actions" that trigger U.S. trade litigation. The "nullification and impairment" clauses in NAFTA effectively require compensation if the Mexican government takes action that reduces current or potential benefits to corporations from the other country. These and other provisions have far-reaching implications since they effectively restrict many types of government intervention.
9. Judith Teichman, "The Dismantling of the Mexican State and the Role of the Private Sector," in Grinspun and Cameron, eds., *The Political Economy of North American Free Trade*, 184.
10. "Union chief approves change to labor law," *El Financiero International*, 29 June 1992, 4. Opponents argue the objectives of the proposed changes were "to eliminate fixed wage scales, give preferences to non-union employment, and restrict the right to strike."

11. Noteworthy was the wildcat work stoppage and police-enforced lockout at Volkswagen de México. The Federal Labor Arbitration Board granted the firm's petition to cancel its union contract and fire its nearly 15,000 union members. Talli Nauman, "Is Labor Law Losing Teeth in Face of Free Trade?" *El Financiero International,* 7 September 1992, 12.

12. John Sheahan, *Conflict and Change in Mexican Economic Strategy* (La Jolla: Center for U.S-Mexican Studies, University of California at San Diego, 1990), 9.

13. Office of Technology Assessment, U.S. Congress, *U.S.-Mexico Trade: Pulling Together or Pulling Apart?* ITE-545 (Washington, D.C.: Government Printing Office, October 1992), 69.

14. Quoted in William Schomberg and Ted Bardacke, "Doing Business With the Big Boys," *El Financiero International,* 19 October 1992, 14. The anonymous government official does not see an inconsistency between concentration and competition. Schomberg and Bardacke inform us that the twenty-five largest companies in Mexico account for a 47.1 percent share of the nation's GDP. In the United States, the top twenty-five produce just 4.3 percent of GDP.

15. Clearly, many and more productive jobs can address inequality *only* if wages are linked to productivity and provide for a decent living standard. This is a far cry from the Mexican reality, however. Even the more productive new industrial sectors, such as the automobile sector, pay appalling wages.

16. Office of Technology Assessment, *U.S.-Mexico Trade,* 69. The official statistics of unemployment in Mexico are useless, among other reasons because they count anyone who works an hour or more per week among the employed.

17. Agustín Escobar Latapí and Mercedes Gonzáles de la Rocha, "Introduction," in M. Gonzáles de la Rocha and A. Escobar Latapí, eds., *Social Responses to Mexico's Economic Crisis of the 1980s* (La Jolla: Center for U.S.-Mexican Studies, University of California at San Diego, 1991), 9.

18. Secretariat of Commerce and Industrial Development (SECOFI), *The Mexican Program for the Modernization of Industry and Foreign Trade, 1990-1994* (Mexico City: Government of Mexico, circa 1989), 38-39.

19. Merilee S. Grindle, "The Response to Austerity: Political and Economic Strategies of Mexico's Rural Poor," in Gonzáles de la Rocha and Escobar Latapí, eds., *Social Responses to Mexico's Economic Crisis,* 132.

20. Quoted from Jorge Calderon S., in Kathryn Kopinak, "The Maquiladorization of the Mexican Economy," in Grinspun and Cameron, eds., *The Political Economy of North American Free Trade.*

21. Manufacturing employment in Mexico fell from 2.51 million jobs in 1982 to 2.36 million in 1991. *El Financiero International,* 8 June 1992, 12.

22. Kathryn Kopinak, "The Maquiladorization of the Mexican Economy" in Grinspun and Cameron, eds., *The Political Economy of North American Free Trade.*

23. See the chapters by K. Kopinak and E. Velasco Arregui in Grinspun and Cameron, eds., *The Political Economy of North American Free Trade.* An important aspect is agricultural productivity, which depends on government assistance for new infrastructure (such as irrigation and draining projects) as well as technical and financial support to small farmers. However, current Mexican policy is gradually eliminating this type of support to agriculture.

24. Canadian opponents of free trade argue that the free trade agreement with the United States restricts the Canadian government's ability to intervene in the marketplace, through, for example, industrial or trade policies. See chapters by Bruce Campbell, Mel Watkins, and Ricardo Grinspun, in Grinspun and Cameron, eds., *The Political Economy of North American Free Trade.*

25. Judith Teichman, "The Dismantling of the Mexican State and the Role of the Private Sector," in Grinspun and Cameron, eds., *The Political Economy of North American Free Trade.*

26. "Oligopolies Rule," *El Financiero International,* 19 October 1992, 1.

27. Garavito and Bolivar, *México en la década de los ochenta,* 301.

28. Mexico produced about 17.6 million metric tons of grains in 1980, and consumed 22.4. By 1990 Mexico produced 20.4 and consumed 27 million, so the gap widened. See Gary Hufbauer and Jeffrey Schott, *North American Free Trade: Issues and Recommendations* (Washington: Institute for International Economics, 1992), 282. According to this data, grain consumption grew at an average annual rate of 1.8 percent during the 1980s. Population grew during the same period at 2.0 percent per year, so there was a fall in per capita consumption during the period.

29. The important question of food self-sufficiency and rural development is analyzed in David Barkin in "About Face," *NACLA Report on the Americas,* vol. 24, no. 6 (May 1991); and in more detail in his *Distorted Development: Mexico in the World Economy* (Boulder: Westview, 1990).

30. "The 1992 reforms substantially changed the rules for land ownership and use. *Ejidatarios* will get title to their lands. While individuals are still limited to one hundred hectares, foreigners can purchase land on much the same basis as Mexican citizens. Corporations, domestic and foreign, may own up to 2,500 hectares (about 6,200 acres)." Office of Technology Assessment, *U.S.-Mexico Trade,* 201.

31. The number is taken from Office of Technology Assessment, *U.S.-Mexico Trade,* 67.

32. David Barkin, "State Control of the Environment: Politics and Degradation in Mexico," *Capitalism Nature Socialism* 2, no.1 (February 1991): 86-108.

33. About half the foreign investment that came in 1991 went into the *Bolsa* (stock market). Janet Duncan, "Foreign Investment to Slow in 1992," *El Financiero International,* 27 January 1992, 3.

34. The deficit may reach $25 billion in 1994—an unprecedented amount in historical terms. See Banamex, *Review of the Economic Situation of Mexico* 50 (March 1994): 120.

35. "The main question confronting Mexican companies is whether these [foreign] investors are willing to become long-term investors in Mexico, or whether they will flee at the first sign of trouble." See "Taking Stock of the Companies," *El Financiero International,* April 1992, 14.

36. "In macroeconomic terms, this has been the most successful administration in decades," said Mexico City analyst David Carrera. "What is lacking is the microeconomic reform, which will benefit consumers and small businesses." UPI, Mexico City, 29 November 1994.

"The Old Strategy"

1. Rosa Albina Garavito and Augusto Bolívar, *México en la década de los ochenta: la modernización en cifras* (Mexico: UAM-Azcapotzalco, 1990), 117; and Judith A. Teichman, *Policymaking in Mexico: From Boom to Crisis* (Boston: Allen & Unwin, 1988), 153-54.
2. More than $11 billion left the country in 1981, and perhaps $40 billion during the period from 1980 to 1984. Estimates for the decade as a whole range up to $80 billion. U.S. Congress, Office of Technology Assessment, *U.S.-Mexico Trade: Pulling Together or Pulling Apart?* ITE-545 (Washington, DC: Government Printing Office, October 1992), 68.
3. Robert Kaufman, "Economic Orthodoxy and Political Change in Mexico: The Stabilization and Adjustment Policies of the de la Madrid Administration," in Barbara Stallings and Robert Kaufman, eds., *Debt and Democracy in Latin America* (Boulder: Westview Press, 1989), 114.

"A Lesson from Southeast Asia?"

1. René Villareal, "The Latin American Strategy of Import Substitution: Failure or Paradigm For the Region?" in Gary Gereffi and Donald L. Wyman, eds., *Manufacturing Miracles: Paths of Industrialization in Latin America and East Asia* (Princeton: Princeton University Press, 1990), 316.
2. These issues are discussed at length in different chapters of Gereffi and Wyman, eds., *Manufacturing Miracles*.

4

Flexibility and Repression: The Chilean Model Explained

Duncan Green

It hits you from hundreds of yards away, the rich sweet smell of fermenting wood floating through the crisp air of a Chilean night. The scent emanates from several huge mounds of wood chip, silhouetted against the dockside floodlights. Dwarfing the wooden houses and shops of the southern port of Puerto Montt, the mounds steam gently as they await loading onto the Japanese ship which rides at anchor in the bay. Each pile contains the remnants of a different species of Chilean tree, hauled from the country's dwindling native forest.

Along the southern coast, the wire-mesh tanks of innumerable salmon farms dot the picturesque fjords and inlets. On the beaches, the black strings of pelillo seaweed lie drying, before being sent to Japan for processing into food preservative. In the ports, the fishmeal factories grind mackerel into animal fodder. All these products will be shipped overseas as part of the Chilean export boom, a vast enterprise which has turned the country into the fastest-growing economy in Latin America and a showcase for neoliberalism's "silent revolution" in the region.

The figures are eloquent: economic growth of nearly 6 percent in 1993, and over 10 percent in 1992, making Chile the third fastest growing economy in the world that year; low inflation; a government which runs a fiscal surplus of nearly a billion dollars a year; the highest rate of investment in Latin America, most of it financed by local savings; the next in line for a free trade agreement with the United States. Its supporters trumpet Chile as the first Latin American economic tiger, ready to take its place alongside the *tigres asiaticos* of Taiwan, Singapore, and South Korea.

Moreover, the Chilean economy is doing better now under a democracy than during the Pinochet dictatorship. Taken over the whole seventeen years of the dictatorship, the economy was far from being a success story, even in macroeconomic terms. Two enormous recessions in 1975 and 1982, followed by periods of high-speed growth, averaged out at a miserly annual per-capita growth rate of less than 1 percent from 1973 to 1989. The first boom, which ran from 1977 until 1981, foundered as the "Chicago Boys"—free-market zealots placed in charge of the Chilean economy—deregulated private banks. The banks promptly went on a borrowing spree and then collapsed in 1981 in a private-sector version of the debt crisis. Pinochet had to forget his neoliberal aversion to the state and bail out the banking sector the following year by temporarily renationalizing it.

Emerging from recession in the mid-1980s, however, the government adopted a more pragmatic approach, concentrating on balancing the books and promoting exports and investment. By 1990 it was able to present incoming President Patricio Aylwin with a fairly stable platform for an economic take-off. Above all, the dictatorship had turned Chile into an export-oriented economy. Aylwin picked up the ball and ran with it. Over the course of his presidency, per-capita GDP grew by almost a fifth, exports by 14 percent, and investment rose from under 19 percent of GDP to an impressive 27 percent, unmatched anywhere except by the Asian tigers.

The *Economist* is impressed, but what about the Chileans? It depends on whom you ask. The Chilean yuppies marvelling at the giant new Alto las Condes shopping mall seem well pleased. Opened in September 1993, the biggest mall in Latin America is a monument to the new Chile, a temple of consumerism set in the plushest of Santiago's suburbs. The mall has three floors of gleaming boutiques in cream and gold, a vaulted glass roof, palm trees, silent escalators, and muzak. In the window of the World Book Center, Pinochet's memoirs share pride of place with Martha Stewart's *Gardening Month by Month*, the perfect Christmas presents in the new Chile. The Chilean elite vastly increased its wealth under Pinochet, and then did even better during the Aylwin boom.

Outside the middle-class enclaves, however, the flaws in the model start to appear. Chile's neoliberal success has been built on past repression and current hardship. In the fruit farms near Santiago, life is hard. "They work you like a slave here, squeeze you dry, and then throw you out," says Roxana, a smartly dressed thirty-year-old woman. She can only find work during the harvest and packing seasons, seven months of the year. The few permanent jobs all go to men, she explains.

Roxana's house is a wooden hut with a tin roof, a few sticks of furniture, no heating, and no glass in the windows. The family bakes in summer and freezes in winter. Roxana picks and packs kiwi fruit, peaches, and apples for export, all grown on land that used to belong to peasant farmers growing food for Chileans. Under Pinochet the farmers were bought out by banks and fruit-growers. Now they are casual laborers on their old lands.

"Casualization" is central to Chile's economic "miracle," and has accelerated since the end of the dictatorship. A labor force once accustomed to secure, unionized jobs has been turned into a collection of anxious individualists. Pinochet's bloody repression of the trade-union movement played an essential part in the process. "If he hadn't killed all those people, the economy wouldn't be where it is today," says Luz Santibañez, who spent seven years in exile in Scotland and now runs her own clothing workshop in Santiago. The military espoused a particularly brutal form of economic Darwinism. When asked about the high bankruptcy rate, Pinochet's colleague in the junta, Admiral José Toribio Merino, replied: "Let fall those who must fall. Such is the jungle of... economic life. A jungle of savage beasts, where he who can kill the one next to him kills him. That is reality."

The Aylwin government corrected some of the worst abuses of the Pinochet labor code. It did nothing, however, to challenge the underlying free-market model which relies on the "flexible" labor practices established under the dictatorship, such as subcontracting, short-term contracts, piecework, and management's right to hire and fire almost at will. Aylwin's team of economic technocrats was convinced that Pinochet's legacy of a compliant labor force and a self-exploiting sweatshop economy was essential to the Chilean boom and could not be touched.

Although the number of unionized workers increased by about a third to 700,000 in the first years of the Aylwin presidency, the Christian Democrats used their control over the trade-union leadership to keep a tight rein on labor. In late 1993, during the height of the election campaign, the government was both able and willing to face down a rare strike by healthcare workers. Aylwin refused to negotiate while the 55,000 low-paid members of the National Federation of Health Workers were on strike. Wages are only just getting back to the levels of twenty-five years ago, while around 40 percent of the workforce is now estimated to be operating in the dirty, dangerous, and unregulated world of the informal economy.

In purely material terms, even the poorest Chileans have become less poor since the restoration of democratic rule, but the loss of job security and the dismantling of the welfare state have exacted a heavy human price. According to a recent World Health Organization survey, over half of all visits to the public health system involve psychological ailments, mainly depression. "The repression isn't physical anymore, it's economic—feeding your family, educating your child," says María Peña, who works in a fishmeal factory. "I feel real anxiety about the future," she adds. "They can chuck us out at any time; you can't think five years ahead. If you've got money, you can get an education and health care. Money is everything here now."

The increased stress and individualism have also affected Chile's traditionally strong and caring community life. According to press reports, suicides have increased threefold between 1970 and 1991, and the number of alcoholics has quadrupled in the last thirty years. Community leaders in Santiago's working class *poblaciones* say family breakdowns are increasing, while opinion polls show the current crime wave to be the most widely condemned aspect of life under Aylwin. "Relationships are changing," says Betty Bizamar, a twenty-six-year-old trade-union leader. "People use each other, spend less time with their family. All they talk about is money, things. True friendship is difficult now. You have to be a Quixote to be a union leader these days!"

Pinochet's combination of neoliberal economic surgery and the repression of dissent turned Chile from one of the most equitable societies in Latin America into one of its most unjust—by some reckonings second only to Brazil. Average wages in 1989 were still 8 percent lower than in 1970. The minimum wage was drastically reduced and casualization, in any case, rendered it meaningless in large sectors of the economy. The numbers living in poverty—defined as those in households with an income of less than twice the cost of a minimum food basket—had risen from 20 percent to 40 percent of the population, and the richest 20 percent of the population had increased their share of total consumption from 45 percent in 1969 to 60 percent in 1989. These wealthiest were the only people who experienced a real increase in their income between 1969 and 1988. Despite growing poverty and inequality, the dictatorship cut per-capita social spending by a fifth over the course of the Pinochet years.

Aylwin inherited an economy primed for growth, but with much-increased inequality. He chose to avoid redistribution, and bank on growth to reduce poverty—everyone kept the same proportional slice of the pie, but the pie got steadily bigger. In the short term the trickle-down strategy produced results unparalleled anywhere else in the region. Growth lifted perhaps as many as a million Chileans out of poverty during the Aylwin years. His newly elected successor, Eduardo Frei, has sworn to eradicate extreme poverty—currently affecting nearly one in ten Chileans—by the end of the century.

Aylwin had good reasons for putting continuity before change, and an excellent alibi in the old patriarch himself. Pinochet remains head of the armed forces and a jealous defender of his legacy. He also bequeathed a Congress with an built-in majority for the right designed to block radical reform or any attempt to call the military to account for any of the three thousand political killings under the dictatorship. Aylwin's other reason for caution was economic. Any serious attempt to redistribute wealth would have led to political and economic warfare with the Chilean elite, a slump in investment, and a swift end to neoliberal growth. Don't-rock-the-boatism became the hallmark of the Aylwin presidency.

One of the least publicized and perhaps most positive aspects of the Pinochet legacy is Chile's success in solving Latin America's historic inability to generate domestic savings. The main vehicle has been the radical pension-fund reform introduced in 1980. The reform replaced the ramshackle state pension schemes with private pension funds (AFPs), and made membership compulsory for all workers entering the labor force from 1983, obliging them to contribute a minimum of 10 percent of their salaries. AFPs currently manage capital of $13 billion, equivalent to one third of Chile's GDP.

Any new pension scheme has a honeymoon period while it accumulates capital before having to start paying out pensions as its members start to retire. During this period, the AFPs have not only generated far higher returns for their members than the old schemes, but have been instrumental in increasing Chile's domestic savings rate to 21 percent of GDP, the highest in Latin America. As a result, Chile has been able to finance investment with its own resources, allowing it to impose restrictions on speculative foreign capital, something that other Latin American countries would not dare to do, given their desperation for foreign investment. The experiment is now being repeated elsewhere; Peru introduced a similar system in 1991, and Argentina is now following suit.

Is the Chilean model sustainable? It certainly seems more stable than other supposed neoliberal success stories such as Mexico and Argentina, which are both relying on massive inflows of fickle foreign investment to cover large trade deficits. In Mexico and Argentina, the influx of foreign investment has included both direct investment lured in by privatization programs, and a growing component of portfolio investment attracted by high interest rates and rich pickings on the local stock markets. Now, however, alarm bells are ringing since there is not much left to privatize—especially in Argentina—and speculative investment can leave as easily as it enters. Both countries are exacerbating their trade problems by running highly overvalued currencies to hold down inflation. In comparison, Chile has so far been a model of prudence, running government and trade surpluses until a large trade deficit appeared in 1993.

But in the long term, the Chilean model's Achilles' heel is that, underneath all the hype, Chile's recent success has been based on the old developing-country recipe of exporting raw materials. Last year, only 20 percent of its exports were manufactured goods. Granted, products have diversified from the days when copper made up 80 percent of Chilean exports—it now accounts for around 40 percent—with dynamic new "non-traditional" sectors in fruit, forestry, and fisheries. Globally, however, agricultural products are the most sluggish backwater of the world economy. Successful developing countries get into computers, not kiwi fruit, yet the Chilean government shows a massive indifference to the country's technological base. While the business courses are packed, in 1992 only three students graduated in math and four in physics from the University of Chile.

This latest twist to the old commodity-export story is already showing signs of coming to an unhappy ending. As more and more developing countries leap aboard the bandwagon, the increased competition floods the market. As one author asked: "How many macadamia nuts or mangoes can North Americans be expected to eat, even at lower prices?" In the Aconcagua Valley near Santiago, growers are hacking down hectares of kiwi-fruit trees because of a world glut. Chile's apple growers have suffered a different kind of setback. By competing with European producers, they have triggered a bout of first world protectionism. In 1993 the European Community responded to a bumper apple crop at home by virtually closing the doors to Chilean apples. In the same year, in a sign of the limits to its export drive, Chile ran up a $1 billion trade deficit after years of surplus, reflecting sharp price declines in a number of key exports.

Up to now the response has been that of a hamster on a treadmill, as the Chilean economy churns out ever greater quantities of raw materials to try and compensate for the falling prices. In the end, the ceiling on such a rapacious model is the land itself. In the deforested hills around Puerto Montt, the fished-out shorelines of the South, and the chemical-ridden fields of the fruit belt, even Chile's abundant ecosystem is starting to protest, and some of the results are horrific. In the Regional Hospital of Rancagua in the lakes region of Southern Chile, investigations show that of the 90 babies born with a range of neural tube defects in the first nine months of 1993, every one was the child of a temporary worker on the fruit farms. The Rancagua figure is three times the national average, leading investigators to blame the tragedies on the indiscriminate use of pesticides on the farms.

Government economists acknowledge the limitations of a purely natural resource-based model, and argue for a new kind of industrialization, based on natural resources and destined for export rather than import-substitution. Chile, say the economists, should export wine, not grapes, and furniture instead of wood chips. In the longer term, they argue, the country should try and mimic Finland, which successfully found a niche in the world market when it developed timber processing and paper machinery on the foundations of its forestry sector.

To date, however, the Chilean government has failed to shake off its neoliberal inferiority complex, believing that the state can only harm the economy by stepping in to protect and nurture this process. So far, President Frei has said nothing to suggest a change of direction. There has been sharp growth in a few areas—wine exports have grown over 50 percent a year for the last five years. But critics argue that without a coherent industrial policy, the leap to a broader resource-based industrialization will never happen. Furthermore, if Chile succeeds in its efforts to join NAFTA, the government may find that any attempt to encourage fledgling Chilean industries becomes illegal under clauses requiring equal treatment of local and foreign investment.

Aylwin's success has been based on an unprecedented level of political consensus, in part a reaction to the horrors of military rule, in part the result of fast growth which has been able to keep almost everyone happy without raising divisive issues of inequality and redistribution. The danger for his successor is that, as memories of the dictatorship fade, different sectors will become more willing to rock the boat. The first could be the Socialist Party, which may grow tired of playing second fiddle to the Christian Democrats in the governing coalition, first under Aylwin and now under Frei.

Disputes over the skewed distribution of wealth will probably emerge if the Chilean boom runs into trouble, and there are already signs of a slow-down. Growth in 1993 was 5.7 percent, down from an unsustainable 10.4 percent in 1992, and was forecast to reach only 4 percent in 1994. Most Latin American governments would be delighted with such a rate, but once the pie stops growing, Chile's poor might become more dissatisfied with the tiny slice they have been allocated by Pinochet and Aylwin. In 1992 the poorest fifth of the population received just 4.5 percent of national income, the same percentage as in 1987.

Despite the rhetoric, Chile is a long way from being a pure neoliberal showcase. Foreign investors complain about the new government's insistence on retaining tighter controls on foreign capital than almost any other Latin American country. General Pinochet showed his own double standards towards the free market by insisting that the Chilean Copper Corporation (Codelco) remain in state hands; indeed copper revenues subsidized the state during the restructuring of the 1980s. The military as an institution also showed some aversion to its own free-market medicine. By law 10 percent of Codelco revenues—currently around $190 million a year—goes to the armed forces. The armed forces also declared itself the only group in Chile exempt from joining the new private pension funds.

Some aspects of the Chilean experience could usefully be copied elsewhere, notably the creation of a local capital market, the tradition of honest government (which long preceded Pinochet), and a concern with avoiding large fiscal or trade deficits and excessive openness to foreign speculators. Others, such as Chile's unique endowment of natural resources (copper, forests, excellent farmland, and a two-thousand-mile coastline, all in a country of just 14 million people), are just Chile's good fortune and the envy of others.

But Chile's macroeconomic success under Aylwin has only been possible because of the brutal social and economic surgery carried out under Pinochet. In Chile, the rise of the market has relied on dictatorship and repression. The return to democracy has seen a move to "neoliberalism with a human face," but the social and environmental costs of the model remain so severe that they undermine many of its gains. Moreover, even on its own terms, the model is flawed in its dependence on raw materials, and the government's aversion to taking a real role in directing the economy. The Chilean experience may contain some lessons for other developing countries grappling with the market, but it is certainly not the neoliberal nirvana painted by its supporters.

5

Costa Rica: Non-Market Roots of Market Success

Marc Edelman and Rodolfo Monge Oviedo

From 1980 to 1982, Costa Rica was battered by its worst economic crisis since the great depression. Inflation soared, and the normally complacent citizens of Central America's most prosperous nation were shocked by unprecedented scenes of children singing for coins on buses, beggars going door to door, and homeless families huddled under bridges. As the heavily indebted country went into a tailspin, it appeared that Central America's model democracy might slide into chaos or authoritarianism.

In 1993, however, just a decade later, President Rafael Angel Calderón Fournier could trumpet the "stability" of Costa Rica's "transformed" economy and boast that "the World Bank, the Inter-American Development Bank and the International Monetary Fund... describe us as a human and economic miracle."[1] Foreign Minister Bernd Niehaus claimed that Costa Rica was becoming a "locomotive pulling the other economies of Central America toward... development."[2] Echoing Oscar Arias—president from 1986 to 1990—and Eduardo Lizano—Central Bank director between 1984 and 1990—Niehaus maintained that this small Central American republic of less than 3 million people could soon be the first developed country in Latin America.[3]

Indeed, Costa Rica has become something of a showcase of market-oriented economic development, and is now a regular stop on the U.S.-sponsored neoliberal tour of the Americas. When the Bush administration attempted to convince Bolivian peasants to stop growing coca, for example, it arranged to have a few farmers sent to Costa Rica to learn how to grow and export macadamia nuts. Hilario Claros, one of those farmers, made the switch after his Costa Rican tour. "The Costa Rican trip convinced us that this can work," he told a *New York Times* reporter upon his return to the Andes. Costa Rican macadamia trees soon began growing across Bolivia's Chapare rain forest.[4]

Costa Rica's "agriculture of change"—based on the export of macadamia nuts, pineapple, citrus concentrates, coconut oil, and other tropical products—is part of a radical turn to free-market economics that has endeared the country not only to a handful of favored Bolivian peasants like Claros, but to U.S. policymakers and champions of neoliberalism throughout the hemisphere. Even the United Nations' International Labor Organization (ILO), hardly a bastion of right-wing zealots, points to Costa Rica, together with Chile and Mexico, as a Latin American success story that demonstrates how free-market economics may actually improve the situation of workers.[5]

Advocates of neoliberal policies point to the country's moderate inflation, healthy growth rates, and booming nontraditional export sector as evidence that stabilization and adjustment programs can work wonders in dependent, heavily indebted Latin American economies. But the recent economic history of Costa Rica contains lessons that are a good deal more ambiguous. Much of Costa Rica's recent economic "success" has hinged on its strategic geopolitical position, on the legacy of the social democratic and statist model that preceded the free-market "revolution," and on the redefinition of key indicators and statistics.

Costa Rica's 1980s crisis has roots both in the downturn of the world economy and in a thirty-year reformist experiment that gave the country the highest living standards in Central America and health and literacy indices approaching those of developed, industrialized countries.[6] In 1942, Social Christian President Rafael Angel Calderón Guardia, father of the current chief executive, alienated his elite backers by implementing a labor code and a broad social reform program. He sought support from the country's progressive archbishop, and from the Communist Party, which had gained strength during the 1930s depression. In 1948, however, an alliance of social democrats and upper-class conservatives, angered by official corruption, and suspicious of electoral fraud and communist influence in the government, launched an armed insurrection that toppled Calderón's successor, Teodoro Picado. The social democrats under José Figueres, who controlled the weapons of the winning side, ruled by decree for eighteen months. Figueres's junta, while persecuting its vanquished Social Christian and Communist foes, also took measures that deepened the reforms the latter had initiated in the period 1942 to 1948. In an effort to limit the strength of the traditional upper class, the junta nationalized the banks. It also abolished the army in order to forestall a conservative restoration and to free up resources for social programs.[7]

In subsequent decades, even though the social democrats in the National Liberation Party (PLN) usually alternated in power with the conservative opposition, the nationalized banks channeled massive flows of subsidized credit to regions of the country and sectors of the economy where loans had previously been scarce. The state invested in energy, transport and communications infrastructure, housing, education, health and nutrition services, and generous pension and savings programs for public and private sector employees. These policies spawned a burgeoning, affluent class of professionals, small-scale entrepreneurs, and state functionaries, as well as a large number of peasant and artisan cooperatives. In the 1960s, the Central American Common Market spurred industrialization, as local and transnational corporations sought to supply expanding regional demand for consumer goods while safely ensconced behind high tariff walls. In the 1970s, when rapidly rising oil prices slowed expansion, the state increasingly made direct investments in manufacturing and agroindustrial enterprises. During the 1950s and 1960s, Costa Rica's economic growth rates were the highest in Latin America, and even during the 1970s they were still among the continent's four highest.[8]

The Costa Rican model, though, had growing costs. Industry relied on imported inputs and technology, exacerbating a chronic trade imbalance. Subsidized prices for food staples combined with high farm support prices fueled the public-sector deficit. National Banking System loans at below-inflation rates encouraged speculation and consumption instead of investment. While the state's expenditures rose from 15 percent of gross domestic product in 1970 to 22 percent in 1980, its income remained constant at roughly 13 percent of GDP.[9]

In the 1970s, commercial banks were recycling petrodollars, and Latin American governments eagerly sought short-term credits to cover budget shortfalls. But the loans often had variable interest rates that unexpectedly skyrocketed when oil prices soared again in 1979. Costa Rica was caught in the debt trap: its terms of trade fell by one-third and its debt service quadrupled between 1977 and 1981. By mid-1980, dollar reserves covered only one week's imports and the colón began a rapid downward spiral that in eighteen months resulted in a 500 percent devaluation.[10]

Costa Rica declared a moratorium on debt payments in July 1981, over a year before Mexico caused world consternation with its announcement that it could not meet its interest obligations. Although Costa Rica had one of the highest per capita debts in the world ($2,021 in 1980), as a "small debtor" its problems attracted little attention or sympathy in the international financial community.[11] Commercial banks were initially reluctant to negotiate at all with Costa Rica for fear of establishing precedents that might influence talks with Mexico and Brazil.[12] Yet sandwiched between Sandinista Nicaragua and Noriega's Panama, Costa Rica combined small size with a pivotal position in Washington's geopolitical strategy for the region. Even before the country emerged from the severe economic crisis of 1980-1982, it started to receive favored treatment from USAID, which began to provide large amounts of "economic support funds" intended to shore up its balance of payments. As the decade progressed, this partiality was also reflected in the policies of U.S.-dominated multilateral lenders, especially the IMF and the World Bank.

In 1980-1981, two IMF accords with President Rodrigo Carazo's government broke down in the face of public opposition. But by late 1982, as inflation neared 100 percent, the newly-elected PLN government of Luis Alberto Monge had little alternative but to sign a $100 million IMF stand-by accord, committing itself to a package of measures intended to reduce inflation, cut the public sector deficit, and bring order to the foreign exchange market. To free up resources for paying the foreign debt, the IMF required Costa Rica to slash public sector spending and investment, and to raise taxes, interest rates, and utility rates.

IMF actions in Costa Rica, however, suggested uncharacteristic sensitivity to the importance of political stability in the economic stabilization process. In a striking departure from monetarist orthodoxy, the IMF allowed National Banking System interest rates to remain below inflation and permitted the Central Bank to maintain a monopoly of foreign exchange transactions. Unification of the overvalued official exchange rate with the free market one was to occur gradually, rather than through sudden, disruptive "shocks."

Washington was setting out to build a democratic, prosperous and stable "showcase" next to Sandinista Nicaragua. Given the severity of the economic crisis, it had to move fast. Between 1983 and 1985, the

$592 million in U.S. economic aid was equivalent to a staggering 35.7 percent of the Costa Rican government's budget, one-fifth of export earnings, and about 10 percent of GDP. By 1985, Costa Rica was the second highest recipient of U.S. assistance in Latin America, after war-torn El Salvador, and the second highest per capita recipient in the world, after Israel.[13] To stem "non-productive" social welfare spending and losses from oversized publicly-owned enterprises, USAID insisted on sweeping changes in the country's economy: an expanded role for private banks, the auctioning off of state companies, and the creation of new non-public organizations—from agricultural schools to export promotion offices—that intentionally duplicated functions of public-sector institutions, thus weakening the state and accelerating Costa Rica's embrace of neoliberalism.[14]

Washington put intense pressure on Costa Rica to comply with these demands. In 1984, for example, USAID said it was holding up disbursement of desperately needed funds until the legislature—sequestered during an exhausting twenty-hour debate—approved banking and currency reforms that permitted loans in dollars and that allowed private financial institutions to receive credit from the Central Bank. U.S. money also went towards founding a new Coalition for Development Initiatives (CINDE)—staffed by Costa Ricans and North Americans, with offices in San José and several U.S. cities—which provided funds for nontraditional export projects, training, private sector "educational" activities, and opening new markets abroad. CINDE and USAID in turn played key roles in establishing and staffing a new Ministry of Exports. In 1985, USAID created the Transitory Investments Fund (FINTRA), a trust that was to support the buy-out of state-sector companies.[15] Washington also pushed for and received reductions in Central American extraregional tariffs and generous incentives for producers of nontraditional exports. Meanwhile, the IMF, alarmed that Costa Rica was not fully complying with promises to slash public spending, conditioned continued support on the signing of a structural adjustment agreement with the World Bank.

In 1985, Costa Rica signed a new IMF stand-by accord, new agreements with the commercial banks and the creditor nations in the Paris Club, and its first structural adjustment loan (SAL) with the World Bank. Thanks in part to the huge flow of U.S. assistance, the economy had stabilized since the debacle of 1980-1982: inflation had dropped below 20 percent, growth had been positive for two years in a row, and the public-sector deficit stood at about 6 percent of GDP—short of the IMF target, but less than half the 1982 level. The adjustment phase initiated with SAL I meant a continuation of measures adopted in the 1983-1985 stabilization period. But it also portended a series of more profound, long-term changes in Costa Rican society.

SAL I—an $80 million long-term loan from the World Bank—sought to redirect Costa Rican industrial development from domestic and Central American markets to new international ones.[16] According to World Bank officials, this shift would allow Costa Rica to sustain the recovery initiated in 1983. Lower tariffs would force local industries to be "competitive" and would facilitate the technology imports necessary for modernizing manufacturing, more tax breaks would encourage retooling and investment, and continued "mini-devaluations" of the colón would boost exports, dampen consumption and keep trade deficits in check.

In agriculture, the World Bank program required the reduction and eventual elimination of crop price supports, subsidized production credit, restrictions on food, input, and machinery imports, and subsidized consumer prices for maize, rice, and beans. It also called for a reorientation of investment and research away from food crops for domestic consumption and toward "nontraditional" exports like those that had so impressed the Bolivian coca growers who had toured Costa Rica at U.S. expense. In order to encourage new exports—agricultural as well as industrial— producers were urged to take advantage of Washington's Caribbean Basin Initiative (CBI), which provided greater access to the U.S. market.

The World Bank also prescribed a fundamental transformation of the Costa Rican state. Rather than intervening directly in the economy, as in the 1970s, the state was to divest itself of unprofitable enterprises, slash its deficit, improve the efficiency of its administrative activities, and limit itself as much as possible to guaranteeing social stability and facilitating the activities of the private sector. The nationalized banks, which previously budgeted credits to meet the needs of specific economic sectors and social groups, were told to make loans only according to profitability—not social development—criteria.[17] Finally, the World Bank sought to reduce the growth of the foreign debt, to restrict new loans to those with favorable, "concessionary" terms, and to assure that "fresh" loans were not used for paying debt service.

SAL II, signed in 1988, was a $200 million loan agreement with the World Bank and Japan that contained an extensive list of measures designed to continue the "reassignment" of resources to the private sector and to export activities and the "reordering" and slimming down of the state that began under SAL I.[18] The accord committed the Costa Rican government to bring domestic prices for grains, sugar, milk, and other basic foods into line with lower international ones, thus encouraging "efficiency" but also opening the market to a flood of imports and undermining many peasant producers. It also called for improving cold storage facilities, containerized ports, and transport and irrigation infrastructure—all necessary concomitants of the "agriculture of change." Public sector services were to be transfered to the private sector when they were "not indispensable for the functioning of the government." Key policymakers, such as Central Bank head Lizano, argued that state enterprises had to be privatized even when, as with the telephone company and the oil refinery, they were running "healthy" surpluses.[19]

Within two years of SAL II, Costa Rica, Japan, and the World Bank began discussions for a third structural-adjustment loan linked to further economic liberalization. New IMF accords in 1991 and 1992 kept the free-market juggernaut on track, commiting the Costa Rican government to a complete liberation of exchange and interest rates. In late 1992, Costa Rica and the World Bank finally hammered out the details of SAL III, a continuation of the free-market restructuring initiated in the mid-1980s.

It has not been easy to achieve consensus about the adjustment process—as the lengthy discussions over SAL III suggest. Measures to "privatize," "correct distortions," and "improve the allocation of production factors" have created new winners and losers and forced virtually every group in society to redefine its strategies for survival. These processes also raise questions about how closely structural adjustment actually conforms to neoliberal concepts and how effective it has been in meeting its professed goals.

The main beneficiaries of the rush to the free market have been the export and private banking sectors and foreign investors, especially those who have come to dominate key parts of the "agriculture of change" and the flourishing *maquila* assembly industry. By the late 1980s, almost half of Costa Rica's foreign exchange came from "non-traditional" exports—those other than the established mainstays of coffee, bananas, and sugar. Nonetheless, all the tax breaks, financial backing, new industrial parks and free trade zones, and support for foreign marketing and promotion have not brought high-value-added industries or vertical integration of production (linkages between suppliers, producers, and distributors) to Costa Rica.

The key tax break did aim at generating more value-added, a necessity for a more dynamic and autonomous accumulation process. But it set the required level rather low, and was costly. Producers of nontraditional exports to non-Central American markets receive tax-credit certificates called CATs if their output contained 35 percent national value-added in the form of local raw materials, labor, or energy. Established in 1972 during the heyday of the social democratic model, CATs cost the government $150,000 to $200,000 for each $1 million worth of exports. Ironically, this "statist" subsidy has been crucial to the "success" of the new, supposedly free-market strategy. But by 1990, with the export fever generated by structural adjustment, CATs ate up 10 percent of the government budget and contributed significantly to continuing deficits.[20] Their distributional effect has also been highly regressive. In an eighteen-month period in 1988-1989, 27 percent of the approximately $72 million in CAT subsidies went to only eight firms; a mere twenty-six companies received over half the CAT subsidies; and a single transnational—PINDECO, the pineapple subsidiary of Del Monte received almost 10 percent of the certificates.[21] In recent surveys, a majority of exporters indicate that if CATs were eliminated, they would reduce or cease their activities.[22]

Since the crisis broke in the early 1980s, diverse social groups have opposed free-market stabilization and adjustment policies. Industrialists who produced goods for the domestic and Central American markets, large and small grain farmers, the urban poor, government employees, and students, faculty, and workers at the public universities have all been on the losing end, as the radical restructuring of Costa Rican society assigned resources to other sectors.

Each of the last three administrations has faced major protest movements that forced modifications in particularly draconian policies. Costa Rica's first "letter of intent" to the IMF, in late 1982, specified that the state utility company would boost electricity rates 90 percent, a measure intended to raise revenue for debt service and to eliminate wasteful "distortions" caused by artificially cheap energy.[23] By early 1983, Monge's government had to contend with demonstrations and highway blockades by outraged consumers, many of whom publicly burned their electricity bills and announced their inability to pay the increases. In June, the government caved in and signed an accord with the protesters that, IMF notwithstanding, rescinded many of the rate hikes and provided generous payment terms for those consumers who had fallen into arrears.[24]

Between 1986 and 1988, after SAL I slashed resources for grain producers, peasant organizations, allied at times with wealthy rice farmers, staged marches, road blockades, and building occupations to call for the restoration of price supports and credit and extension programs. President Oscar Arias, though he won the 1987 Nobel Peace Prize for brokering the Central American peace accords, found the political problems generated by structural adjustment in agriculture an impossible challenge. During his four-year term, two of his three ministers of agriculture quit, squeezed from both sides by pro-free-market policymakers and agriculturalist organizations.

In 1991, the administration of Rafael Angel Calderón Fournier trimmed budgets at the four public universities and tried to shift much of the cost of higher education to students. The expansion of public postsecondary education had been a major accomplishment of the social democratic development model; by 1980, a remarkable 27 percent of the population of university student age was enrolled in institutions of higher learning.[25] Calderón's budget cuts prompted a wave of student protest that caused the government to retreat and the treasury minister—who had advocated a hard line against "pressure groups"—to resign.

Although economic policymakers championed free-market ideology, in practice their attainments owed much to Costa Rica's social democratic legacy. Together with CATs and other subsidies, the availability of a literate, disciplined workforce and a large corps of highly trained managers and technicians—the product of the social democrats' thirty-year-long public investment in "human capital"—constituted one of Costa Rica's main attractions for the export-oriented investors that flooded in after 1982.

The continued capacity of the Costa Rican state to absorb discontent and the worsening divisions within opposition forces have also been crucial to the "success" of the model. The labor movement—riven by doctrinal disputes, debilitated by poorly planned strikes in the early and mid-1980s, and facing growing competition from employer-worker *solidarista* associations—has lost much support and largely ceased to be an effective defender of workers' standard of living. Housing movements, which in the early 1980s led land invasions in the cities, weakened after the Arias administration promised to build 80,000 new homes, giving priority to the most militant squatter settlements. Peasant organizations, whose militant actions contributed to the resignation of two of Arias's three ministers of agriculture, nonetheless signed agreements with the Arias administration to secure social-security health coverage for their members.

Under Calderón, the peasant movement, boosted by significant aid flows from foreign governments and nongovernmental organizations (NGOs), has shifted from challenging free-market policies to attempting to carve out "economic space" for its members within the new system. Even industrialists, once adamant defenders of protectionism and overvalued exchange rates, have been lured into backing the free-market model by generous subsidies for plant reconversion and export promotion and by the possibility of buying discounted CATs from producers of nontraditional exports.

The absorption of opposition has been part of a state and lending agency strategy to blunt the negative social impact of structural adjustment policies. Foreign aid agencies, NGOs, and even the multilateral lenders began to provide "social compensation" funds to ease the crisis caused by large-scale dismissals of public employees, declining real wages, and cutbacks in state services. As early as 1983, USAID, European governments, and Catholic charities helped the Monge government to begin indexing public sector salaries to inflation and to institute a food distribution program that benefited 42,000 of the poorest families.[26] Soon after, the European Economic Community launched a major aid effort directed at the poorest sectors of the population throughout Central America. By the mid 1980s, NGOs and foreign aid organizations proliferated in Costa Rica, incorporating personnel dismissed from the public sector and attempting, albeit with mixed results, to mitigate the social hardships brought on by the rush to the free market. In 1990, the Calderón government introduced a "food bond" for needy families which, despite its good intentions, reached less than half of those in the "extreme poverty" category.

Economic adjustment in Costa Rica has had a "trickle down" effect, but largely in the form of low-paying jobs in assembly industries or agroindustrial export enterprises. After a decade of stabilization and adjustment, per capita GDP, a key indicator of living standards, had not regained its 1980, pre-crisis level. The real minimum wage (i.e., adjusted for inflation), an important gauge of the living standards of the poor, jumped in 1983 as the country recovered from the devastating devaluation-inflation of 1981-1982. But it has declined every year since, with the exception of 1985 and 1989, both pre-election years, when governments in Costa Rica typically expand spending to garner votes and good will (knowing too that their successors will have to pick up the tab).[27]

And, to make matters worse, employers increasingly flout wage legislation, knowing that the state's enforcement capacity has been weakened by budget cuts and dismissals of public employees. By 1991, an estimated 37 percent of workers were paid less than the legal minimum.[28] In agriculture, industry and construction, the percentage of the workforce receiving below-minimum wages has risen well above 1980 pre-crisis levels; a particularly large number of complaints come from women employed in new garment assembly plants.[29]

Average real wages recovered to pre-crisis levels in 1987, though the gain largely evaporated by 1991. Even the initial post-crisis rise likely reflects increased upward skewing of the income distribution.[30] Real private consumption per head, often a better indicator than real wages of the burden of adjustment, has not recovered from the 1980-1982 downturn and has fallen nearly one-quarter from its pre-crisis level. Many categories of social spending fell sharply in the mid-1980s, although some have since recuperated. Measured as a percentage of GDP, the budgets of the ministries most critical to basic well being—among them, health and education—remain considerably below 1980 levels.[31]

The percentage of the population below the poverty line has also climbed over the last five years, from 18.6 percent in 1987 to 24.4 percent in 1991.[32] The rise, however, is not simply quantitative; living in poverty is increasingly precarious in today's Costa Rica, with the unravelling of the social safety net.

The recent ILO report that celebrates Costa Rica's adjustment experience notes that between 1980 and 1990 the country conducted the second-sharpest reduction of public sector employment in the hemisphere (after Chile). In contrast to the rest of Latin America, it claims, the expansion of the informal sector—street vendors, sidewalk food and shoe repair stands, and so on—has been negligible. The report lauds the large increase—from 14 percent to 22 percent of the urban workforce—in employment in "small private enterprises."[33]

These conclusions highlight one way in which changing, politically influenced definitions of key indicators have been used to cast a favorable light on troubling economic processes. The entrepreneurial energy embodied in "microenterprises" has been an article of faith for neoliberal theorists at least since the publication in 1986 of Peruvian economist Hernando de Soto's influential treatise *The Other Path*.[34]

Microenterprises have become a cornerstone of neoliberal strategies for economic recovery and growth. In Costa Rica, interest in charting this new sector led to changes in 1987 in the surveys used to measure employment, income and living standards. After holding virtually constant between 1980 and 1986 at around 17 percent, the "self-employed" category was broadened to include more kinds of informal sector workers and, not surprisingly, leaped 3.6 percent in 1987 to 22.9 percent of the labor force, and climbed to 24.8 percent by 1991. Yet these "independent workers" are hardly something for neoliberals to crow about—53.5 percent were below the poverty line in 1991, in contrast to 39.8 percent of workers who were wage earners.[35]

Changes in definitions of other indicators have also affected understanding of the impact of adjustment. This is most evident in data on social spending. In 1987 methods were modified for recording some transfers of funds and services between public sector agencies. These accounting shifts tend to "consolidate" certain kinds of public spending, an effect consonant with IMF and World Bank objectives, since funds sent by one ministry to another did not count twice as income. But some key kinds of social spending, such as the Family Aid program, which involved disbursements to numerous other public-sector organizations, continued to be counted with the old methods. This makes it difficult to tell to what extent the apparent recuperation of some kinds of social spending is real and to what degree it simply reflects accounting changes.[36]

In some cases too, apparent fiscal health obscures disquieting realities. The budget of the social security system, for example—responsible for public clinics and hospitals, as well as old-age and disability pensions—recovered its pre-crisis share of GDP by 1987 and has retained it through 1991. The institution nonetheless increasingly suffers from severe shortages of equipment, medicines, and personnel, as the central government delays disbursement of promised funds in an effort to hold down its deficit.[37] The greatest "success" of economic structural adjustment in Costa Rica has been the boom in nontraditional exports. Yet this expansion hardly resulted from giving free play to market forces. Indeed, the traditional neoliberal tools—lowered tariffs on imports, interest rate liberalization, privatization, and cuts in public spending—have been less important in fueling the growth of new exports than the huge subsidies given exporters, the expansion of U.S. quotas for key products under the CBI, and the constant currency devaluations demanded by the international lending institutions and pro-export lobbies in Costa Rica. The fragility of the new strategy is highlighted by the exporters' anxiety after Bill Clinton's election about increased U.S. protectionism and by the candidate's promises that taxpayers' money will not be used to modernize companies abroad which are potential competitors of U.S.-based industries.[38]

Moreover, the boom shows signs of slowing—nontraditional export growth was only 3.8 percent in 1991, dramatically less than the 7.4 percent of 1990 or the 27.7 percent of 1989. This slowdown is linked to the world recession, but it also arises from a number of other factors. In February 1991, Costa Rica's Constitutional Court halted the CATs program, arguing that the subsidies violated "the principle of equality in public taxation."[39] Suddenly, a critical incentive for nontraditional exporters evaporated. Although it was soon restored, it is set to expire within the next two years.

Costa Rica's early "success" with nontraditional exports also paradoxically threatened its edge over neighboring countries in attracting new investment. The country's new insertion in international markets is based on abundant cheap labor and fertile soil, as well as on an institutional context that hinders labor organization, provides guarantees for capital, and fails to regulate the intensive agrochemical use that accompanies the "agriculture of change." But as other Central American countries follow Costa Rica's lead, they compete to develop the same comparative advantages and to supply foreign markets with the same kinds of products. Instead of fostering comparative advantages based on human capital investment and the constant technical innovation necessary to survive and prosper in the global economy, Costa Rica has become—at great cost to its people—a tragically passive player in an increasingly integrated and competitive world.

The crowning irony of Costa Rica's experience with neoliberalism is that it has not brought more than a momentary reduction of total debt. Faced with slackening growth rates and an ongoing balance of payments deficit—themselves signs of the model's limits—the Calderón government has contracted or sought almost $2 billion in new obligations since the 1990 Brady Plan canceled most of Costa Rica's outstanding commercial bank debt. One-half of the proposed loans is for balance of payments support and much of the rest is intended for ambitious hydroelectric and geothermal energy projects that could eventually permit Costa Rica to sell electricity to Mexico, and Central and South America.[40]

But the World Bank generally recommends that a country's debt not exceed 50 percent of its GDP or 150 percent of its annual exports, and that its debt service not go beyond 15 percent of exports. If Costa Rica, in addition to its new $300 million SAL III, receives all of its $1 billion Inter-American Development Bank energy loan and the other credits contemplated by Calderón, its foreign obligations will reach an all-time high of $5.67 billion. This would be over 60 percent of 1992 GDP and would require almost one-third of export earnings to service.[41] Proponents of the new loans argue that most are low-interest, medium- and long-term multilateral credits, with generous grace periods. But with debt at record levels, many macroeconomic targets unfulfilled, a majority with diminished access to social services, rising poverty, and slackening growth after a decade of stabilization and adjustment, Costa Rica is hardly good material for a free-market success story.

Notes

1. Advertisement, *New York Times,* 5 October 1992, A12.
2. *Tico Times* (San José), 25 May 1990, 1.
3. Antonio Alvarez Desanti, *Agricultura de Cambio* (San José: Imprenta Nacional, 1988), 9; Eduardo Lizano, "Los principales problemas de la política de ajuste estructural," *Actualidad Económica* (San José) 5, no. 3 (November 1988): 48.
4. *New York Times,* 20 May 1990, 12.
5. *Latin America Weekly Report* (London), 29 October 1992.
6. See Marc Edelman and Joanne Kenen, eds., *The Costa Rica Reader* (New York: Grove Weidenfeld, 1989), chaps. 3-5.
7. Although security-related expenditures grew significantly in the early to mid-1980s, Costa Rica still had one of the lowest ratios of military to social welfare spending of any country in the world.
8. ECLAC data cited in Ennio Rodríguez, "Costa Rica: en busca de la super- vivencia," in Stephany Griffith-Jones, ed., *Deuda externa, renegociación y ajuste en la América Latina* (Mexico: Fondo de Cultura Económica, 1988), 219.
9. Adrián Rodríguez V., "La deuda pública externa de Costa Rica: crecimien- to, moratoria y renegociación," in José Roberto López and Eugenio Rivera, eds., *Deuda externa y políticas de estabilización y ajuste estructural en Centroamérica y Panamá* (San José: Secretaría General del CSUCA, 1990), 257.
10. Joan M. Nelson, "The Politics of Adjustment in Small Democracies: Costa Rica, the Dominican Republic, Jamaica," in Joan M. Nelson, ed., *Economic Crisis and Policy Choice: The Politics of Adjustment in the Third World* (Princeton: Princeton University Press, 1990), 183; Humberto Jiménez Sandoval, "La deuda pública externa: teoría y práctica [II]," *Banca, Bolsa & Seguros* (San José) 2 (July-August 1990): 44; E. Rodríguez, "La supervivencia," 221.
11. Per capita debt from Centro de Estudios Para la Acción Social (CEPAS),

Costa Rica en el umbral de los años noventa: deterioro y auge de lo social en el marco del ajuste (San José: CEPAS, 1992), 18.

12. Costa Rica was, nonetheless, the first country in the 1980s to negotiate a multi-year repayment schedule with the private banks. Vargas Peralta, 205-6.

13. Marc Edelman, "Back from the Brink: How Washington Bailed Out Costa Rica," *NACLA Report on the Americas* 19, no. 6 (November/December 1985): 42.

14. Lezak Shallat, "AID and the Secret Parallel State," in Edelman and Kenan, eds., *Costa Rica Reader*, 221-27.

15. Privatization, however, often meant giveaways to the already well-off. When publicly-owned cotton gins and sugar mills were put on the auction block, they were sold for only a tiny fraction of their assessed value. See Marc Edelman, *The Logic of the Latifundio: The Large Estates of Northwestern Costa Rica since the Late Nineteenth Century* (Stanford: Stanford University Press, 1992), 299, 321-22.

16. For the text of the plan, see "Programa de ajuste estructural," in Víctor Hugo Céspedes, Alberto Di Mare, and Ronulfo Jiménez, *Costa Rica: recuperación sin reactivación* (San José: Academia de Centroamérica, 1985), 199-225.

17. The only exceptions were monies for the new Export Finance Fund (FOPEX) and Industrial Development Fund (FODEIN).

18. For the text of SAL II, see "Programa de ajuste estructural," *La Nación* (San José), 5 May 1987.

19. Eduardo Lizano, "Programa de ajuste estructural," in Luis Paulino Vargas Solís, ed., *Crisis económica y ajuste estructural* (San José: Editorial Universidad Estatal a Distancia, 1990), 46.

20. CEPAS, *Costa Rica en el umbral de los años noventa*, 58. In late 1990, the IMF and the World Bank, which had long been dissatisfied with CATs, pressured Costa Rica to reform the system, so that tax credits would be based on a percentage of the local value-added rather than the total value of the exports.

21. René Vermeer, *El cambio en la agricultura: el caso de los granos básicos durante la Administración Arias* (San José: Centro Nacional de Acción Pastoral, 1990), 53-54.

22. Isabel Román, "Efectos del ajuste estructural en el agro costarricense," *Polémica* (San José) 16 (January-April 1992): 20.

23. "Carta de Intenciones al FMI," *La Nación*, 1 December 1982.

24. CEPAS, *La lucha en contra del alza de las tarifas eléctricas: junio de 1983* (San José: CEPAS, 1985).

25. World Bank data cited in Haydée Mendiola, "Expansión de la educación superior costarricense en los 1970s: Impacto en la estratificación social y en el mercado de trabajo," *Revista de Ciencias Sociales* 42 (1988): 82.

26. Jorge Rovira Mas, *Costa Rica en los años '80* (San José: Editorial Porvenir, 1987), 68-69.

27. CEPAS, *Costa Rica en el umbral de los años noventa*, 18.

28. MIDEPLAN data cited in *Esta Semana* (San José), 24-30 May 1991, 5.

29. CEPAS, *Costa Rica en el umbral de los años noventa*, 26, 43.

30. Ministerio de Planificación Nacional y Política Económica, *Costa Rica: indicadores sociodemográficos período 1975-1989* (San José: MIDEPLAN, 1990), 14.

31. CEPAS, *Costa Rica en el umbral de los años noventa*, 73.

32. *Inforpress Centroamericana* (Guatemala) 995 (13 August 1992): 6; CEPAS, *Costa Rica en el umbral de los años noventa,* 46-47. These data are from the U.N. Economic Commission for Latin America and the Caribbean.

33. *Latin America Weekly Report* (London), 29 October 1992.

34. Hernando de Soto, *The Other Path: The Invisible Revolution in the Third World* (New York: Harper & Row, 1989).

35. CEPAS, *Costa Rica en el umbral de los años noventa,* 41, 49.

36. CEPAS, *Costa Rica en el umbral de los años noventa,* 91-92.

37. CEPAS, *Costa Rica en el umbral de los años noventa,* 73; *Inforpress Centroamericana,* vol. 976, 26 March 1992.

38. USAID's creation of an endowment for CINDE, intended to shield it from the budget appropriation process, is another indication of concern about the political vulnerability of the "free-market" strategy.

39. *Tico Times,* 8 February 1991, 1, 22.

40. The Costa Rican Electrical Institute, the public sector agency charged with carrying out this scheme and only a few years ago a target of privatizers, is now praised for having little debt and for operating in the black.

41. *Inforpress Centroamericana,* vol. 996, 20 August 1992; *Tico Times* (San José), 24 July 1992.

6

Puerto Rico:
Lessons from Operation Bootstrap

Hector Cordero-Guzmán

When Puerto Ricans participate in debates over the North American Free Trade Agreement, they do so with a feeling that they have been there before. In the 1950s, Puerto Rico underwent the same kind of economic restructuring that Mexico is undergoing now, tying its development strategy to market-oriented reforms and to the U.S. economy. Puerto Rico's on-going reform package has proved neither a cure-all for the economic ills facing the island, nor an unmitigated attack on social well-being. The plan has brought benefits to some, and very real costs to most. The mixed results of the experience may offer some clues to what Mexico can look forward to in a NAFTA-dominated future.

The Puerto Rican development model was launched after World War II under the name Operation Bootstrap—or, in Puerto Rico, *Manos a la Obra* ("Let's Get to Work!"). It promoted the island's industrialization through the establishment of export-oriented, U.S.-owned manufacturing operations. The model is a showcase of development strategies based on an openness to foreign investment and the free movement of consumer goods, capital, and labor power.

Bootstrap was the precedent-setting forerunner of the principal U.S. hemispheric economic initiatives launched over the past three decades: the Alliance for Progress of the Kennedy years, the establishment of Mexico's *maquiladoras* during the 1970s and 1980s, the Caribbean Basin Initiative and the enterprise-zone proposals of the Reagan administration, and now NAFTA, which is clearly part of more ambitious designs for further hemispheric integration. Bootstrap's pillars were low wages, the lack of trade barriers between the island and the mainland, a policy of population control, and Section 936 of the U.S. Federal Tax Code, which leaves the profits earned by Puerto Rican subsidiaries of U.S. companies relatively untaxed. These four conditions, formulated under the umbrella of the Commonwealth of Puerto Rico, have created a formidable magnet for U.S. investment, and triggered the sustained circulation of people between the island and the mainland United States.

Stateside investors in Puerto Rico enjoy several key advantages. First, they benefit from a relatively cheap and skilled labor force. Second, they operate in sectors (mainly pharmaceuticals and electronics) where research and development expenditures—partly subsidized by the federal and commonwealth governments—translate into relatively high prices for consumers, and hefty profit margins for company stockholders. Third, Puerto Rico offers companies a modern subsidized infrastructure that reduces their costs of production, thus further increasing their profits. All these advantages are multiplied by very low tax rates both in Puerto Rico and for parent companies in the mainland. Recent calculations by the U.S. General Accounting Office, for example, indicate that in 1987, U.S. pharmaceuticals doing business in Puerto Rico obtained more than $3 billion in Section 936 tax credits. This translates into $70,000 for each job created in Puerto Rico. In other words, the government gives about $2.67 in credits to the pharmaceutical industry per dollar paid out in wages.

The evidence commonly cited by Bootstrap's supporters is familiar, but nonetheless bears highlighting. Puerto Rico had economic growth rates averaging 6 percent in the 1950s, 5 percent in the 1960s, and 4 percent in the 1970s. Even with subsequent reversals and some stagnation during the 1980s, this pace of economic expansion looks very good when compared with the record of the rest of the Caribbean and Latin America. These growth rates have given Puerto Rico the second highest per-capita income in Latin America, impressive for a tiny Caribbean island with limited resources and a population of only 4 million. In addition, modern port facilities and an extensive highway complex that accommodates over a million vehicles reflect Puerto Rico's infrastructural modernity. The island's industrial/occupational profile—except for a somewhat bloated public sector—has a decidedly modern cast as well, with high-tech manufacturing, financial services, and trade and commerce the dominant economic activities. Agricultural wage-workers, by contrast, represent a minuscule proportion of the labor force. The literacy rate is above 90 percent, and life expectancy is on a par with that of the most advanced nations.

All these indicators of progress are tied to Puerto Rico's close economic relationship with the United States. Well into the 1980s, Puerto Rico boasted the highest index of per-capita imports from the United States, served as host to about a third of total U.S. direct investment in Latin America, and was the world's fifth largest exporter of goods to the mainland United States.[1] But there is a difference between economic progress and economic development—a difference suggested by the human costs of this progress, both in Puerto Rico and for the Puerto Rican population on the mainland. This difference is not lost on members of the Puerto Rican labor movement, local environmentalists, and industry leaders in labor-intensive, import-sensitive sectors. These sectors have not been well served by the penetration of Puerto Rico's economy by U.S. capital, and the consequent subjugation of native interests brought about by Bootstrap-generated progress.

Most families in Puerto Rico have seen their incomes and wages stagnate over the last twenty years. Federal transfers—such as Aid to Dependent Children and Food Stamps—make up a growing portion of their income. In some years, the level of transfers has surpassed the profits generated in the island by U.S. businesses. Despite the full application of federal minimum-wage standards on the island, average wages there remain at about the same relative distance from average mainland wages as they did in 1973, and real personal income per capita is the same percentage of the mainland figure as it was at the start of Operation Bootstrap, some forty years ago. In 1990, about 60 percent of the population on the island and 40 percent of the Puerto Rican population the mainland were living in or near poverty.[2]

The prolonged and privileged flow of U.S. capital into Puerto Rico seems to have brought more rather than less unemployment, and more rather than less emigration. Labor's efforts to secure greater social equity and to improve the material conditions of Puerto Rican workers are continually met with stiff resistance from the business community. Mainstream economic theory, in fact, provides a veneer of legitimacy to this resistance. Some economists, for example, argue that relative to international market conditions—and despite twenty years of stagnation—Puerto Rican working hands are overpriced.[3] Bootstrap's proponents blame this "overpricing," not the export-oriented development plan, for the island's high unemployment rates, long duration of unemployment, and marginal and unstable connections to formal employment. These harsh labor market conditions persist despite massive emigration (nearly half the potential workforce of Puerto Rican descent is on the mainland) and despite determined policies of population control (by the late 1970s one-third of Puerto Rican women of childbearing age had been sterilized).

Another troubling feature of Puerto Rican development is the island's inappropriately high level of dependence on the U.S. economy—from the standpoint of Puerto Rico's future development. Reflecting this dependence, the gap between the gross *national* product and the gross *domestic* product has increased steadily over the last two decades. This means that native capital formation has been thwarted by the penetration of U.S. firms. North American companies effectively monopolize banking, transport, tourism, and high-tech manufacturing. U.S. transnationals have also made steady incursions into the growing service sector of the economy. As a consequence, Puerto Rico faces an uphill battle in its efforts to build a self-reliant national economy.[4] By the mid-1980s, this lack of self-reliance meant that 85 percent of Puerto Rico's production was for export while 45 percent of food consumption was imported from the continental United States.

The battle is even more uphill with the passage of NAFTA. The agreement places Puerto Rico, other Caribbean states, and Mexico in direct competition with one another, especially in labor-intensive sectors like apparel, footwear, and electronics assembly. This will force governments to provide yet more attractive conditions to the absentee owners of capital—basically lower wages, and fewer labor and environmental regulations.

Political developments on the island—necessarily quite different from developments in sovereignty-conscious Mexico—have to be understood within this economic context. Puerto Rico was granted commonwealth status in 1952 to provide a semblance of decolonization for the Bootstrap design of "associated development." Over recent decades, however, a powerful movement advocating U.S. statehood for Puerto Rico has emerged. This movement now competes on fairly even terms with pro-commonwealth forces. Both principal political camps—the independence movement is now a distant third in all public-opinion polls—see the massive U.S. economic presence in Puerto Rico as a benediction rather than a problematic aspect of the island's development.

Commonwealth supporters argue that a "perfected commonwealth" would give Puerto Rico even more freedom to court foreign capital and sell its labor power at rates below those currently sanctioned by federal overseers. The current pro-statehood offensive is based on the argument that the solution to Puerto Rico's socioeconomic crisis resides in the island's further absorption into the U.S. economic and "social support" apparatus. A large part of statehood's popular appeal derives from the argument that under this formula the unemployed and the poor will never lose their welfare benefits on the island, nor their capacity to relocate to the mainland whenever economic conditions deteriorate.

Among many Puerto Ricans and U.S. Latinos, there was an uneasiness about NAFTA, frequently accompanied by an element of fatalism—a fatalism that saw the structural and political forces behind the agreement as overwhelming. Many felt the only realistic alternative for the present was to go along with the agreement, try to carve out a beneficial niche or two, and hope to reshape its design at some future date.[5] Some government officials, and a number of activists and business people, see the treaty as an opportunity to develop Puerto Rico as a regional "financial center," as long as Section 936 continues to generate extraordinary profits for U.S. companies and banks. In their minds, Puerto Rico could—with permission from the U.S. Treasury— become a source of financing NAFTA-spawned investment opportunities. Hence, diverse Puerto Rican interests came together to orchestrate a largely successful defense of Section 936 when this tax haven was threatened by President Clinton's deficit-reduction program.

Many of NAFTA's original promoters also moderated their positions. They recognized the limitations inherent in the agreement's design, and urged Puerto Rican policymakers to support the treaty because its effects on Puerto Rican and other U.S. workers were likely to be minor and would take a long time to manifest themselves. They no longer encourage any expectation that genuine breakthroughs against joblessness and poverty are in the offing. It is generally recognized that, if anything, NAFTA is likely to exacerbate Puerto Rico's unemployment problem. Indeed, the promises that the treaty now holds out to Mexican workers—when seen through the lens of the Puerto Rican experience—take on a different cast. Despite the new enthusiasms for free markets, free trade, incentives to capital, deregulation, and privatization, NAFTA supporters cannot claim to have any well-founded proof of the capacity of capital—in combination with compliant states—to nurture and develop the human resources at its disposal.

Notes

1. See Frank Bonilla and Ricardo Campos, "A Wealth of Poor: Puerto Ricans in the New Economic Order," *Daedalus* 110, no. 2 (1981): 133-76; Ricardo Campos and Frank Bonilla, "Industrialization and Migration: Some Effects on the Puerto Rican Working Class," *Latin American Perspectives* 3, no. 3 (1976): 66-108; and Emilio Pantojas-García, *Development Strategies as Ideology: Puerto Rico's Export-Led Industrialization Experience* (Boulder, CO: Lynne Rienner Publishers, 1990).
2. National Council of La Raza, *Poverty Project Newsletter,* vol. 4, nos. 2 and 4 (1992).
3. See Carlos E. Santiago, *Labor in the Puerto Rican Economy* (New York: Praeger, 1992); and Health and Migration Taskforce, Center for Puerto Rican Studies, *Labor Migration Under Capitalism: The Puerto Rican Experience* (New York: Monthly Review Press, 1979).
4. See the U.S. General Accounting Office, "Puerto Rico and the Section 936 Tax Credit," report nos. 93-109 (June 1993); and Pantojas-García, *Development Strategies.*
5. See Annette Fuentes, "Bad Table Manners: Latinos and NAFTA," *Dialogo,* vol. 7 (June 1993).

7

Venezuela:
The Temperature Rises
in the Crucible of Reform

Fred Rosen

In January 1994, the old colonial city of Barcelona, near the Caribbean coast, the adjacent resort town of Puerto La Cruz, and dozens of smaller cities in the interior of Venezuela were burned and looted in spontaneous uprisings that began as protests over increases in local bus fares. These disturbances broke out in the month leading to the inauguration of the new president, Rafael Caldera. Spontaneous demonstrations and scuffles also broke out throughout the country as merchants attempted to collect the country's new value-added tax (VAT) which, on most goods, amounted to a 10 percent sales tax. The short-lived VAT (it was suspended soon after the disturbances), coupled with the abolition of price controls on all but a handful of goods, had led to a wave of speculative price hikes. The population, following a decade and a half of declining incomes, responded violently.

Venezuela is wracked by increasing violence, not all of it political. On Christmas day, 1993, more than one hundred homicides were committed in Caracas, and according to news reports twenty or thirty Caraqueños are killed on virtually every weekend.[1] While the homicides are frequently attributed to the lack of any police presence in the poorer neighborhoods of the city, police chief Orlando Hernández blames the killings on "the city's advanced state of social decomposition."[2] Social decomposition, in turn, may be linked to deteriorating living standards. Average real incomes peaked in Venezuela in 1978, midway through the country's oil boom. They have steadily declined ever since, and the daily struggle to make ends meet is becoming more and more difficult for the vast majority of the population.[3] Meanwhile, the conspicuous consumption of a small minority of Venezuelans—many enriched by the country's recent market-oriented reforms—provides a telling contrast. As the gap between rich and poor continues to widen, resentment and frustration build, tearing the country's social fabric.[4]

The VAT and the higher gasoline—and therefore transportation—prices were two of the cornerstones of the past administration's program of market-oriented reforms, known to Venezuelans as the "*paquete.*" The VAT is a frankly regressive tax, which operates just like a sales tax. International lending agencies push it because it is supposedly easy to collect, and hence a reliable way to balance fiscal budgets. Defenders of the tax argue that if the government were to eliminate the VAT and not raise the domestic price of state-produced gasoline, it would remove up to $2 billion from the 1994 budget. Caldera has indicated he will do just that. He proposes to make up the lost revenue with progressive alternatives, such as a luxury tax, selective wholesale taxes, and a collectible income tax.[5] So as Caldera's center-left coalition settles in, Venezuela's fiscal balance remains caught in a standoff between the country's haves and have-nots. Just as the wealthy always announce their intentions by sending "market signals," the poor have let it be known by "disturbing the peace" that it will not be easy to balance the budget on their backs.

Political-economic questions are increasingly being taken to the streets. The January riots are in keeping with Venezuela's precarious social and political situation over the last five years. The most dramatic disturbances of this period have become iconographic reference points, known simply as 27F, 4F, and 27N to the traumatized citizens of South America's longest-standing constitutional democracy. 27F refers to the spontaneous nationwide rioting and looting that broke out on February 27, 1989, following the rise of bus fares and then-president Carlos Andrés Pérez's announcement that the country had accepted the IMF's deficit-reduction austerity measures. The official death toll was 276 in those riots. Unofficial estimates run well over a thousand.

4F and 27N refer to the two unsuccessful coup attempts—the *intentonas*—led by middle-level, "populist" officers, on February 4 and November 27, 1992. Though the uprisings were quickly put down by the loyal officer corps, and the coup leaders remain in jail, most Venezuelans agree that the *intentonas*—especially 4F—proved successful in slowing down the country's neoliberal economic reforms. While the February coup attempt failed, says Pérez's first minister of industry,

Moisés Naím, it "mobilized other individuals and groups that had not been very active in the political debate, and soon thereafter, traditional politicians were put on the defensive."[6] Soon, the *paquete*, and not the coup, became the hotly debated issue. Many Venezuelans believe that then-president Pérez might not have been impeached for misappropriating $17.2 million in May 1993, were he not associated with the pain inflicted by his economic reforms.[7]

There are many explanations for the existence of Venezuela's economic crisis, which have more or less credibility depending on one's social situation and ideological predisposition: dependency on oil and consequent lack of planning; the foreign debt; corruption and the bloated state agencies; dependency on transnational capital; neoliberal export-oriented strategies. Several explanations are unique to Venezuela, but many are shared with other Latin American countries.

The explanations unique to Venezuela tend to revolve around the way the country had become accustomed to living off its oil rents, and the consequent creation of a "rentier mentality"—the generalized expectation of living off someone else's work and investment. In the old "rentier political model," the centralized state—frequently through its agents, the major political parties—distributed the national rent, and promoted national industrial development. While rentier politics created the important political expectation that the state should function as a repository of rights for the poor, these rights were accepted passively, without the active participation required of a truly democratic citizenry. The parties dominated political and social life, civil society was weak, and a "client-oriented style of politics became the rule."[8] Neoliberal economist Ricardo Hausmann's critique of this brand of "populism" is not without justification: "Citizens had a positive claim on the state to a decent standard of living, but no duties to contribute to collective spending.... Populism amounted to entitlements without duties, absolute rights with no trade-offs, redistribution without a budget constraint."[9] As state resources declined in the 1980s, the traditional parties lost credibility when they could no longer perform the only function expected of them: to deliver the goods.

In the 1950s, the rentier political model became associated with the import-substitution industrialization (ISI) model of development. ISI was an attempt to develop an internal market. It called for selective subsidies for industries which would produce for that internal market; the creation of popular purchasing power through policies that encouraged higher wages and salaries; and the broadening of that market through integration with other economies at similar levels of development. According to former industry minister Naím, the old ISI model "did create an industrial base, but it also created fertile conditions for major economic distortions to emerge."[10] More to the point, in a rentier setting, it created fertile conditions for the emergence of a state based on patron-client relations—the clientelistic state. By combining state planning with private profit-seeking, the Venezuelan model of ISI created a set of state-sanctioned oligopolies which were immune from competitive pressures, social responsibility, and democratic accountability.

More than anything else, it was the debt crisis of the 1980s that signalled the exhaustion of the rentier state. "More than fluctuating oil prices," says economist Luis Zambrano, "it's the excessive external debt, incurred in the 1970s, that forms the origin of Venezuela's economic problems."[11] Falling oil prices, together with rising international interest rates, transformed Venezuela's debt problem into a crisis. With export earnings falling and the cost of debt service rising, Venezuela transferred an estimated 54.8 percent of the country's export earnings to the exterior in the form of service payments on its $30 billion debt between 1982 and 1986. As investor confidence flagged, the Central Bank of Venezuela estimates that private investment fell from 24.1 percent of GNP in 1982 to 17.2 percent of (a lower) GNP in 1986, and that nearly $20 billion left the country over that period as capital flight.[12]

Venezuela, of course, was not alone in its mountain of debt. "The debt crisis," says Mexican political scientist Jorge Castañeda, "and its endless negotiations, together with the stepped up conditionality that each new agreement brought had dramatically weakened the so-called welfare state."[13] In any case, the well-being of Venezuela's rentier state—and its clients—was mortally damaged during the debt crisis. When oil prices collapsed in 1986, its fate was probably sealed.

Venezuela's State Office of Statistics and Information (OCEI) reports that in 1993, 8 million Venezuelans—about 40 percent of the population—were living in poverty, of whom nearly half were living in extreme poverty.[14] According to OCEI's figures, this is a jump from a poverty rate of 34 percent in 1986. Many studies put the number of the poor at about double the OCEI estimate. At a recent forum sponsored by the independent National Academy of Medicine, for example, it was estimated that Venezuela's "critical" poverty rate—those suffering from serious malnutrition—was about 40 percent, with another 40 percent living in more bearable, "relative" poverty.[15] While there are many ways to define and measure poverty, every estimate is dramatically rising.

The country's symptoms of poverty do not stem solely from falling revenues. Some may well stem in part from the inefficiencies of a corrupt and client-centered public sector. The World Bank reports, for example, that while Venezuela spends 20 percent of its central government budget on education—the highest percentage in South America—70 percent of those expenditures are for payroll and bureaucratic operations. Crumbling, dangerously overcrowded public schools have become emblematic of the bloated, inefficient state. The results are an 11 percent school-dropout rate, and a first-grade failure and repetition rate of 28 percent.[16]

Those children who remain in school have fewer teachers and less physical equipment to work with. The Caracas daily *El Nacional* reports that 42,000 teachers recently left their jobs, mostly to seek work in the country's burgeoning informal—off the books—sector. The shortage of nurses in public hospitals is a result of the same phenomenon. Nannies hired off the books, for example, earn higher salaries than the average $170 per month paid to public school teachers, or the similar amount paid to nurses in public hospitals.[17] By the most conservative estimates, 2.6 million people—about 38 percent of the labor force—work in the informal economy, about two thirds in the "commercial sector," mostly selling in the street.[18] While the *paquete* has exacerbated the situation, it is by no means to blame. When Carlos Andrés Pérez was elected in 1988, the swollen informal sector already accounted for 35.8 percent of Venezuela's workforce.[19]

By the mid-1980s, it had become clear that the country's political-economic crisis demanded a strong response. Two reform movements—having dramatically different consequences—found support within the government: decentralization of the political system, and privatization and deregulation of the economy. The one empowered politically, just as the other disempowered economically. This was—and remains—a volatile mixture: on the one hand, greater democracy and participation; on the other, fewer social rights and protections. Both were critiques of an increasingly closed and corrupt political-economic system. Neither was, however, a critique of the class determinants of that system. As Venezuela searched for a way out of its social crisis, it became a crucible—within the limits imposed by its class structure—of economic and political reform.

The Presidential Commission for the Reform of the State (COPRE), created in 1984, successfully pushed for reforms which opened up political culture: among them, the decentralization of powers to local communities, direct election of local and regional officials, the election of (some) congressional representatives by name instead of party slate, and democratic party primaries. These reforms have opened the political culture to the participation of outsiders, and have closed the divide between "civil" and "political" society.

The other major response to the crisis was the neoliberal *paquete*—officially called "*el gran viraje*," the great turnaround—introduced by the government of Carlos Andrés Pérez in 1989. The *paquete* sought to stabilize the economy at the same time as it opened and privatized it through restructuring. Stabilization measures fell in three categories: "getting prices right," balancing the fiscal budget, and establishing an "autonomous monetary authority." Getting prices right meant leaving things to the market: eliminating exchange-rate controls, interest-rate controls, and most private sector price controls. Balancing the budget meant cutting public spending, establishing the VAT, and raising the domestic prices of publicly produced goods.[20] Establishing an autonomous monetary authority meant separating the country's Central Bank governors from the direct political control of the electoral cycle. The idea was to "depoliticize" the use of monetary policy in order to accomplish some "necessary but unpopular" tasks—initially to slow the growth of the money supply—impose a regime of "tight money"—in order to stabilize and build confidence in the bolívar.[21] Taken as a whole, these measures amounted to an austerity program: the working population saw its purchasing power cut, while fewer services were provided by the state.

The major structural reforms attempted to make the economy more export-oriented and driven by private capital. To this end, trade rules were liberalized, financial markets deregulated, direct foreign investment welcomed and promoted, and many state companies privatized.[22] The elimination of exchange-rate controls led to a devaluation of the bolívar, a further reduction of internal purchasing power, and a boost to the export sector.[23] The *paquete* also abandoned subsidies in favor of "more focused efforts directly targeting the most vulnerable groups of society."[24] In many cases, this has meant the privatization of social services to religious groups and nongovernmental organizations (NGOs).

The popular sectors were the hardest hit by the price rises. Because of the oligopolistic structure of Venezuela's private sector, the elimination of price controls sent prices not to market-driven competitive levels, but to company-set oligopoly mark-up levels. In the most egregious example, the average price of medicines rose 513 percent between 1989 and 1991.[25] The Pérez government never developed adequate policies to cushion the impact of the *paquete* on the poor, or to distribute fairly the burdens of sacrifice. Its "trickle-down" assumption was that "social equity was a subproduct of economic growth."[26] Most Venezuelans had been so hard hit by the declining incomes of the 1980s that even the slightest increases in prices stretched their family budgets—and political tolerance—to the breaking point.

The *paqueteros* had always said that their reforms would exacerbate some hardships in the short run, but that the resulting economic growth would benefit everybody in a few years' time. Now, however, perhaps linked to the country's unrest, the *paquete's* short spurt of impressive economic growth has come to a grinding halt. After three years in which economic growth averaged about 8 percent—the highest rate of growth in Latin America—Venezuela's GNP declined in 1993 by 2.2 percent, the fiscal deficit grew to $1.9 billion, and the rate of inflation rose to 46 percent, the second highest level in the country's history.[27]

The *paquete* failed because it began to destroy the social protections that must accompany the development of capitalism. Pérez, an international figure always mindful of the winds of history, positioned himself on what he perceived to be the winning side of late-twentieth century global politics. His announcement to the world was that "painful transitions toward free markets pay off, and that a democratic regime can indeed survive the unpopular decisions required by economic reforms."[28] But if *painful* transitions are to pay off in a *democratic* setting, the pain must be perceived as somehow shared, and be accompanied by some perceptible benefits. If the center-left is to administer capitalism any differently from the right, it must do so in a way that builds and maintains not just a safety net for the poorest, but the bonds of solidarity that come from sharing the hardships and benefits of daily life. The free market—for all its dynamism—destroys those bonds. The *paquete* may have been technically impeccable, but it didn't emphasize distribution, and ignored popular expectations and the lack of real political consensus.[29]

The *paquete* also failed because it misinterpreted the fall of Soviet socialism. At the end of the cold war, the *paqueteros* thought they saw the unambiguous victory of "free markets" and "democracy" over state intervention and authoritarian/totalitarian governments. According to this simplistic reading of events, Germany, (Thatcher's) England, and Japan all rose to power on the backs of autonomous private investors supported by states which only set the rules of the game and then went away, while

Poland, (the Labor Party's) England, and Venezuela remained bogged down in the old state-run, inefficient economies. Not only in Venezuela, but throughout Latin America, says Jorge Castañeda, obvious historical distinctions were lost "in the ideological fervor of the early 1990s."[30]

Naím confirms this conflation of models, even though he denies its ideological ramifications. He says of Pérez that following the collapse of the Eastern bloc, "profound disillusionment with the possibilities of state action in a developing country, more than trust in the workings of the free market, seemed to be the underlying thrust of his... economic thinking."[31] Aided by the proliferation of U.S.-supported free-market think tanks, Pérez's thinking was not atypical in late 1980s/early 1990s Latin America. All the models which involved some state intervention were—in a neoliberal sleight-of-hand—lumped into one, and that one model was declared a failure.

The conflation of the problem leads, of course, to conflated solutions. Economist Victor Fajardo persuasively argues that one of the *paquete*'s problems was that it was designed not for Venezuela, but for a textbook country: a country with autonomous, risk-taking entrepreneurs, perfectly competitive markets, and abstract, malleable poor people.[32] The problem is, while each Latin American country's development strategy had its own internal contradictions, the collapse of each economy in the 1980s was part of a continental trend, in large part due to the debt crisis. The continental trend provided an opening for the continental solution—sometimes referred to as the "Washington consensus"—of the market-oriented adjustment of each country's economic structure.[33] The Washington consensus—"structural adjustment"—is cut from very general, abstract cloth, seldom taking local conditions into account. Pérez' ministers frequently argued the specific conditions, but typically applied the generic rules.

In this ever-worsening economic climate, the maverick, grandfatherly Rafael Caldera was elected president; Causa R, the workers' party, captured 22 percent of the presidential vote, and dissidents in general made strong showings in the congressional races. Caldera had campaigned on an anti-*paquete* platform launched by his dramatic televised indictment of the hardship-generating reforms on the day the first coup attempt was put down. But it will not be enough for Caldera to oppose the neoliberal programs of his predecessor. He must make good on his inaugural promises to institute a progressive set of alternatives to the VAT. He must figure out a way to cut deficits without making the price of gasoline—estimated to be well below the cost of production—and everything that flows from oil too expensive for the population. And above all, he must stimulate growth and development under the aegis of social solidarity and protection.

As reforms are devised, floated and put into practice, the roles of the state, private capital, local self-government and civil society are all up for grabs. In a country where the majority of the population is poor, and with socialism off the agenda for now, there are currently three positions in the national debate. From right to left, the first position calls for the imposition of a neoliberal program *à la* Pinochet or Fujimori. This position is usually expressed *sub rosa*, but one cannot avoid it in conversations with members of the country's business community. The second position is neoliberalism with a human face: a better safety net, more efficient targeting of social services to the neediest, and a convincing explanation to the poor of the virtues of market-oriented reform. This position is associated with the country's traditional parties, AD (Acción Democrática) and COPEI. These two positions conform to the neoliberal logic that the pain is inevitable, and that in order to attract private investment, the pain cannot be directed to the wealthy. Thus, the reasoning goes, the pain must either be explained or imposed upon the poor by a strong and determined state.

That leaves a third, social democratic project: the incorporation of the poor not simply for purposes of dialogue, but in the logic of the plan itself. If a genuine neoliberal program can only be imposed by authoritarian means—on a continuum running perhaps from Salinas to Pinochet—the only democratic alternative currently on the table is some form of "protected capitalism," or social democracy. This is the position taken by most of the socialists and dissident social Christians in the coalition around Caldera, and by his likely congressional allies, Causa R. If some version of a social democratic strategy does emerge from the Caldera Administration, the model will inevitably draw upon the past "structuralist" ISI models: incorporation of the poor through wage-led growth, development of the internal market, and selective protection of nationally critical firms and industries. It will also draw upon some elements of the *paquete*: the development of micro-industry, selective privatization, and a much greater openness to the international economy. Because of the small size of Latin American markets, ISI always implied a model of Latin American economic integration, and this will remain on a social-democratic agenda. The model will recognize private capital as the motor force of the economy, but a force to be guided and reined in by a democratic, decentralized public sector. Guided by the belief that growth will produce a better distribution if it goes into the formation of human capital, the model will attempt to increase productivity by supporting education, training, and health care.[34]

In contrast to other Latin American experiences, Venezuela's political reforms have produced *more* democracy, precisely at the time the austerity-producing economic measures were introduced. This has resulted in continuing social and political clashes. The active involvement of popular organizations, independent unions and political parties not controlled by elites may yet yield a democratic and popular solution. Much depends on the political role played by the incoming Caldera coalition, and by Causa R. The center-left must find creative, humane, and democratic solutions to the short-run problems of fiscal balance and inflation, and to the long-run problem of economic growth. The old paradigm of the populist rentier state has not yet been fully superceded. This "paradigm crisis" may become a creative one as decentralization creates a new sense of the public sector. The shape of the new political system will play a major role in determining how Venezuela's—and Latin America's—ongoing development crisis is resolved.

Notes

1. "22 muertos este fin de semana," *El Nacional*, 17 January 1994; and "Mas muertes violentas que en cualquier guerra," *Inter Press Service*, 27 December 1993.
2. "Mas muertes violentas que en cualquier guerra," *Inter Press Service*, 27 December 1993.
3. Victor Fajardo, "Colapso del Paquete Económico: Causas, Efectos y Perspectivas, Venezuela 1989-92," *Cuadernos del CENDES*, vol. 20, May-August 1992.
4. See Gustavo Márquez et al., "Fiscal Policy and Income Distribution in Venezuela," in Ricardo Hausmann and Roberto Rigobón, eds., *Government Spending and Income Distribution in Latin America* (Washington, DC: Johns Hopkins Press, 1993), 152-56.
5. Rafael Caldera, quoted in "El país requiere de un país que gobierne dentro del estado de derecho," *Venpress*, 2 February 1994.
6. Moisés Naím, "The Political Management of Radical Economic Change: Lessons from the Venezuelan Experience," in Joseph S. Tulchin and Gary Bland, eds., *Venezuela in the Wake of Radical Reform*, (Boulder, CO: Lynne Rienner Publishers, 1993), 161.
7. See Steve Ellner, "A Tolerance Worn Thin: Corruption in the Age of Austerity," *NACLA Report on the Americas*, vol. 27, no. 3, November-December 1993.
8. Carlos Blanco, "The Reform of the State in Latin American Perspective," *Venezuela in the Wake of Radical Reform*, 100.
9. Ricardo Hausmann, "Venezuela," in John Williamson, ed., *Latin American*

Adjustment: How Much Has Happened? (Washington, DC: Institute for International Economics, 1990), 224.

10. Moisés Naím, "The Launching of Radical Policy Changes," *Venezuela in the Wake of Radical Reform*, 34.

11. Luis Zambrano Sequín, "Sobre lo que hemos hecho y aún podemos hacer en política económica," in Andrés Serbin, et al., eds., *Venezuela: la democracia bajo presión* (Caracas: Editorial Nueva Sociedad, 1993), 89.

12. Luis Zambrano Sequín, "Sobre lo que hemos hecho," 91.

13. Jorge Castañeda, *Utopia Unarmed: The Latin American Left After the Cold War*, (New York: Alfred A. Knopf, 1993), 245.

14. "Venezuela: pobreza agobía a mas de ocho millones de personas," *Inter Press Service*, 22 December 1993.

15. "Al 40% aumentó cifra de pobreza crítica," *El Nacional*, 25 November 1993.

16. For World Bank findings see "Venezuela: sistema educativa es caro e ineficiente," *Inter Press Service*, 29 December 1993. Also see Jere R. Behrman, "Investing in Human Resources," Inter-American Development Bank, *Economic and Social Progress in Latin America: 1993 Report* (Washington, DC: Johns Hopkins Press, 1993), 214 and 218.

17. "42 mil docentes han desertado de la profesión," *El Nacional*, 15 January 1994.

18. See, for example, OCEI statistics cited by Victor Fajardo, "Colapso del paquete económico," 51.

19. Ibid.

20. Naím, "The Launching of Radical Policy Changes," 53; also see Hausmann, "Venezuela," 224-244.

21. Ruth de Krivoy, "The Changing Role of Central Banks in Latin America: the Venezuelan Case," address to the Council of the Americas, New York City, 10 November 1993.

22. For the full range of measures, see Hausmann, "Venezuela"; Naím, "The Launching of Radical Policy Changes"; and various bulletins published by CONAPRI, the Council for the Promotion of Investment (Caracas).

23. Luis Zambrano, "Sobre lo que hemos hecho," 93.

24. Naím, "The Launching of Radical Policy Changes," 53.

25. Victor Fajardo, "El colapso del paquete económico," 41.

26. Ibid.

27. Inter-American Development Bank, *Economic and Social Progress.*

28. Pérez speech to business and political leaders in Davos, Switzerland on 3 February 1992, the eve of the first attempted coup. Quoted in Naím, "The Political Management of Radical Economic Change," 147.

29. Luis Zambrano, "Sobre lo que hemos hecho," 94-95.

30. Jorge Castañeda, *Utopia Unarmed*, 246.

31. Naím, "The Launching of Radical Policy Changes," 52.

32. Victor Fajardo, "Colapso de paquete económico."

33. See John Williamson, "The Washington Consensus," in Williamson, ed., *Latin American Adjustment.*

34. See, for example, Victor Fajardo, "Colapso del Paquete Económico"; Luis Zambrano, "Sobre lo que hemos hecho," 97; and Jere R. Behrman, "Investing in Human Resources."

8

Brazil:
Cardoso Among the Technopols

José Luiz Fiori

In January 1993, almost two years before Mexico's economic drift became every financial risk analyst's worst nightmare, Washington's prestigious Institute for International Economics (IIE) brought together more than one hundred specialists from the United States and a number of Asian, African, and Latin American countries to discuss a document by one of the institute's senior fellows, John Williamson, "In Search of a Manual for Technopols." The discussion took place in the context of an international seminar on "The Political Economy of Policy Reform."

The two-day gathering brought together executives from governments, the multilateral banks, and private businesses as well as a select handful of academics. Discussions of economic stabilization and reform programs turned on the need for "the most favorable conditions and action-guidelines enabling 'technopols' to garner the political support needed to make such programs work," the delicate terms implicit in what Williamson years ago termed the "Washington consensus."

This illustrative catch phrase, in common use today internationally, refers to a single adjustment plan for the world's peripheral economies, formulated by International Monetary Fund (IMF) and World Bank strategists. So far, the plan has been implemented in sixty-plus nations. The plan seeks to attain uniformity in national economic policies, sometimes by placing those policies under the direct management of IMF and World Bank technical staff. This has happened in many African nations, beginning with Somalia in the early 1980s. Elsewhere, in countries like Bolivia, Poland, and even Russia, the strategy has been broadened to include participation by leading economists, mostly from U.S. universities.

A third option applies to nations with more fully developed bureaucratic structures. These countries employ native economists, Williamson's "technopols," who are not only capable of ensuring proper administration of their free-market policies, but also able to garner popular support for the same consensus agenda. These have included Mexico's Pedro Aspe, Carlos Salinas, and Ernesto Zedillo; Argentina's Domingo Cavallo; Russia's Yegor Gaidar; Taiwan's Lee Teng-hui; India's Manmohan Singh; and even Turkey's Turgut Ozal. There has also been a long line of Brazilian technopols, beginning with Zélia Cardoso and Antônio Kandir, followed by Pedro Malan, Persio Arida, Edmar Bacha, and Gustavo Franco.

The foundation of this "New Colonialism," as *Newsweek* solemnly termed it in its August 1, 1994 issue, is a three-step strategic plan. First, national macroeconomic stabilization must be assured, with absolute priority given to producing a fiscal surplus. Invariably, this implies reorganizing inter-governmental fiscal relationships, and restructuring government social welfare mechanisms. The plan's second phase stresses what in World Bank parlance are termed "structural reforms," encompassing financial and commercial reforms, deregulation of markets, and the privatization of state-run enterprises. The third stage is supposed to bring renewed investment and economic growth.

By the early 1990s, a host of pessimistic policy evaluations by both the IMF and the World Bank singled out the crucial importance of the "political factor" in the success or failure of programs. This new concern on the part of intellectuals and managers of the "Washington consensus" explains not only the timeliness of the Williamson seminar, hailed as a benchmark in the treatment of the issue, but also the participation of two political scientists, Joan Nelson and Stephan Haggard, the authors of the most complete comparative studies in the United States on the implementation of such adjustment programs.

In his introductory document, Williamson clearly acknowledges the perverse economic and social consequences of austerity and liberalization policies on target nations' economies and populations, as well as the logic that makes it difficult to elect a minimally stable government. Working from these premises, Williamson suggests several political tactics and pretexts for making the electorate accept the social devastation invariably wrought by the neoliberal program as both temporarily necessary, and undertaken for the greater long-term good. The programs are deemed more likely to succeed when their implementation follows some catastrophe, such as war or hyperinflation, of a magnitude capable of undermining any and all resistance; when technopols are pitted against a discredited or disorganized opposition; and where, in addition, strong leaders can "insulate" the programs from social issues.

In all of the cases it has been necessary to form a political coalition strong enough to take power at the most favorable moment, and to wield it over long periods at the head of governments with solid parliamentary majorities. Indeed, such legislative majorities are now considered essential to the "credibility" required by the risk analysts at the handful of giant financial consulting firms which in effect control global movements of capital.

Fernando Henrique Cardoso, Brazil's recently elected president, came to power with the backing of a neoliberal elite determined to enforce precisely this hegemonic stabilization program. Midway through his campaign for the presidency, Cardoso, then finance minister, launched a tight-money anti-inflation program called the Real Plan, named after the new currency. The plan brought inflation under control for the first time in years, and gave Cardoso the momentum he needed to capture the presidency. Considering the umbilical linkage between the Real Plan's stated long-term strategic objectives—obligatory reforms to a gamut of fiscal and monetary policies, liberalized commercial and financial regulations, privatization of state-run concerns, economic opening, and renewed economic growth—and the implied corollary requirement of long-term political stability, the plan appears to most observers to be simply another offspring of the larger family of stabilization packages discussed at IIE's Washington seminar.

Though Cardoso achieved prominence as a Marxist sociologist in the 1960s and 1970s, it can be argued—even though his early works contain a vehement, well-reasoned indictment of the course he has come to take as president—that the trajectory of his intellectual career contains no major breaks. His early scholarship includes some of the seminal work on dependency theory, written from the mid-1960s to the early 1970s, when he was exiled in Chile, and associated with the UN's Economic Commission on Latin America (ECLA). One can trace the logical path that led him from his theoretical contributions on the nature of Brazilian industrialists, and the fundamentally dependent nature of Brazilian capitalism, to his current position in political and ideological struggle.

Cardoso's academic work can be summarized as a tireless search for the connections between the interests and objectives which exist under given "historico-structural" situations, and the political strategies that are constructed by social groups and their political coalitions. With this aim, Cardoso was one of the first to examine and conclude forcefully, as early as 1963, that Brazil's "national industrial bourgeoisie was precluded by structural impediments from playing the role assigned it by nationalist-populist ideology." He argued that the industrial bourgeoisie had abdicated any pretensions to exercising full hegemony over society, accepting its role as junior partner to Western capitalism. This finding enabled Cardoso to discover very early on that while the Brazilian bourgeoisie may be associated, depending on the circumstances, with a broad range of ideological positions, in the end it always supported enhanced capital mobility, and the geopolitical and economic developments which led to the increasing internationalization of capital.

This discovery was directly responsible for Cardoso's next and most original step. For Cardoso, peripheral capitalism was defined by the lack of convertible currencies and the lack of endogenous capability for technological innovation. "Dependent status," on the other hand, was defined by the specific way in which national entrepreneurs were associated with international capital and with the state. This three-way relationship among national and international capital and the state cushioned the "internationalization of the domestic market." By the 1970s, multinational corporations had taken the lead in almost all sectors featuring state-of-the-art technologies, coming to account for approximately 40 percent of Brazil's industrial output.

It would hardly be a stretch to extend and properly update Cardoso's analysis to fit the current "structural situation," defined by a more advanced internationalization of capitalism, associated with an increase in Brazil's internal "sensitivity" to changes in the world economy. Indeed, the new economic conjuncture goes beyond—though does not invalidate—the essence of Cardoso's writings of the 1960s and 1970s. In a recent article called "Reform and Imagination" which appeared in the daily *Folha de São Paulo* on July 10, 1994, Cardoso exuberantly displays his historical materialist sensibilities when he states that he continues "to believe that globalization of the economy is a direct consequence of a new mode—flowing from a new technology—of production." His concrete grasp of the facts, however, surprisingly ignores any political and power dimension in the globalization process. He calls any conceptual resistance to the dominant model "devoid of any practical application." He decries charges that he has a political connection with the so-called "new colonialism" as "conspiratorial stereotypes." He recognizes that he places conditions on his ability to govern by adopting a policy of uniform stabilization, reforming the state, and attempting to attain a "social democracy capable of reducing the inequalities of a mass society." Finally, he refuses to admit his obvious swing to the right, seeking to explain away, in particular, the most hardcore members of his coalition, the Liberal Front Party (PFL), principal heir to the spoils of the successive military governments. In his view, the PFL has freed itself from its past, and no longer represents traditional clientelism.

The key issue is that, contrary to what Cardoso thinks, globalization of the economy is not just a consequence of technological development or the competitive evolution of markets. Globalization is increasingly proving to be a political, cultural, and economic reality whose origins and consequences are more complex because of its many noneconomic dimensions. While globalization emerged behind the backs of many producers and governments, it is also the result of political and economic decisions made, in an increasingly focused manner, by a relatively small number of global oligopolies, banks, and a few national governments. It appears, however, that neoliberals, for obvious reasons, as well as some of the old structuralists and traumatized leftists, have tremendous difficulty assimilating the importance of the political factor in the origin and unfinished history of this process of change that capitalism is undergoing.

In many ways, therefore, Cardoso is right when he says that at no point has he renounced or cast aside his sociological analysis. What he has done is perhaps more profound. He has chosen a new ethical and political option by abandoning his reformist idealism to embrace the position of his former object of study, the Brazilian business class. Simultaneously, he assumes as an unquestionable fact the current international relations of power and dependency. After two decades of critical political life, Cardoso is offering himself as the "*condottiere* of the industrial bourgeoisie," capable of redirecting it to its manifest destiny as the lesser, dependent partner of Western capitalism, with new life breathed into it by the third technological revolution and by financial globalization.

His painful letting go of his old idealist and reformist positions, expressed in his frequent discomfort with the foibles of neoliberalism and his irritation whenever the issue is raised, may be less a move to the right than a hitherto unimaginable naivete. This naivete, in turn, is the result of an even more unimaginable mistaken assessment of the process and programmatic content of the Spanish social democracy of Felipe González, which was always the great model that has guided Cardoso's political history. Cardoso may believe that the "infallible combination" of his capacity for political wizardry and the materialist forces of historical inevitability make it possible to avoid having to first reach par with Mexico or Argentina before attaining the level of Spain. To analyze Cardoso's future, it is therefore important to be familiar with the history of Spain's "real social democracy." A close look at that history indicates that Cardoso is mistaken in his idealized vision of what Spain was and still is.

From the standpoint of policies and consequences, the "real social-liberalism" achieved by Spain's "socialist" government after twelve years of *pactación social* is indistinguishable from the neoliberalism of Great Britain under Margaret Thatcher. The Spanish "economic miracle" is summarized, in chronological terms, in eight years of recession (1977-1985) and four years of growth (1986-1990) with a common objective: reducing inflation and promoting economic growth. The issue of renewed growth, however, was left almost entirely to the vagaries of the marketplace. From 1982 to 1986, the dominant orthodoxy suggested devaluation of the exchange rate, high interest rates, clamps on wages, and fiscal and monetary austerity. These policies were implemented so rigorously that the recession dragged on until 1985, when inflation slowly receded into the single digits.

The entry of Spain into the European Economic Community (EEC) in 1986 reoriented González's political-economic strategy towards the new global orthodoxy: economic opening and deregulation, which provoked an overvaluation of the exchange rate. This was responsible for Spain's mounting trade deficit, financed by the import of short- and long-term capital attracted by extremely high interest rates in relation to the average in the EEC. This situation of external disequilibrium was further aggravated with the entry of Spain into the European Monetary System (EMS) in 1989, which was the Spanish equivalent of adopting dollarization in Brazil. In addition to working towards the goal of stanching inflation, the government under González embraced new orthodox policies: structural reforms of the labor market and social security, together with deregulation, liberalization, and reduction in the size of the public sector.

What were the lessons of the rapid economic growth Spain experienced from 1986 to 1990? First, this growth was above all an effect of entering the EEC and the consequent explosion in external—mostly speculative—investment. From 1986 to 1990, 10 billion pesetas flowed into Spain, ten times more than in the previous five-year period. Of this sum, 30 percent was used to buy local firms; 58 percent for investments in portfolios of stocks, bonds, and public debt on the securities markets; and the rest was earmarked mainly for the purchase of real estate. This process brought about a revaluation of real and financial assets, increased the personal wealth of their owners, and multiplied urban housing costs, but did little in the way of contributing to activities capable of generating lasting and stable economic progress. In the same period, Spain spent less on human resources—about 0.08 percent of GDP—than any other country of Europe, except Luxembourg; and its investment in research and development was no more than 0.68 percent of GDP, superior only to Portugal.

The figures show that Spain ceased being an industrial economy. During this period, and increasingly in the 1980s and 1990s, industry's share of GDP in Spain fell from 32.9 percent to 24.2 percent, employing just 27 percent of the labor force, while the participation of services increased from 47 percent to 63 percent of GDP, today employing about 60 percent of the population. What industry remains is divided between small and medium enterprises, which account for about 90 percent of industrial output, and a dynamic core of multinationals, which accounts for the lion's share of exports. According to data published by the *Economist* in October 1994, Spain, of all the countries belonging to the Organization of Economic Cooperation and Development (OECD), sold the largest number of firms to foreigners between 1989 and 1993, because as the economy opened up, Spanish capital migrated to the service sector. According to the World Economic Forum, Spain is now among the least competitive nations of the OECD.

This scheme that has provoked the deindustrialization of Spain without attaining greater competitiveness, is an essential part of the strategy adopted by the González government. It is also automatically accepted as part of the logic of Cardoso's plan. Spain has been a pioneer, for more than a decade, of this "orthodox swindle." The *tucanos brasileiros*—Brazilian social democrats—should learn from the experience of Spanish socio-liberalism that inflation never decreases to levels capable of halting deindustrialization and denationalization. The Spanish economy, hindered as it was by high interest rates and an overvalued currency, was unable to achieve competitiveness.

Now if that was the economic result of "real social liberalism," what can be said about its social facet? Here too the facts are eloquent. In twelve years of rule by Felipe González, social spending increased from 19.42 percent to 21.37 percent of GDP, a minimal increase that keeps Spain among the lowest ranks of the OECD countries. As for income distribution, the poorest 10 percent of all families increased their share from 2.41 percent in 1980 to 2.85 percent in 1992, and the highest 10 percent of all incomes saw their share decline in the same period from 29.23 percent to 28.01 percent. Nevertheless, the wage share of GDP fell from 51.2 percent in 1980 to 46.1 percent in 1991, while unemployment, about 6 percent at the outset of the González administration, has skyrocketed to 24 percent of the adult labor force today, reaching the imponderable level of 37.9 percent among people under twenty-five years of age. Of the population between the ages of 30 and 55, 800,000 of the 3.4 million unemployed are illiterate or have little if any training, which makes it very difficult for them to hold jobs offered in the "restructured" sector of the economy. To round out the social picture of the "Spanish miracle," one should recall that beginning in 1992, the Economic Plan for Convergence, which was designed to complement the Maastricht agreements, brought to the forefront of Spanish political debate the "de-universalization" of social security. This new situation led a high-ranking member of González's party to note recently that "Spain has begun to turn back without ever having gone forward."

This journey through the history of "real social liberalism" in Spain demonstrates that the current hegemonic model has a long history and has been clothed in a variety of garbs. It also suggests that from the standpoint of his personal political strategy, Cardoso has proven to be an applied and rigorous disciple of González. He got ahead of himself on just one point: from the outset, notwithstanding his sleight of hand, he has been allied with the right. This alliance led Antônio Carlos Magalhaes—the conservative PFL leader who is one of the pillars of Cardoso's coalition—to remark with sarcastic pleasure to the president's chorus of Penelopes, that they are weeping over someone who never existed. "Behind the brilliant Marxist sociologist," suggests Magalhaes, "was always an elitist and a man of the right."

Cardoso wanted to leap straight to the stage of the idealized and seductive elite of socialist technopols commanded by González without going through the Mexican experience, disregarding the fact that except for the pomp, the formula was essentially the same as Mexico's. But the irresistible emanations from Washington and the need to win international trust required that he sing praises to the glory of Carlos Salinas de Gortari. In the key statements of his political history, for example his farewell speech as he left the Senate in 1994, Cardoso elevated Mexico and to a lesser extent Argentina to the status of models pointing the way to possible success. Mexico was brought in as a partner to the North American bloc, and had a single-party government for more than sixty years, making it the darling of ten out of ten risk analysts specializing in the "emerging" countries. In the end, of course, the country led the "credibility" formulation into a paroxysm.

The cherished ideal of the technopol community turned out to be a house of cards built on a seismic foundation. The Mexican collapse has been a sort of chronicle of a death foretold, in which the same variables touted as indicating the success of the stabilization program—total financial deregulation, controlled overvaluation of the currency (the narrow-band floating regime), absolute trade opening, and a deficit in the external current accounts (8.5 percent of GDP) increased according to the formulaic recommendations of the new globalizing order—are now crucified as the cause of death. Actually, Mexico was already agonizing socially and politically—Chiapas did not come out of thin air—when the bubble of prosperity ephemerally provided by the dominant model of stabilization burst. Statistics and reality were back-to-back; the debacle was only a question of time. But neither the intellectuals of the Washington consensus nor the pragmatic social liberals were capable of recognizing it in time.

Now there is no turning back. The end of the Mexican dream will inevitably condition the path taken not only in the short run, but also in the medium and long term in all the adjustment programs, including Brazil's. This will occur despite the understandable effort of opinion makers to try to convince the risk analysts that even though their stabilization programs are strikingly similar, their countries are different: Mexico is not Brazil; Brazil is not Spain; Spain is not Mexico, etc. At the nerve center of the consensus, the tendency is to forge full speed ahead with the adjustments. Rolling back now would be a disaster. In this regard, IMF Director Michel Camdessus affirmed that the choice is between "advancing or advancing." In Brazil, Cardoso and his tech-nopols indicate that they understand Camdessus's message and will shorten the time period for undertaking the "structural reforms" like the rest of the herd. What took over twelve years in Mexico must be done in two years in Brazil in the name of "credibility."

As of this writing, however, a very discreet tone can be heard that is out of tune with the resounding neoliberal symphony, bringing some encouragement to those who believe that history is far from reaching its end. At ECLA, where Cardoso wrote—with Enzo Faletto—the classic *Dependency and Development in Latin America* in 1971 during his Chilean exile, he recognized, in a speech this past February, "the arrogance, insensitivity, political dimension, and lack of understanding on the part of the IMF for the democracies, values, and beliefs of our society." Perhaps it was just the Chilean air, or perhaps even a spectacular artifice of illusion. But I prefer to think that under the emotional outpourings of his re-encounter with the land where he made his most important theoretical contributions, Cardoso rediscovered some unfeigned part of his idealism and was moved to dance a last tango of rejection of the neoliberal onslaught.

Note

The author would like to thank Luiz César Faro for his collaboration.

9

Feeding the Global Supermarket

Lori Ann Thrupp

Growing global trade is bringing North American shoppers a year-round supply of fresh mangos, artichokes, broccoli, and roses, flown in from Latin America and the Caribbean. In the countries of origin, production of these fashionable "nontraditional" agro-exports (NTAEs) is booming. Hoping to overcome economic stagnation and to add diversity to "traditional" agro-exports like bananas, coffee, and sugarcane, international aid agencies and local governments have been promoting these products in Latin America over the last decade. The NTAE strategy is a key part of trade liberalization and structural-adjustment policies.

The growth of nontraditional exports has had bittersweet outcomes. Among the positive effects, these products have proven very profitable for foreign investors, some enterprises in the South, and transnational food corporations. At the same time, they satisfy the appetites of Northern consumers. On the "bitter" side, NTAEs have considerable economic, social, and environmental costs, repeating patterns of previous agro-export sectors. The problems are particularly serious for small-scale farmers. Although the NTAE boom has been called a "success" using macroeconomic indicators, a closer look reveals symptoms of unsustainability and inequity.

The region's agrarian structure has historically been characterized by an inequitable distribution of resources. Large numbers of people, especially indigenous peoples, have been excluded from the benefits of economic growth and marginalized on unproductive lands. In Central America, for example, large farms (more than one hundred acres), although representing only 7 percent of the total operations, control about 73 percent of the total agricultural land; by contrast, small farms (under five acres), although representing 78 percent of the total number of farms, occupy only 11 percent of the total land.[1] In some areas of Latin America, this dualism is being broken down, yet the polarity still prevails in the region.

Agriculture has formed the foundation for Latin American and Caribbean economies for centuries. Coffee, bananas, and sugarcane were the main agricultural exports for most countries. Large plantations of these commodities date back to the 1700s and 1800s. Over time, countries expanded into cotton, beef, and cacao for export. During the 1960s and 1970s, although most countries adopted an inward-oriented model of import-substitution industrialization (ISI), they continued to depend largely on export agriculture, even into the 1980s and 1990s.

In many countries, agro-exports occupy the largest portions of agricultural land. Much of this agribusiness is foreign-owned, especially in Central America. The main features of the agro-export economy include dominance of large-scale monocultural plantations, high inputs of chemicals, dependency on volatile Northern markets, and the exploitation of both natural resources and low-wage labor. While traditional exports have enjoyed dynamic growth and high profitability over time, these conditions have left a legacy of short-lived export "booms" followed by economic "busts." They have also caused degradation of natural resources, exploited labor, and exacerbated inequities.

During the early 1980s, the region suffered a serious economic crisis. Dependency on a small set of traditional exports made the Latin American and Caribbean economies vulnerable and unstable. Declining commodity prices, global recession, declining terms of trade, and trade protectionism cut into the region's economic earnings. In response to the crisis, most of the region diversified into nontraditional, high-value products.

The purpose of NTAE promotion policies and programs, from the perspectives of development agencies and governments, is to generate foreign exchange for repaying the debt, diversify the economy to reduce dependence on low-priced traditional exports, increase agribusiness and export earnings, generate employment, and in general, revitalize economic growth. In Colombia and Bolivia, where narcotics production is prevalent, development agencies are eager to develop NTAEs as high-value alternatives to coca.

Chile and Mexico were pioneers in the NTAE sector. Their movement into this sector preceded the regional diversification of the 1980s and 1990s. Between 1962 and 1988, Chile's fruit exports expanded twenty-six-fold, with earnings growing from $19.9 million to $473 million (in constant 1985 dollars).[2] Following a similar model, Mexico's fresh vegetable sector was developed by U.S. transnational companies in the 1960s. This was followed by the rapid expansion in the country of large agribusinesses in strawberries and tomatoes for export to the United States in the late 1970s. Recently, the most remarkable agricultural growth in Latin America has been in such high-value crops as flowers, fresh and processed fruits (particularly mangos, melon, pineapples, passion fruit, and berries), and vegetables (such as broccoli, snow peas, asparagus, mini-squash, and artichokes).

The growth of NTAEs since the first half of the 1980s in Latin America and the Caribbean has been strongly supported by international financial agencies, particularly the World Bank and the International Monetary Fund, and by the U.S. Agency for International Development (USAID). For example, in fiscal year 1992, USAID spent nearly $119 million on agribusiness worldwide, the large majority of which was for nontraditional crops.[3]

Local governments have also established a variety of policy reforms and institutional support for NTAEs since the late 1980s. These include export facilitation procedures, new tax policies intended to stimulate NTAE growth, and with the assistance of international financial agencies, increased credit for NTAEs.[4] Policies and programs have also been developed to improve capacities for marketing, transport, and infrastructure for NTAEs. These include advertising and publicity campaigns, trade fairs, quality control, provision of price information, setting up joint ventures or trading companies, and helping to establish cold-storage facilities and port warehouses.

Innovations in products, production processes, and distribution systems (mainly through investments of foreign capital), and the increasing globalization of transnational agribusinesses have also favored growth in this sector.[5] International information and communication systems also facilitate efficient product turnover and help minimize losses mainly for large producers who have access to such networks. Additional supply-side inducements for investment in NTAEs are the conventional conditions of "comparative advantage" in tropical countries, including relatively low labor and land rent costs compared to those in Northern countries, and favorable climatic conditions and tropical soils.[6]

International and regional trade agreements, particularly the Caribbean Basin Initiative, established in 1983, the Generalized System of

Preferences of 1976, and the Andean Trade Preference Act, passed in 1991, provide influential export incentives. They allow products to enter the U.S. market duty-free or under reduced tariffs.[7] The provisions of the North American Free Trade Agreement and General Agreement on Tariffs and Trade also encourage expansion of agricultural exports, mainly by reducing trade barriers that affect vegetable and fruit markets.

The growth rate of the nontraditional agro-export industry has been impressive. From the mid-to-late 1980s, NTAEs grew 222 percent in Chile, and 348 percent in Costa Rica.[8] In Paraguay, the value of NTAEs nearly tripled during the 1980s, and in Guatemala, the value of NTAEs more than doubled between 1986 to 1990.[9] Of course, NTAEs still represent a relatively small proportion of exports compared to the traditional exports from Latin America. It is unlikely that they will ever (nor are they intended to) approach the values of coffee, cotton, beef, and bananas. The net revenues and returns per acre of NTAEs are, however, remarkably high, especially compared to traditional staple foods. For example, world prices for sorghum, maize, and wheat in recent years have ranged from $75 to $175 per metric ton, while many NTAE fresh fruit and vegetable products have international prices of $500 or more per metric ton.[10]

Many producers have enjoyed unprecedented revenues from these new crops, which has translated into increased foreign-exchange earnings and rising GDP. These economic benefits appear to be working towards structural-adjustment aims. The growth of NTAEs has also spawned the growth of numerous businesses for transport, supplies, packaging, marketing, and intermediary brokers for NTAEs.

The main beneficiaries of NTAE growth are large companies, which include both transnational corporations and large national and foreign investors. Many of the crops are highly technology- and capital-intensive, which usually limits them to wealthy enterprises. In Central America, for example, multinational corporations account for approximately 25 percent of the total production of NTAEs.[11] They also handle distribution and transport for a large percentage of the exports. The transnational business is strongest in fruits and vegetables. For example, Del Monte in Costa Rica and Dole in Honduras market almost all of the pineapple exported from these countries.[12] These companies directly produce the majority of the pineapple, and contract the rest with medium and large national growers.

Besides the transnational corporations, another important category of NTAE enterprises are large and medium-sized businesses. They include foreign entrepreneurs mainly from the United States, large and medium-sized national producers, and shippers who are not directly involved in production. These *empresarios* account for an estimated 40 percent of the NTAEs from Central America. Foreign investors have a highly prominent role. In Costa Rica, foreign investors dominate the production of flowers, ornamental plants, citrus fruits, and macadamia nuts. Of the fourteen largest flower growers, only two are Costa Rican.

The scale issue in certain NTAE crops, especially flowers and specialty vegetables, poses a paradox, because the average farm size for many of these crops is generally quite small. For example, the average size of Ecuador's flower plantations is under twenty-five acres. Yet, contrary to what might be expected, these producers are not typical "small-scale" resource-poor farmers. Rather, they are highly capitalized entrepreneurs. Each flower plantation requires a capital investment of at least $80,000 per acre, as well as very costly marketing and sophisticated transport systems.[13]

Resource-poor farmers usually have considerable difficulties competing in the NTAE market. In nearly all countries, they lack access to the credit, capital, and information required for success in the business. They also tend to be unfamiliar with the crops and the production technology. Gaining entry in the market is very difficult for poor farmers in many countries like Chile, Ecuador, Paraguay, and Costa Rica, where NTAE programs have given very little attention to such matters. Even if resource-poor farmers do get involved in NTAE production, they often get squeezed out of the competition over time.

On the other hand, small-scale resource-poor producers have benefited considerably from NTAEs in certain countries and contexts, especially where they are organized in cooperatives or groups. Guatemala provides a unique illustration of substantial involvement of such farmers in NTAEs. In that country, 90 percent of snow peas are grown by relatively poor farmers on very small farms—typically less than two acres.[14] The competitiveness of small farmers in these crops is largely due to relatively low labor requirements, low land rent, the use of family labor, and the fact that these producers are more likely to be organized into associations.

Bolivia also has substantial involvement of small-scale resource-poor farmers in NTAE production. Bolivia has a history of communal traditions among the indigenous communities, which can serve as a social basis for management and organization of small farmers to successfully market NTAEs. Many Bolivian smallholders are involved in the production and marketing of organic quinoa, a traditional high-protein grain crop that has been grown by the indigenous peoples for centuries.[15] In recent years, this grain has been rediscovered and increasingly demanded by natural-food consumers in North America and Europe. This new taste for quinoa has opened up a niche market and export opportunities for Andean smallholders. The farmers have traditionally produced it without chemical inputs; therefore organic production comes "naturally."

In most Latin American countries, however, small-producer organizations for poor farmers do not exist, or when they do exist, they generally do not have sufficient resources for success in NTAEs. Moreover, they are usually dependent on external donors. Therefore, inequity in the distribution of benefits remains a serious predicament in the NTAE sector.

The nontraditional export sector is also subject to significant economic uncertainties. NTAEs are vulnerable to the risks and vagaries of the market. Prices fluctuate greatly in the NTAE market, not only over the year, but also from week to week, or even from day to day. This volatility is associated with seasonal changes, varying consumer preferences, regulations, and competition from other countries and national rivals.

The NTAE business is highly competitive, not only among national producers within a country, but also among different countries of the region and in Africa and Asia. Everyone is vying for dominance in relatively narrow niche markets. Producers also sometimes face competition with producers in the North. Related to this is the risk of market saturation. With the rapid growth of NTAEs, significant price declines have already occurred in some sectors such as snowpeas as a consequence of oversupply. The result is direct losses for exporters, and especially for producers.

Poorer NTAE farmers and businesses are especially vulnerable to these price fluctuations and declining terms of trade. They suffer greater proportional losses compared to more affluent large businesses. They also tend to face more difficulties in responding to the market windows and changes in demand. This is partly because the smaller enterprises tend to have less bargaining power, and have less collateral or capital to buffer against downturns or losses. Moreover, small local producers tend to lack access to information, credit, and other services.

NTAE farmers also suffer from a lack of diversification. At the national level, the diversity of NTAE products has increased significantly in all countries but farmers in the NTAE sector usually plant entire farms with a single monoculture. For small farmers, this generally means converting from mixed farms with a diversity of subsistence crops into farms planted with a single export commodity. Over time, this uniform conversion can bring serious economic risks and other disadvantages. By contrast, maintaining diversity of crops within individual farms has proven benefits including spreading risks, reducing vulnerability to fluctuating prices, reducing pests and diseases, and other agroecological advantages for soils and resource nutrients.

Another important issue to consider is the distribution of economic benefits at different levels in the market chain of NTAEs. Producers ultimately receive a very small percentage of the final sale. For example, a U.S. shopper spends on average ninety-nine cents per pound on mangoes, of which about eight cents per pound goes to the producer. The producer's costs are often very high, and the net profits are usually low. The profit margins for small poor farmers are particularly low. While this pattern is true for all crops, the price gaps in the NTAE market chain are particularly wide.[16]

NTAE growth does generate employment throughout the cultivation, packaging, and marketing process. The labor requirements in different NTAEs vary considerably, but many NTAE crops entail much more labor per acre on average than traditional crops. This labor intensity is beneficial in most rural areas of Latin America, where jobs are needed. In Guatemala, for example, a recent analysis of employment generation in NTAEs, based on estimates from the Bank of Guatemala and two field studies, showed approximately 14,000 jobs in agribusiness processing firms, and about 21,000 full-time jobs in production. Adding to this, jobs in the "spin-off" industries were estimated at about 5,000, putting the total at around 40,000 full-time jobs.[17] By 1991, the estimated total full-time jobs in NTAEs reached 12,400 in Costa Rica and 11,890 in Honduras.[18] Many of these jobs in NTAEs enable workers to acquire new skills, especially in processing. Certain specialization of skills can sometimes bring workers a daily wage 5 to 10 percent more than other workers' wages.[19]

Throughout Latin America and the Caribbean, a large proportion of workers in nontraditional agro-export sectors are women, in both production and processing.[20] This trend of increasing feminization of the rural wage-labor force is a ubiquitous change that has accompanied the globalization of food systems. Of course, women have traditionally been actively involved in subsistence farming, but the agro-export industry gives women increasing wage-based work. In Ecuador, for example, an estimated 69.3 percent of workers in Ecuador's NTAE production were female in 1991.[21] Managers interviewed in an Ecuador study said they preferred women laborers because they were better suited to and dexterous at pruning, harvesting, sorting, selecting, and packaging. The managers also stressed that women were "more submissive, obedient, capable, and honest" than men in such jobs.[22] In many cases an important reason why managers prefer women is that they are paid lower wages than men for equivalent work, work longer hours often without overtime pay, and are rarely promoted.

Workers in the NTAE sector tend to have unpredictable hours and very long working days during peak periods. In most of the NTAE-growing countries, a high proportion of employees are temporary workers. For example, in Costa Rica and Honduras, over two-thirds of the employees in fruit and vegetable NTAE farms and processing plants are temporary workers. This means that they lack security and are subject to dismissal unexpectedly, especially during times of market declines. Furthermore, workers are rarely unionized and are discouraged from organizing. In Guatemala, the use of child labor in NTAEs has become very common among smallholders.[23]

The production of NTAEs is also characterized by the heavy use of chemical inputs and pesticides. Doses of pesticide applications per unit of land greatly exceed those used in subsistence crops, and are also greater per acre than in many of the traditional export crops.

Although pesticides can bring short-term benefits in controlling pests, heavy pesticide use has several adverse impacts. First, pesticides are expensive. For example, an average flower producer in Ecuador spends an estimated $12,000 per year per acre on chemical inputs, which is over half of the total production costs.[24]

Secondly, when pesticides are applied excessively or too close to harvest time, the residues accumulate in foods in levels that exceed the tolerance standards established by the governments of importing countries. Pesticide-residue violations and detentions have been a major problem for Latin American and Caribbean NTAE exports to the

United States. They have occurred more than 10,000 times in the last ten years in U.S. entry ports.

Violations have resulted in millions of dollars in losses for the exporters and producers.[25] The most serious and frequent residue-detention problems in the region have occurred with products from Guatemala and Mexico. In Guatemalan NTAEs during the late 1980s, detention rates reached 27.3 percent of the total shipments.[26] Between 1990 and 1994, Guatemala's exports were detained 3,081 times because of residue violations, resulting in total losses of about $17.7 million.[27] Mexican export crops were detained 6,223 times in the 1980s, resulting in losses of $49.5 million, and 1,391 times in the 1990s, resulting in losses of $5.9 million.

Pesticide residues also pollute the environment, particularly water sources, soils, and vegetation. This contamination can raise costs for producers or lead to social costs, though most are never calculated by producers.

Another negative impact from the continual use of pesticides in all crops is pest resistance. Through genetic selection, pests evolve to tolerate the effects of pesticides over time. As pesticides become ineffective, high economic losses ensue. Farmers then become trapped into increasing pesticide inputs in an attempt to regain control. Resistance is sometimes accompanied by the death of natural pest enemies, leading to outbreaks of secondary pests. The resulting "pesticide treadmill" has affected many traditional agro-export crops in Latin America, leading to major crop losses.[28] In NTAEs, heavy use of pesticides has provoked a major problem of resistance and resurgence of white flies in Colombia and Central America. In recent years, the incidence of these insects has reached crisis proportions in some areas.

Pesticide use also puts workers' health at risk. Increasing numbers of people are being exposed and impaired, and more are suffering acute poisonings and chronic damage. Most of the victims are agricultural workers—the poorest of those involved in NTAE production. Women workers are particularly vulnerable to problems from pesticide exposure.[29] In a survey of workers in Ecuador's NTAE sector, 62 percent said that they had suffered health disorders from exposure to pesticides while working.[30]

The growth of NTAEs has inevitably involved changes in the use of natural resources, particularly land, vegetation, and water. Preliminary appraisals suggest that significant areas of forest cover have been cleared for NTAEs in a few areas—such as the Northern region of Costa Rica for citrus plantations and in the Central Valley in Chile for vegetables and flowers. Perhaps more common than forest removal, the agroecological changes with NTAEs involve conversion to monocultural farming systems and to standardized foreign varieties and uniform genetic stock, as required by Northern markets. This change often displaces the genetic diversity of indigenous varieties, and exacerbates other economic and agroecological risks.

Most of the products in the NTAE sector are highly perishable and have short shelf-lives. This elevates risks and requires specialized agricultural technologies, rapid transport systems, refrigerated storage, and sophisticated packaging procedures. These requirements raise questions about the institutional and technical capacities of Latin American and Caribbean countries to sustain NTAE production and marketing. Meeting strict market demands present an overarching, sometimes insurmountable, challenge as well.

Current services for NTAEs are largely dependent on foreign aid, but this support is being cut back. Moreover, even though some market studies suggest that Northern demand for NTAEs will increase, the market may not expand enough to absorb the growing supply.[31] Since many of these products are "trendy" luxury foods susceptible to instabilities, economic recession in the North, as well as changes in consumers' tastes, can reduce the demand and thus curtail market opportunities. Given these uncertainties, some analysts predict that the present fervor surrounding NTAEs will soon fade.

Last, but certainly not least, one of the crucial issues noted by several analysts and numerous farmers is that nontraditional agro-export growth and the associated land-use change reduce food availability locally and therefore can hinder food security, both at local and national levels. In nearly all countries, fiscal policy changes to stimulate NTAE growth have entailed reductions of funding for local food production. Likewise, analysts have noted that the increasing investments by aid organizations in export-directed development have come at the expense of attention to domestic food needs.

When taking into account the "bitter" aspects—the social and environmental costs—one is forced to reassess the supposed "success" of the nontraditional agro-export development strategy. The expansion of this "new" sector is repeating deleterious patterns and risks in past agroexport booms. Meanwhile, local food production in Latin America stagnates, and hunger and insecurity among the majority of the region's rural people continue to grow.

Notes

1. Secretaría de Integración Económica Centro Americana (SIECA), *VIII Compendio Estadístico para Centroamerica, 1978,* cited in Tom Barry, *Roots of Rebellion: Land and Hunger in Central America* (Boston: South End Press, 1987), 8. This data is based on estimations from the 1970s, because updated censuses have not been undertaken throughout the region. The land distribution patterns, however, have remained similar in recent years.
2. Shawki Barghousi et al., "Trends in Agricultural Diversification," World Bank Technical Paper 180 (Washington, DC: World Bank, 1993).
3. USAID data cited in Margaret Lycette, "Women, Poverty and the Role of USAID," *Poverty Focus,* Bulletin 2 (Washington, DC: Overseas Development Council, 1994): 5.
4. Martin Raine, "Strategy for the Promotion of Nontraditional Agricultural Exports," Internal Discussion Paper, Latin America and Caribbean Region (Washington, DC: World Bank, 1989), 15.
5. S. Jaffee, *Exporting High-Value Food Commodities: Success Stories from Developing Countries,* World Bank Discussion Papers 198 (Washington, DC: World Bank, 1993), 38, and William Friedland, "The Global Fresh Fruit and Vegetable System: An Industrial Organization Analysis," in Philip McMichael, ed., *The Global Restructuring of Agrofood Systems* (Ithaca, NY: Cornell University Press, 1994).
6. Luis Llambi, "Latin American Nontraditional Exports," in Philip Mc-Michael, ed., *The Global Restructuring of Agrofood Systems,* 195.
7. U.S. International Trade Commission, *Report on the Impact of the Caribbean Economic Recovery Act on U.S. Industry Consumers,* Seventh Report of 1991, U.S. ITC publication 2553, Washington, DC, September 1992.
8. Michael Carter, Bradford Barham, Dina Mesbah, and Denise Stanley, "Agroexports and the Rural Resource Poor in Latin America: Policy Options for Achiving Broadly-Based Growth," draft paper (Madison: University of Wisconsin, Land Tenure Center, 1993), 5.
9. PROEXAG data cited in Marteen Immink et al., *Nontraditional Export Crops Among Smallholder Farmers and Production, Incomes, Nutrition, and Quality of Life Effects* (Washington, DC: International Food Policy Research Institute, 1993), 42.
10. S. Jaffee, *Exporting High-Value Food Commodities,* 1.
11. Joseph Collins, "Nontraditional Agroexports, Basic Food Crops, and Small Farmers in Central America," unpublished paper (Arlington, VA: Interamerican Foundation, 1992), 7.
12. Joseph Collins, *Nontraditional Agroexports.*
13. William Waters, "Rosas y Claveles: Reestructuraciones de la agricultura ecuatoriana y el sector de productos notraditionales," presented in Argentina at the Third Latin American Congress of Rural Sociology, 1990.
14. James Fox et al., "Agribusiness Assessment: The Case of Guatemala," draft paper (Washington, DC: USAID, 1994), 30.
15. Kevin Healy, Interamerican Foundation, personal communication, May 1994.
16. Michael Conroy, "Problemas y alternativas económicas a las EANT," in World Resources Institute/INCAP, *Memorias del taller "Sostenibilidad de la producción agrícola notradicional de exportación por pequeños productores en Guatemala"* in Antigua, Guatemala, 20-22 September 1993.

17. James Fox et al., "Agribusiness Assessment: The Case of Guatemala," 30.

18. Jurgen Weller, "Las exportaciones agrícolas notradicionales y sus efectos en el empleo y los ingresos," in Jurgen Weller, ed., *Promesa o Espejismo?* (Panama: PREALC, 1992), 142.

19. Amalia Alberti, "Impact of Participation in Nontraditional Agricultural Export Production on the Employment, Income, and Quality of Life of Women in Guatemala, Honduras, and Costa Rica," unpublished report (Guatemala City: ROCAP/USAID, 1991), 32.

20. The impacts of NTAEs on women have been analyzed in a comprehensive surveys. See, for example, Lucia Salamea, A. Mauro, M. Alameida, and M. Yepez, *Rol e Impacto en Mujeres Trabajadoras en Cultivos Notradicionales para la Exportación en Ecuador* (Quito: CEPLAES, 1993); and Rae Blumberg, "Gender and Ecuador's New Export Sectors," Report for USAID, draft paper (Washington, DC: GENESYS Project, 1992).

21. *PROEXANT 1993 Annual Report,* unpublished (Quito: Programa para Exportaciones Agrícolas Notradicionales, 1993).

22. Lucía Salamea et al., *Rol e Impacto en Mujeres Trabajadoras,* 24.

23. Wayne Williams, personal communication, 1993; and discussions with smallholders in workshops as part of author's field studies, 1993.

24. An Ecuadorian flower producer, June 1992, quoted by Brian Riley, Appropriate Technology, Inc.

25. World Resources Institute analysis of U.S. Food and Drug Administration unpublished detention data, 1983-1994.

26. Douglas Murry and Polly Hoppin, "Recurring Contradictions in Agrarian Development: Pesticide Problems in Caribbean Basin Nontraditional Agriculture," *World Development* 20, no. 4 (1992): 603.

27. Calculation of World Resources Institute, based on analysis of FDA primary data.

28. See, for example, Lori Ann Thrupp, "Entrapment and escape from fruitless insecticide use: Lessons from the banana sector in Costa Rica," *International Journal of Environmental Studies* 36 (1990): 173-189; and D. Bull, *A Growing Problem: Pesticides and the Third World Poor* (Oxford: Oxfam Books, 1982).

29. World Health Organization, *Public Health Impact of Pesticides Used in Agriculture* (Geneva: WHO, 1990).

30. PROEXANT/University of San Francisco at Quito (USFQ), unpublished results of 1992 survey of NTAE producers. See also Jorge Rodriguez in William Waters, ed., *Deafíos de los Cultivos Notradicionales en Ecuador* (Quito: USFQ, 1992).

31. See, for example, N. Bonis, "The Nontraditional Agricultural Production Strategy in Central America" (Masters thesis, University of Texas at Austin, 1990).

10

A Note from
the Polish-Bolivian Border

Lawrence Weschler

Jeffrey Sachs arrived on the scene in Poland in the early fall of 1989, within weeks of Solidarity's overwhelming triumph in the June parliamentary elections—a veritable blast of can-do American energy and self-confidence. The country's economy was careening wildly, veering inexorably toward hyperinflation, and Solidarity's new legislators were utterly unprepared for the powers and responsibilities which were suddenly and unexpectedly being thrust upon them. Young Dr. Sachs—only 34 and already a full professor at Harvard—presented himself as the proverbial Man with a Plan. A plan—and a resumé.

Two aspects of that resumé particularly commended themselves to the floundering Poles: he had been centrally involved a few years earlier in helping to formulate an emergency shock rescue in Bolivia which succeeded in bringing hyperinflation to a dead halt, virtually overnight. Secondly, although in many ways a straightforward neoliberal, he had no use for the banks and regularly advised his clients on how to defer debt payments and concentrate instead on their own economy's domestic needs (which, granted, might turn out to be increasing foreign investment and exports).

He was, in short, no simple Chicago boy. He insisted that the short-term shock reforms he was proposing would be necessary whether one eventually wanted to end up with a Swedish-style social democracy or a Thatcherite model—and he often implied a preference for the former. I interviewed Sachs at length at that time for several articles I was writing on Poland. Leafing back through my notes, I find that he had much to say about Bolivia.

Poles were as surprised as anyone to find themselves suddenly focusing their national debate on fantasies about what might have happened in such a far distant land. Thus, for example, to those who doubted the ability of average Poles to master the sudden complications of the capitalist system, Sachs insisted that such a system was as natural as common sense: "The peasant Indians in the Bolivian market were able to operate the free exchange rate perfectly well within one day." Further rhapsodizing on the effects of that transition, Sachs averred as to how "in Bolivia, they went from a rationed exchange rate to a convertible currency in a single day, stabilizing their currency in the process. When I leave Bolivia, I'm happy to take it home for a month because when I get back I know it's going to have the same value. And it's legal for me to do so."

Poles were understandably dazzled at the prospect. But Sachs insisted that the transformation had to be sudden and almost convulsive. Addressing Solidarity's parliamentary caucus, he recalled approvingly how at one point Bolivia's finance minister, suddenly seeing the light, had commented, "Stemming hyperinflation is like cutting the tail off a cat: it's better to do it in one fell swoop than through a succession of tiny slices." A few days later a prominent Warsaw columnist opined to the effect that "Professor Sachs is proposing to cut off the tail of the Polish economy—at the neck!"

At one point around the time, I asked Sachs how, irrespective of any favorable macroindicators, the poorest classes were doing back in Bolivia. "To tell you the truth," he replied, "no one knows. And it's all so complicated because Bolivia happens to be a country that is at 14,000 feet, that isn't in the center of Europe, and that produces three things—tin, natural gas, and cocaine. Tin prices collapsed at the beginning, no one buys Bolivian tin anymore. Natural gas no one pays for anymore because it goes to Argentina, and Argentina is bankrupt, so they don't pay for Bolivian gas. And cocaine—everyone is doing the best they can to cut off that source of income, including the Bolivian government. So you have an intrinsic deep economic problem there."

On another occasion he commented in passing that 6 million people had no business trying to eke out a living upon such tragically impoverished terrain—that that was the country's fundamental problem. "I always told the Bolivians, from the very beginning, that what you have here is a miserable, poor economy with hyperinflation; if you are brave, if you are gutsy, and if you do everything right, you will end up with a miserable, poor economy with stable prices. But there's a reason you have to do that, and that's because only with stable prices do you have any sort of chance at surviving into the future."

"Now, here," he continued, "the situation is completely different...." And he went on to count the ways: Poland, he insisted, was a country with all sorts of natural advantages—a skilled workforce, superb location, considerable resources, and so forth. He saw no end to its potential, once it got its house in order.

Two years have passed, and the results have been, well, mixed. Hyperinflation was averted, though inflation has recently been creeping back. The currency did stabilize, markets filled with all manner of goods, exports boomed. At the same time, however, the country experienced a harrowing recession, far worse than anyone predicted and from which it has yet to emerge. And with prices rising and wages held down (a key element of the plan), the standard of living for many has dropped significantly though a good quarter of the population is doing quite well. If things have not gone as badly as some had warned, this is in part because the various Solidarity-configured governments have been hesitant to push the plan all the way. They still claim to be intending to do so in the months immediately ahead.

I'm reminded of an incident which occurred during Lech Walesa's first triumphant tour of the United States, back in November 1989. One morning during that week, a story buried deep in the *New York Times* was headlined "Bolivia Declares State of Siege after Breakdown in Strike Talks." It went on to detail the mass arrests of union leaders and their incarceration in Amazonian internment camps. I showed a clipping of the piece to a senior official in Walesa's entourage—a longtime oppositionist and supporter of Poland's workers. "Oh dear," he smiled grimly. "Oh dear. Do you mind if I keep this?" He slid the clipping into his coat pocket. "I want to be able to show it to the prime minister back in Warsaw so he'll know what to do when we get to that stage of the plan."

Sachs himself, meanwhile, has continued to support and consult with Poland's leaders. When last seen in print, however, he was deeply involved in discussion with Soviet planners and government officials, this time mapping out a Bolivia-style rescue plan the size of a virtual continent.

11

Neoliberalism
and Its Discontents

Germán Sánchez Otero

Despite some of their claims, proponents of neoliberalism in Latin America have no real interest in reproducing the free market of the nineteenth century. Though even if the interest were there, it would not be possible. Transnational corporations—with their centralized control of money, their regulation of prices and profits, and their centrally planned management—now dominate the world economy. This domination, along with the relentless pace of the ongoing techni-cal-scientific revolution, has irreversibly transformed the character of competition in the global marketplace, introducing new forms of cooperation and integration among industrialized countries. It is in this "new world order" that we have to understand the neoliberal model.

Neoliberalism promotes, above all, total freedom of movement for capital, goods, and services. It advocates the opening of economies, and competition in the world market in conditions of absolute freedom. To achieve this, it attempts to remove controls on prices. Labor, in contrast, is the only commodity which is not considered free in the market, due supposedly to the need for permanent extra-economic state regulation to reduce its cost. This regulation can include everything from legal measures, to the repression of strikes and the co-optation of union leaders.

Neoliberalism would eliminate the regulatory functions of the state and promote the denationalization and privatization of its goods and services. Instead of the state, it favors using the market to determine distribution and stimulation. The invisible hand of the market is to take care of the movement of resources, the growth in productivity, the renovation of technology, and the reinforcement of comparative advantages. However, once the state is reduced and weakened, the national economy's capacity to withstand external economic pressures is diminished, because only the state could have sufficient control over resources and regulatory mechanisms to soften the blow. To attenuate the negative social consequences of the model, neoliberals have designed certain instruments and escape valves, such as the negotiation of conflict (firm or flexible, according to the case), the growth of the informal economy, and programs of social assistance which are more propagandistic than effective.

The neoliberal discourse emphasizes the ideological neutrality of state management and the "de-ideologization" of the notions and principles underlying the economic system. Among these notions—which are held to be universally valid—are competition, iron work discipline, pragmatism, realism, asceticism, and the replacing of social groupings with individuals as the principal intermediaries and interlocutors in society.

The reformulation of the world economy according to the new interests and needs of the great capitalist corporations is explained by proponents of neoliberalism as the natural result of historical evolution, a process all countries must inevitably join. This logic is used to justify the denationalization of states in the dominated countries of the South, with the pretext that it is the cost they must pay to form part of this new world order, which supposedly offers interdependence among all nations.

The concepts of sovereignty, development, social justice, and democracy have also been redefined. The so-called new interdependence among nations sets the limits for national sovereignty. Development is conceived of as a goal which all countries can achieve if they join in the neoliberal process (it's just a question of time and sacrifice). Social justice becomes a function of the opportunities created by individual effort, while democracy is a universal value with no class or political qualifications whatsoever.

To date we can identify three stages in the implementation of the model in the region. The first period was really an antecedent, undertaken without the express rationality of neoliberalism. This was characterized by the openings of the end of the 1960s. These policies criticized the developmentalist process of industrialization based on state protectionism. Its proponents claimed that stagnation was the result of inefficiency due to lack of foreign competition, and inflation caused by government efforts to stimulate employment and growth. Such "openings" were not attempted in all countries, nor did they lead to any real reduction in the role of the state. By the mid-1970s, their most enduring legacy was to open the economies to foreign investment and credit.

During the second stage, the neoliberal model was applied in a radical and obvious way in several countries. The necessary pre-condition seems to have been military rule, as in Pinochet's Chile after 1973 and Argentina after 1976. In those countries, particularly in Chile, the economy was opened completely to foreign capital and services, and the state's roles as economic regulator and social benefactor were rapidly diminished.

Squeezed by the foreign debt, the new democratic governments of the Southern Cone tried to pursue a more social democratic model of development, in part because neoliberalism was so closely associated with military rule, but also because the governments feared neoliberalism's negative social consequences might affect their chances for reelection, or even the survival of the new and fragile democratic regimes.

But the economic crisis of the 1980s, in particular the deepening problem of the foreign debt, led these countries to eventually abandon these social democratic plans, which the United Nations' Economic Commission on Latin America and the Caribbean had principally developed. On the one hand, governments could not find a way to spread the growing costs of adjustment fairly. On the other, they fell prey to pressure from international finance capital and its powerful hold through the debt. Neoliberalism in its most savage forms was therefore adopted throughout the region by the end of the 1980s and the beginning of the 1990s.

The roots and context of the crisis of the 1980s are well-known. From the 1950s to 1980, the transnationalization of capitalism brought annual economic growth of 5 percent in Latin America. The price of that induced expansion was the structural incorporation of the region's economies into the global division of labor of that period. Import-substitution industries lost their national character. The agrarian sector was partially modernized to fit foreign markets. And the principal basis of the economy came under the control or hegemony of foreign capital, creating a nearly total subordination in the areas of technology and science as well.

In the 1960s, national populist movements led by the industrial bourgeoisie since the early 1930s were snuffed out by the new system of foreign domination. Sectors of that bourgeoisie put up some resistance, but most jumped on the bandwagon and accepted the role of junior partners. In most countries, save a few temporary and partial exceptions, governments tried to avoid the negative effects of the new subordination by borrowing money, which was readily available during the 1970s.

Thus, the countries of Latin America and the Caribbean turned to massive foreign credit to confront the deterioration of the terms of trade, the overvalued dollar, and the other effects of transnationalization. Indebtedness allowed several countries to artificially maintain certain elements of the import-substitution industrialization model for several more years. Thus the crisis of that model was worsened by the diabolic trap of debt, which, from the end of the 1970s through the 1980s, generated a vicious cycle of crisis-debt-crisis.

From then on, international financial institutions and the governments of the Group of Seven industrialized countries helped reproduce and accentuate this spiral by demanding that debtor countries apply onerous adjustment measures. During the first stage, these measures were intended to allow them to collect—at least in part—on the debt. Later, when it became clear that no more liquid capital would be forthcoming, institutions of the North began sucking out natural resources, and goods and services of the state in return for reductions in the debt.

The consequences of the current "savage" round of neoliberal policies have been dramatic. To begin with, we are in the midst of a profound and accelerated process of economic restructuring and foreign takeovers of Latin American productive systems. Industries characterized by low productivity and outdated technology, nearly all of them owned by midsized national capital, have been destroyed and replaced by speculation and imports. While the desperate opening of the economy to foreign interests often responds to the immediate desire to obtain favorable terms for repaying the foreign debt, the dismantling of the state—including privatization and drastic budget cuts—has caused faster rises in both unemployment and the relative and absolute levels of poverty than at any other time in the region's history.

Governments throughout Latin America have virtually abandoned their efforts to win national independence and economic development—goals which to one degree or another they had pursued in past decades. Never before have government policies been so directly managed by the International Monetary Fund, the World Bank, USAID, and other well-known institutions of transnational capital. Neoliberalism is synonymous with the definitive neocolonization of the subcontinent. Neither can the new dynamics of subregional, regional, and hemispheric integration be termed a victory for sovereignty. The principal beneficiaries of the current market-oriented integration will once again be the transnational corporations.

From neoliberalism grows neomarginality, euphemistically called the informal economy. This change of name seeks to recategorize the causes, the attributes, and the perspectives of this enormous sector of society that the model generates. It is an escape valve in which private and familial solutions replace social ones. In reality, the informal economy is one of the most prominent and harmful effects of neoliberalism, both in its human dimensions and its economic, ideological, and political ones.

Since full employment is excluded from the model, this "informal" route is designed not only to compensate for the steep rise in unemployment, but to thwart the efforts of the working class to resist, by pressuring the most exploited to seek out private solutions. The model preaches that informal workers stand at the base of a ladder of bourgeois accumulation. Now they have to resolve as individuals their problems of health, education, and social security. Neoliberal ideology has inverted people's expectations. Before, poor people considered themselves wage earners, and their hope lay in the power of their class. Now, informal workers are told to believe that they are or can become part of the bourgeoisie.

This virtual swarm of poor merchants will become poorer and more marginal, since they number ever more in the same market, and receive ever fewer of the social benefits that used to be the responsibility of the state. Informality is not a step toward wealth, nor even along the road toward wage labor. It is a dead-end social phenomenon, a structural fruit of the model.

Many other social consequences of neoliberalism are visible and well-known, from cholera to the steep rise in crime rates and drug trafficking. More children are in the street; retired people get fewer benefits; urban and rural workers are more exploited if they have work at all; the middle class has become an impoverished petty bourgeoisie; millions of bureaucrats and state employees have become small merchants or "informal" workers; the youth find no work and many turn to crime, become "informals," or emigrate to survive; and women suffer the most, as they try to compensate with personal sacrifice for the lack of basic necessities.

Paradoxically, this picture of social and human suffering has yet to produce significant resistance and struggle. The ideological and political roadblocks that the system has set up have managed to twist the truth, and neoliberalism is not yet perceived as the cause of the problem. Worse yet, many of those affected are convinced the system can work. This false vision produces resignation and apathy both among the marginalized poor and among a sector of the working class who fear for their jobs.

Nonetheless, although we can't know the form it will take, nor the exact moment it will occur in any country, the unravelling of neoliberalism seems inevitable. The design of a viable way out that favors development, integration, social justice, and democracy will contribute to the crisis of credibility of the current model. Such a design would have to take into account the objective international situation and the tendencies that define the current drift of the world economy. But in the new design, a country would insert itself into that economy in order to move toward economic independence.

This supposes several lines of action. First of all, it implies the accelerated development of new high-productivity areas of production, principally in high tech fields. Without state-of-the-art technology it would be very difficult to compete in the world economy or to obtain the large influx of capital necessary for integral social development. Second, efforts to move towards a New International Economic Order (the renegotiation of the global division of labor and terms of trade) must be given high priority. Third, the process of handing the economy over to transnational corporations must be stopped and reversed, beginning with the achievement of some satisfactory resolution of the foreign debt. Regional integration of groups of countries should be pursued, guided by the goals of developing our countries, and achieving independence and equity in the interests of the people.

The entire gamut of economic restructuring should be addressed, from the land question to the transformation of obsolete industries. Existing industrial infrastructure should be utilized wherever possible, while at the same time its renovation and the creation of a material infrastructure capable of satisfying the basic needs of the domestic market should be pursued. Radical change in agrarian structures is indispensable for several reasons, including the need to broaden the internal market and to stimulate food production so that the basic human need for food can finally be met.

New industries should be patterned to fit the consumer needs of the majority, and not only of the top 10 to 20 percent of the population. Along with this ethical/productive transformation, for some time to come it will be necessary to make use of and stimulate people's experience in grassroots economy—the ingenious ways in which the poor survive—by providing the necessary technical, political, and other support needed so that people can continue to get by.

Income distribution must be radically altered to break the pattern which favors (at most) 20 percent of society. The existence of great inequalities and social backwardness is incompatible with the scientific-technological base which must be laid if we are to take charge of the emerging modes of production. If knowledge today is more important than ownership, a crucial factor in development is the guarantee that education, culture, and scientific-technical knowledge are accessible to all. Human capital is today more decisive for development than physical capital.

All of these great tasks will require a state that is clearly legitimate in the eyes of the majority of the population, and capable of taking sweeping measures, firmly defending them, concentrating resources, creating programs, and directing development in all its dimensions. It is not a question of indiscriminate state intervention in the economy nor forced protectionism, which in the past often served only to transfer resources to private businessmen. The objective should be to have the state remain at the helm of the economy, so as to be in a position to resolve the basic problems of education, health care, mass transit, and housing for the poor, along with pursuing specialized development policies in the areas of science and technology. Such a conception supposes, of course, that the state and civil society would share essentially the same interests. This in turn must be assured by means of a democratic system based on popular and national sovereignty.

The fundamental axis of any program which seeks to overcome neoliberalism with real development, equality, and national independence rests on the political and social forces capable of opposing and defeating the economic and political actors who sustain and reproduce the current system of domination. Herein lies the challenge we must take up.

Part II

THE REORGANIZATION OF WORK
AND CLASS RELATIONS

12

The New Women Workers: Does Money Equal Power?

Helen I. Safa

Juana Santana works in the free trade zone of La Romana in the Dominican Republic. She supports her three children on her weekly salary of twenty dollars. She must make this money stretch to cover food, rent, and the babysitter's wage as well as her own expenses such as transportation and lunch. Her husband earns some money driving a taxi (*público*) owned by his family, but like many of the men living with the women workers in the free trade zones, he does not have a steady job. "I have to work, either in the zone or in a private home (as a domestic)," she says. "I cannot be financially dependent on my husband because he doesn't earn enough to help my family and to help me here at home."

Juana's situation is typical of that of many women workers in the free trade zones—low wages, poor working conditions, lack of affordable, adequate childcare, limited job alternatives, partners who offer little or no assistance, and an increasingly high cost of living. These difficult circumstances are the result of recent macroeconomic changes. The Caribbean Basin has historically depended upon agricultural exports such as sugar, coffee, and bananas. Today the region's economies have undergone a profound restructuring away from these traditional commodities toward export manufacturing. Export manufacturing lessens the need to pay sufficient wages to develop the internal market required under import substitution; on the contrary, the external market demand for export manufacturing requires the maximum reduction of production costs, principally wages, in order to compete effectively on the international level. In fact, the availability of cheap labor appears to be the prime determining factor for foreign investment.

Export-led industrialization has intensified dependence on the United States while failing to generate self-sustained growth. It has also contributed to a decline of male labor-force participation. Most of the jobs generated through export manufacturing are for women, who previously represented a small percentage of the industrial labor force under import substitution. Export manufacturers prefer women workers, because they are cheaper to employ, less likely to unionize, and seem to have greater patience for the tedious, monotonous work in assembly operations.[1]

This restructuring of the labor force has profound gender implications at the household level. The increased incorporation of women into the industrial labor force, although in dead-end, low-paid jobs, has given more economic responsibility in the household to women in Puerto Rico and the Dominican Republic, the two countries I will focus on in this article. Men, on the other hand, are increasingly marginalized. Thus, it is not only the increasing employment of women, but the decreasing employment of men that is making women major contributors to family income in both countries.[2] As a consequence, men's authority in the household has declined.

In recent years, spurred on by the debt crisis and growing unemployment, the competition among Latin American and Caribbean countries for foreign investment in export manufacturing has been intense. The state has played a major role in fostering export manufacturing. Governments have attempted to encourage foreign investment by lifting trade barriers and by offering tax holidays, subsidized credit, export subsidies, and freedom from import duties on raw materials and machinery needed for production. Most Caribbean countries also allow unrestricted profit repatriation. Special export-processing zones are constructed at public expense for export-manufacturing plants, complete with such amenities as water, electricity, and roads.

In the 1980s, U.S. Agency for International Development (USAID) made export manufacturing a key development strategy throughout Latin America and the Caribbean.[3] The U.S. government saw export manufacturing as a way not only to provide cost benefits to U.S. manufacturers, but also to improve the stagnant economies of Latin America and the Caribbean, and to promote political stability in the region.[4] Special tariff programs such as items 806.30 and 807 of the U.S. Tariff Codes and the Generalized System of Preferences were instituted to promote the relocation abroad of labor-intensive phases of manufacturing.

Washington's support for export manufacturing in the Caribbean Basin was enhanced by the 1983 enactment of President Reagan's

Caribbean Basin Initiative (CBI). Although textiles and garments are excluded from the CBI, due to opposition from U.S. labor, the United States granted special import quotas to certain Caribbean countries through the Guaranteed Access Levels (GALS) program, sometimes referred to as 807A. Apparel imports to the United States under the GALS program have grown by 76 percent annually since 1987, but they are limited to garments made entirely from U.S.-made and cut fabric.

Tariff restrictions help explain why export-led industrialization in the Dominican Republic has not led to self-sustained growth capable of generating more domestic, capital-intensive forms of industrial production.[5] U.S. tariff restrictions limit Caribbean export-led industrialization to enclave assembly operations. These export enclaves are an increasingly inefficient generator of foreign exchange since they provide no linkages to the domestic economy except for low wages. Domestic investment in the Dominican Republic has declined from 16 percent in the early 1980s to 6 percent in 1990 as state industrial policies favored foreign investment in export manufacturing over domestic industry.[6] Although 37 percent of the firms installed between 1985 and 1990 are Dominican-owned, 68 percent of all firms in the free trade zones are totally reliant on imported inputs for production.[7]

In the Caribbean, the state's principal role in export manufacturing is to create a favorable climate for foreign investment through investment incentives, and the control of wages and labor. Hourly wages vary considerably between countries, with a high in 1988 of $4.28 an hour in Puerto Rico (where the federal minimum wage applies) to a low of $.55 an hour in the Dominican Republic.[8] Labor control can be achieved through the outright repression or prohibition of unions in free trade zones, as in the Dominican Republic, or through cooptation of labor, as in Puerto Rico. Both repression and cooptation lead to a weak and fragmented labor movement that increases the vulnerability of workers in both countries.

Both labor and the state were further weakened by the economic crisis, which hit most of the Caribbean in the mid-1970s and 1980s. The economic crisis has made Caribbean countries even more dependent on export promotion to address the decline in the balance of payments, to service their debts, and to reduce growing unemployment. Many Caribbean and Latin American states have been forced to adopt IMF structural-adjustment policies, which further reduce their control over the economy and usually involve cutbacks in government services. Labor is also weakened by structural-adjustment measures which generally result in higher levels of unemployment and lower real wages.

State policy toward export-led industrialization differs somewhat in Puerto Rico because of its continued colonial status as a U.S. territory. This special status assures Puerto Rico free access to the U.S. market, but restricts the range of permissible economic and political activity, and makes the economy very dependent on federal transfer payments to sustain an increasingly impoverished population. U.S. corporations located in Puerto Rico pay no federal income tax.[9] The Dominican Republic has greater political autonomy, but is increasingly dependent on U.S. market forces to sustain its economy. State economic policy has basically been implemented by a "predatory state" set up by the dictator Rafael Leonidas Trujillo, who ruled the country from 1930 to 1960. Despite elections and lip service to increasing democratic participation, the Dominican state has continued to serve the interests of the agrarian and industrial elite, with little attention to the needs of the poor.

Puerto Rico's export-led industrialization program, known as Operation Bootstrap, started much earlier than that of most countries. It went through three stages, changing in focus from labor-intensive early on to capital-intensive in the mid-1960s, before a third stage of high tech industrialization in the mid-1970s. While each was different in emphasis, no one stage eclipsed the other, so that labor-intensive industries such as apparel continued to be the major source of female employment in manufacturing in the 1980s. Although the industrialization program was initially designed to provide employment to men displaced from agricultural employment, women became the primary labor force in the labor-intensive factories such as apparel and food processing that were attracted to the island in the first stage. While manufacturing output more than tripled from 1950 to 1980, this growth still could not offset the enormous declines in agriculture over this period. Some of this surplus labor was absorbed in services and particularly in public administration. Operation Bootstrap itself tried to remedy the surplus labor problem since it was accompanied by a program of government-sponsored migration to the United States, principally farm labor. Migration peaked in the 1950s, and continued at high levels until 1970.

Since the recession of 1973-1974, unemployment rates in Puerto Rico have hovered around 20 percent, and are higher for men than for women. In a sample survey of Puerto Rican garment workers I conducted in 1980, 90 percent said it was easier for a woman than for a man to find a job. Male activity rates declined significantly from 80.2 to 62.1 percent between 1947 and 1991, reflecting both the precipitous decline in agricultural employment and increasing levels of higher education, which kept young men (and women) out of the labor market.[10] The activity rate for women increased from 25.3 to 32.2 percent during this same period, as women were absorbed into export manufacturing and the growing service industry and the public sector.[11]

Both higher educational levels and lower fertility levels contributed to an improvement in women's occupational profile and to their higher labor-force participation rates. In addition, women are working more because of the rising cost of living, and increasing unemployment and declining real wages among men, which make it necessary for both husband and wife to contribute to the household income. The number of households headed by women has also increased, reaching 19 percent in 1980. The majority of married women in my sample maintain that they share household decisions with their husband, and that husbands no longer have exclusive budgetary control, as was common when the man was the sole breadwinner. Most husbands now accept that their wives work and no longer consider it a threat to their authority, because they realize it is impossible to live on a single wage. "A person who works has rights.... Now her husband is obliged to let her give orders, because she is contributing," says a divorced mother of teen-age children who has worked for several years in the garment industry. "Now it is both of them, before it was one.... In that sense the woman is better off."

However, the increasing incorporation of women into the labor force could not meet the economic needs of many of Puerto Rico's poor. As a result, more and more families depend on transfer payments such as social security and food stamps, which reach over half the population.[12] While seen as subsidies to workers, these transfer payments also aid low-wage industries like apparel that do not pay an adequate wage and might otherwise leave the island because of wage increases or a shortage of cheap labor. By providing alternative or supplementary sources of income, transfer payments further reduce a woman's dependence on a male wage, and also contribute to declining male labor-force participation rates.

These social support measures, in addition to ambitious government programs in housing, education, and health, helped to underwrite the costs of social reproduction for the working class, as well as to contain class conflict. Puerto Rican state policy is directed at containing and coopting the labor movement rather than repressing it. Industrialization also led to a profound recomposition of the working class and, paradoxically, to a weakening of the labor movement. The militant labor union among sugar cane workers was sapped of its strength by the decline of the sugar industry and the increasing fragmentation and diversification of the industrial labor force. The proportion of unionized workers in Puerto Rico as a whole dropped from 20 percent in 1970 to 6 percent in 1988. This can be partially blamed on unions' neglect of women workers.[13]

Though unionized, most women garment workers in my sample regarded the International Ladies Garment Workers' Union as a company union that does little to defend their interests or invite rank-and-file participation. The union is primarily interested in containing worker demands in order to retard the flight of garment plants to cheaper wage areas elsewhere. They have not, however, been very successful. Puerto Rico has lost its comparative advantage as a source of cheap labor to Mexico and other Caribbean countries, who also offer tax incentives and even lower wages. Competition from cheaper wage areas brought about a sharp decline in the Puerto Rican garment industry. This decline particularly hurt older women workers who have worked in the garment industry for twenty years or more, and have no alternative sources of employment. Contrary to global patterns, where most women who work in export manufacturing are young and single, over 75 percent of the women garment workers in my Puerto Rican sample are over thirty years old and two-thirds are married. As in the United States, older women displaced from their jobs due to relocation are not entitled to a union pension unless they are over sixty-two years old and have worked at least ten years in the garment industry.

Although both countries underwent a transformation from an agrarian to an industrial economy, the development process in the Dominican Republic differs considerably from that of Puerto Rico. The Dominican Republic remained dependent on agricultural exports, principally sugar, until the early 1980s, when the United States drastically cut its sugar quotas. Industrialization started much later in the Dominican Republic than in Puerto Rico. It focused largely on import substitution until the massive and rapid expansion of export manufacturing in the 1980s, which resulted largely from the reduction in the cost of labor due to the economic crisis and currency devaluation.

Though manufacturing exports grew 307.4 percent between 1981 and 1988 to $502.1 million, unemployment reached about 27 percent between 1985 and 1990, and continues to be much higher for women than for men. Despite several increases in the minimum wage, the real hourly minimum wage in the Dominican Republic declined 62.3 percent between 1984 and 1990.[14] The economic crisis resulted in higher levels of unemployment, inflation, and cost of living. This, in turn, led to increased migration from the Dominican Republic to the United States and also to Puerto Rico.[15]

Export manufacturing is attracted by the abundance of low-cost female labor in the Dominican Republic. Female labor-force participation rates in the Dominican Republic increased from 25.7 percent in 1970 to 35.5 percent in 1990.[16] Several factors in the development process favored this increase, including urbanization, the growth of the tertiary sector, and the growth of export processing. At the same time, the female population was becoming more employable, as a result of a rise in educational levels (higher than those of men), and a marked decline in fertility.[17] Male labor-force participation rates declined 10 percent over the same period, reflecting both increased enrollment at higher educational levels and men's growing marginalization in the economy, which accelerated with the decline in sugar production. Male unemployment, lower wages, and inflation increased the pressure on women to work in order to add to the household income. Export manufacturing now constitutes the second most important source of urban employment for women after domestic service, and continues to grow with the increase in free trade zones since 1980. As of March 1992, 135,000 workers were employed in twenty-three free trade zones in various regions of the country.[18]

Working women are becoming major economic contributors to the household. In a survey of women workers in export manufacturing in the Dominican Republic conducted in 1981, 38 percent considered themselves to be the major economic provider. As in Puerto Rico, the majority of married women now maintain that they share household decisions with their partners, and say that men no longer have exclusive budgetary control. Their authority in the home is derived from their increased economic contribution to the household, which has taken on major significance in the light of increased male unemployment and its debilitating impact on a man's ability to be the sole breadwinner. In short, it is not simply a question of whether women are employed or not, but the importance of their contribution to the household economy, which gives women a basis of resistance to male dominance in the family.

As in Puerto Rico, the threat to male authority in the household has contributed to an increase in households headed by women, which reached 24 percent in the Dominican Republic in 1984.[19] One 38-year-old supervisor in the free trade zones who now lives alone, although she has had eight children in three consensual unions, says she would not quit working, even if she found another man. "They are machistas," she says. "They think that if the woman works, she will rule too much. When a woman works, men think she is a little too liberal, that they can't mistreat or abuse her. When the woman isn't working, she has to put up with many things from a man. But when she is working, then things change."

Most women workers agree that paid employment has given them greater legitimacy to negotiate with their husbands, even though 80 percent of married Dominican women sampled in the 1981 survey still consider the man the head of the household. In general, more egalitarian relationships seem to be found in those situations where both husband and wife are employed, educated, urbanized, did not marry at an early age, and are legally married rather than living in consensual union. However, the changes are less marked than in Puerto Rico because the Dominican women workers in export manufacturing are younger with young children to support. They also have more children, which increases their dependence on male wages. The rate of consensual unions is much higher among Dominican than Puerto Rican women (twice as many Dominican women surveyed were in consensual unions than legally married), which increases the rate of marital instability. Dominican women also have not been working as long and enjoy less protection on the job. The transfer payments, such as unemployment insurance and food stamps, which cushion the effects of poverty and unemployment in Puerto Rico are also not available in the Dominican Republic. These factors coupled with the pressures of the economic crisis heighten the woman's insecurity and her fear of challenging male dominance.

Differences in Dominican and Puerto Rican state policies also condition the impact of paid employment on women's status. Dominican women workers in export manufacturing are not unionized and receive little support from the government in their struggle for better wages and working conditions, or even to upgrade their skills. Discontent is expressed in high turnover or eventual withdrawal from the labor force, rather than through union organizing. No unions are operating in the Dominican free trade zones, although they are not legally prohibited. Workers are simply fired and blacklisted with other plants if any union activity is detected. Hilda, for example, was fired several years ago along with sixty other women for trying to organize a union in the factory where she works. When she and her co-workers were fired, according to Hilda, the manager told her, "Whoever gets involved in unions here knows she will lose her job and will no longer work in the free trade zone, because as you know the big fish eats the little fish." Complaints of mistreatment or unjust dismissal that women workers have taken to the Ministry of Labor have generally been rejected in favor of management.

Has the growth of export manufacturing benefited women workers in the Dominican Republic and Puerto Rico? Certainly export manufacturing has provided women with an important source of employment at a time when the economic crisis urgently requires households to seek additional sources of income. Though poorly paid and offering few chances of upward mobility, these jobs have provided women workers with a weapon with which to challenge male dominance in the household. This is particularly the case in Puerto Rico, where the man's role as principal breadwinner has been considerably weakened by prolonged unemployment, migration, and increasing rates of female labor-force participation.

The problem is that in both countries, women are being asked to assume increasing economic responsibility for their household because higher rates of labor-force participation for women have coincided with declining job opportunities for men, due both to changes in the economy and to women's need to generate additional household income. This has contributed in both countries to a high rate of marital instability and female-headed households, leading to even greater burdens for women and higher levels of immiseration.

The enclave nature of export manufacturing in the Caribbean thus has negative social consequences for the economy as a whole and for women and their households in particular. The lack of linkages to the domestic economy in all areas but wages has failed to stimulate self-generating growth capable of creating better jobs for women and men. The present pattern of export enclaves places additional burdens on women while marginalizing men. The change in the industrial composition of these enclaves as they move away from garment firms to more highly skilled jobs in electronics and other capital-intensive products appears to have increased the proportion of men employed in export manufacturing in the Dominican Republic and Puerto Rico.[20] These jobs, however, are still heavily dependent on exports as well as foreign investment and inputs. This total dependence on external investment and markets means that these export enclaves may be withdrawn at any time. This state of affairs is underlined by the current fear in the Caribbean that the North American Free Trade Agreement will lead many foreign firms to leave the Caribbean and go to Mexico. The increasing proportion of men in more highly qualified jobs in export manufacturing also demonstrates a continued pattern of gender stratification, despite the increased demand for female labor.

The primary beneficiary of this pattern of export enclaves is the United States, which has promoted this strategy in Mexico and throughout the Caribbean Basin. This economic restructuring makes U.S. firms more competitive in the international market by reducing their labor costs. The Caribbean Basin has thus become a cheap labor pool, increasingly dependent on the United States. Changes in the global economy have also contributed to the increasing marginalization of men and growing dependence on women's wages in the region.

Notes

1. However, with the decline in traditional sectors of male employment such as agriculture and construction, men are beginning to work in the Dominican free trade zones in greater numbers. The percentage of women employed has dropped from about 70 percent in the 1980s to 58 percent in 1990. The growing proportion of men in Dominican free trade zones may be due to a recent increase in firms producing electrical machinery and other products associated with higher-skilled jobs which typically employ more male labor. The earlier figures are drawn from Andrés Dauhajre, E. Riley, R. Mena, and J.A. Guerrero, *Impacto Económico de las Zonas Francas Industriales de Exportación en la República Dominicana* (Santo Domingo, Dominican Republic [D.R.]: Fundación Económica y Desarrollo, Inc., 1989). The 1991 data are drawn from a recent unpublished report on the national labor force by the Inter-American Development Bank, FUNDAPEC, and CIECA, 10. I will henceforth refer to the report as FUNDAPEC.

2. The household-level data presented here are based on a survey of 157 women workers in three Puerto Rican garment plants conducted by the author in 1980, and a survey of 231 women workers in the three oldest

export processing zones of the Dominican Republic in 1981, conducted by Centro de Investigación para la Acción Femenina (CIPAF), a private Dominican women's research center. In 1986 I conducted in-depth interviews with a sub-sample of women working in the garment industry in both countries. A complete analysis of this data, together with a comparison of Cuban women textile workers, is in Safa, *The Myth of the Male Breadwinner: Women and Industrialization in the Caribbean* (Boulder, CO: Westview Press, 1995).

3. This USAID policy of financing and advertising free trade zones has recently come under sharp attack and been subjected to some restrictions by the U.S. Congress as a result of investigations of U.S. labor unions into these practices and their denunciation of the job loss for U.S. workers. See Keith Bradsher, *New York Times*, 4 October 1992, 5.

4. For a fuller discussion of the impact of the economic crisis and economic restructuring on the Caribbean, see Carmen Diana Deere, Peggy Antrobus, Lynn Bolles, Edwin Meléndez, Peter Phillips, Marcia Rivera, and Helen Safa, *In the Shadows of the Sun: Caribbean Development Alternatives and U.S. Policy* (Boulder: Westview Press, 1990).

5. Carmen Deere and Edwin Meléndez provide a critical analysis of the limited benefits of export growth in the Dominican Republic in "When Export Growth is not Enough: U.S. Trade Policy and Caribbean Basin Economic Recovery," *Caribbean Affairs*, vol. 5, no. 1 (1992).

6. FUNDAPEC, 3.

7. FUNDAPEC, 8 and 12.

8. See Deere et al., *In the Shadows of the Sun*, 149. Hourly wages include fringe benefits; the data are for semiskilled labor in export-processing industries.

9. Repatriated profits are subject to a 10 percent Puerto Rican tollgate tax which under Section 936 can be reduced by reinvesting in Puerto Rico or depositing these profits in banks in Puerto Rico.

10. Although the official rate of unemployment is about 20 percent, the actual economic activity rate is around 45 percent. Both the male and female activity rates are drawn from the Puerto Rico Department of Labor and Human Resources, Commonwealth of Puerto Rico, *Serie Histórico del Empleo, Desempleo y Grupo Trabajador en Puerto Rico*, 1991. Activity rates refer to the percentage of economically active women or men as a perentage of the total population over a certain age (ten years in the Dominican Republic, and sixteen years in Puerto Rico) of either sex. I am grateful to Luz del Alba de Acevedo for providing me with this data as well as many other helpful insights.

11. The public sector now constitutes the primary source of employment for both sexes in Puerto Rico.

12. Data for 1981-1983 drawn from Richard Weisskoff, *Factories and Food Stamps: The Puerto Rican Model of Development* (Baltimore: The Johns Hopkins University Press, 1985), 66.

13. Carlos A. Santiago-Rivera presents a fuller discussion of the impact of economic restructuring on the Puerto Rican labor movement in "The Puerto Rican Labor Movement in the 1990s" in Edwin and Edgardo

Meléndez, *Colonial Dilemma: Critical Perspectives on Contemporary Puerto Rico* (Boston: South End Press, 1993), 149.

14. FUNDAPEC, 8. In 1987, the World Bank estimated that the average monthly salary in the Dominican free trade zones was DR $321 (about US $92). See Dauhajre et al., *Impacto Económico*, 82.

15. Dominicans started migrating to New York City in the 1960s, and in 1990 numbered nearly 900,000 according to Annette Fuentes, "Elusive Unity in La Gran Manzana" in *NACLA Report on the Americas,* vol. 26, no. 2 (1991), and in S. Grasmuck and P. Pessar, *Between Two Islands: Dominican International Migration* (Berkeley: University of California Press, 1991). The more recent Dominican migration to Puerto Rico is examined in J. Duany, ed., *Los Dominicanos en Puerto Rico: Migración en la Semi-Periferia* (Río Piedras, Puerto Rico: Ediciones Huracán, Inc., 1990).

16. For the 1960 figure, see Clara Baez, *La Subordinación Social de la Mujer Dominicana en Cifras* (Santo Domingo, D.R.: Dirección General de Promoción de la Mujer/INSTRAW, 1985). For the 1991 figure, see Nelson Ramírez, "Nuevos Hallazgos sobre Fuerza Laboral y Migraciones" in *Población y Desarollo* 2 (Santo Domingo, D.R.: Profamilia, 1992). The 1991 figures are inflated because they include women and men willing to work, but not necessarily actively seeking employment.

17. Isis Duarte, Clara Baez, Carmen J. Gómez, and Marina Aríza, *Población y Condición de la Mujer en República Dominicana* (Santo Domingo, D.R.: Instituto de Estudios de Población y Desarrollo, Estudio no. 6, 1989).

18. This information, provided by the National Council of Export Free Trade Zones, includes ten privately operated free trade zones, eleven administered by the Industrial Development Corporation, two administered by the State Sugar Council (on former state-owned sugar mills) and a special free trade zone. Eighteen firms operated outside industrial parks as special free trade zones. See "Cantidad de Empresas Operando en las Diferentes Zonas Francas del País a marzo de 1992" (Santo Domingo, D.R.: Consejo Nacional de Zonas Francas de Exportación, Secretaría de Estado de Industria y Comercio, 1992).

19. Carmen Julia Gomez explains the increase in Dominican female-headed household in *La Problemática de las Jefas del Hogar* (Santo Domingo, D.R.: CIPAF, 1990), 27.

20. In 1992, 67 percent of firms in the Dominican free trade zones were still in the textile industry. See Consejo Nacional de Zonas Francas, "Cantidad de Empresas," 1992. Palmira Ríos examines the changing gender composition of Puerto Rico's manufacturing sector through 1980 in "Export-Oriented Industrialization and the Demand for Female Labor: Puerto Rican Women in the Manufacturing Sector, 1952-1980" in Edwin and Edgardo Meléndez, *Colonial Dilemma*, 89-102.

13

Bolivia:
The New Underground

Linda Farthing

The day Rafael Ramírez lost the factory job he had held for twelve years, he felt completely uprooted. "The SAID factory was like a family to me," he says. "With so many people out of work, how was I going to make a living?" The next morning he began the rounds of the few factories remaining open in La Paz, only to find that despite his experience as a machinist, no jobs were available.

The severance pay of $300 Ramírez received lasted his family four months. By then he realized that he had little chance of finding a steady job. With $1,000 borrowed from a relative, he bought ground coffee which he took to the eastern lowland city of Santa Cruz to sell, only to find the market flooded with cheaper coffee from Brazil. A year later, having lost much of his capital, he began selling contraband goods in an open-air market in El Alto, the sprawling shantytown city above La Paz. But he was unable to earn enough to make ends meet. His wife took over the stall, and he set up a small folding table and typewriter on a downtown avenue where he works filling out tax forms. "I make about twenty bolivianos a day ($4.25) and with what my wife earns in the market, we just get by."

The closure of the SAID textile factory, high on a hill above La Paz's center, has come to symbolize the de-industrialization Bolivia suffered during the severe economic crisis of the 1980s, which was compounded by the New Economic Policy (NEP), implemented in 1985 as a mechanism of free-market structural adjustment. That the factory is used as a marketplace today reflects the fact that, by the mid-1990s, production is still sluggish in Bolivia. In La Paz, as in every other city in the country, small-scale commercial activities continue to predominate over productive ones.

What Rafael Ramírez's story shows is that Bolivians are exemplary survivors. In the face of acute political instability, an economy dependent on world market fluctuations, and the highest infant mortality rate on the continent, people have developed a remarkable capacity to face economic insecurity. But the NEP, still very much in force through two democratic changes of government, has generated unprecedented levels of hardship.

With one important exception, the NEP was a rehash of initiatives adopted repeatedly since the mid-1950s. Cuts in public spending and deregulation of prices, currency exchange rates, and import restrictions have been tried time and time again, but Bolivia remains, as it was when revolution shook the country in 1952, the poorest country in South America. In the lone exception to the policy rehash, the NEP set in motion a steady reversal of state control of the economy. The current government of Goni Sánchez de Lozada, one of the country's richest men, is in the process of selling off the six largest state-owned enterprises.

Since 1985, an estimated 45,000 jobs in state mining and public administration have been eliminated. Factory closures resulting from free-import policies caused the loss of at least another 35,000. The present government has continued the trend, slashing jobs in state-run firms in order to ready them for privatization.

"I'm really not sure from one day to the next if I'm going to be able to put food on the table for my five children," says Ana de Patino, whose husband worked for thirty-five years in the Colquiri tin mine. "My husband earns eight bolivianos a day ($1.70) when he can find temporary work on construction sites. We still can't believe that this could have happened—that the mines would shut down and we would be left high and dry."

Steady migration away from the countryside has converted what was twenty-five years ago a primarily rural society into one in which just over half the population lives in urban centers, the majority in conditions of extreme poverty. With no state unemployment benefits and social services, limited even before 1985, now virtually nonexistent, shantytown dwellers in the principal cities of La Paz, Santa Cruz, and Cochabamba rely on family and community networks and ingenious survival strategies. The moment the earth is turned on a new construction site, an improvised lunch counter appears nearby, set up by women who haul pots of cooked food from their homes to feed the workers. On La Paz's Buenos Aires Avenue, the clogged traffic provides one ex-miner with the chance to earn two dollars a day changing bills into coins for slow-moving buses.

In the past fifteen years, the percentage of the urban population which supports itself through this type of "informal" activity has grown to 60 percent, largely due to a phenomenal rate of growth during the 1980s. The sector is characterized by its small scale, lack of access to capital and training, and low productivity. Francisco Figueroa of the Confederation of Artisans, Vendors, and Meat Sellers prefers the term "micro-enterprise." "Small vendors lack legal protection, but we pay taxes both to the municipality and to the national government," he says. "So we resent it when people call us informal."[1]

Aside from farming, most formal economic activity in Bolivia has always been in the realm of mineral exports. The small quantities of processed food and textiles produced for the local market never provided many jobs. But the mushrooming of small-scale commercial activities after the application of the NEP has gone hand-in-hand with a steady drop in earnings among informal workers. Silvia Escobar of the Labor and Agrarian Development Studies Center (CEDLA) estimates that only half are able to cover their families' basic food costs.

Over 30,000 vendors, nearly all of them women, fill the streets of La Paz daily, one vendor for every thirty people. The more established sell from fixed stalls, while many peddle minuscule quantities from wraps spread on the sidewalk. With so many now laboring in petty commerce or micro-enterprises, the character of the labor movement and workers' basic values and roles are changing the face of Bolivian society in fundamental ways.

Micro-enterprises often reproduce the complex network of relationships traditional in native culture. A small hand-knit sweater business studied by anthropologist Hans Buechler, for example, is run with the labor of unpaid family members, capital from close kin, and the participation of distantly related kin.[2]

Traditional concepts of reciprocity provide people with some protection against falling incomes. In times of shortage, consumers are assured that their regular vendors will put goods aside for them. Another reciprocal arrangement is found in the *pasanaku* rotating credit system, which allows people with limited resources access to a small amount of capital. Between ten and twenty people each contribute a certain weekly or monthly quota and take turns receiving the total collected.[3]

These types of relationships give income-generating activities in Bolivia a particular logic. Small businesses with close links between family and business earnings reflect a search for subsistence income rather than the rationale of accumulation. Diversification is a strategy widely used to minimize risk. Many vendors knit for the handicraft market while working at their food stalls. Recent migrants to the city often maintain a plot of land in their community of origin for basic foodstuffs.

Aside from perpetuating already low living standards, such work is tremendously unstable; as the informal sector grows, instability has become the norm in employment. According to Silvia Escobar, the work discipline of the labor force has been undermined by the lack of fixed jobs. Alongside factory closures and an undercapitalized and uncompetitive artisan sector, booming micro-enterprises are placing the ability of Bolivia's products to compete internationally ever farther out of reach.

In many countries, informal economic activity depends on a close interaction with the formal economy. In Bolivia, however, the informal commercial sector responds more closely to the dynamics of one of the country's major export activities, the coca/cocaine trade, whose profits are largely laundered through contraband. While unregulated economic activities predate the emergence of the drug business, they were rapidly penetrated, expanded, and strengthened by profits from cocaine.[4]

The influx of cocaine money also spawned informal banking services, operating mostly in dollars. The hyper-inflation of 1983 to 1985, when savings in Bolivian currency could lose 10 percent of their value per day, further strengthened the move to dollars. Today, even in isolated rural areas, peasants will ask foreigners to convert bolivianos into dollars. Flavio Chambi is one of scores of ex-factory workers who change currency on busy La Paz street corners. "People would rather deal with us than with banks," he explains. "We're more accessible and personal."

The explosion of smuggling since the NEP was imposed benefits principally those with government ties who can bring in large shipments using false customs documents. But the trade also provides an income for hundreds of Bolivians who trek across the borders with some savings, and return with a variety of goods over rutted roads in the back of open trucks. Those who work in this "contraband of the ants" have to haggle with wholesalers, haul heavy loads, and face hostile officials who often demand bribes or confiscate merchandise. When they finally get their goods to market, competition is fierce and profits low. "I used to make about twenty dollars a trip," says Berta Calle, fifty-eight, who travels regularly to Chile, "but now I earn as little as seven dollars each time."

Smuggling is not only the domain of the poor. Bolivia's small middle class has also resorted to such strategies to lessen the impact of the economic crunch. Marlene Rodriguez's job as a teacher is so poorly paid that every two weeks she leaves her teenage daughters and hires a substitute teacher so that she can travel to Chile and smuggle back bundles of second-hand U.S. clothing.

The contraband trade is built like a pyramid. A belt of prosperous merchants who market foreign goods is at the top. Below them comes a wide band of intermediaries, which in turn rests upon a mass of peddlers, who manage minuscule amounts of merchandise. "Contraband has become an important vehicle for upward mobility," explains sociologist José Blanes. "Many of those who channel large quantities of capital into contraband were originally working class. Traditional mechanisms for moving up the social scale through the dominant political parties or through professional education are no longer operating. We are witnessing increasing marginalization and poverty on one hand, and the growth of a new wealthy mestizo class on the other."

On my street in downtown La Paz, the two vendors of 1985 have now multiplied to eight. Competition between them is fierce. "When I first started to sell here," says Horencia Menduina, "the woman in the next stall got twenty vendors from the area to come and tell me to leave because I was taking their business away. I moved my stall further away from hers, but I spent two years getting city hall permission, and almost $300 to have the kiosk built, so I'm not leaving. In the end, the vendor's union had to intervene. They told me I should have gotten approval first from the local vendors, but I didn't know that. I thought the city permit and joining the union were enough."

Although half of all informals remain unorganized, union membership is required to sell in fixed street stalls, and the Confederation of Artisans, Vendors, and Meat Sellers has grown to 800,000 affiliates nationally. However, the nature of commerce does little to promote solidarity among union members. "We have constant problems with vendors fighting over space," admits confederation leader Francisco Figueroa.

For former union leader Rafael Ramírez, the contrast between factory and street is striking. "Although in many ways I like the freedom of working in the street, there's a lack of trust here," he says. "In the factory, we all depended on each other for the work to get done, and we knew we had the backup of the union to face our collective problems. Here we each depend on ourselves, so we have very little sympathy for each other. But I try not to forget what I learned in the union: the importance of solidarity with other working class people. Whenever possible, I don't charge people who are very poor, or I charge them very little."

The decline of the traditional proletariat has caused considerable ideological change among the working class, shifting the locus of social and economic demands from the workplace to the neighborhood, and from the search for structural change to single-issue strategies. "The social fabric is changing," explains economist Carlos Torranzo. "These new workers do not have the same tradition of struggle that the miners had." This has brought a steady erosion of the gains won through decades of trade union struggle. Some two-thirds of workers outside the formal economy have no state protection or social security benefits. "Our members aren't on any payroll, so they aren't covered by labor law," says vendors' leader Figueroa.

The shift away from the employer-employee dynamic, while threatening traditional trade unionism, is reinforcing the family as the principal economic unit. Family-run businesses now comprise 76 percent of the informal sector. In La Paz, some 167,000 enterprises provide work for 225,000 people, an average of 1.3 workers per business.[5]

The number of women entering the labor market has skyrocketed. Reflecting Andean women's traditional role in commerce, nearly all street vendors are female, and despite the dominant view that they are "helping" to supplement their husbands' income, many of them support their families.[6] About one-third are heads of households.[7] They work a daily average of eleven hours selling, and five more doing domestic chores. With more women doing a double shift, at least one study has found that traditional gender division of labor is gradually giving way, with more men and boys helping out at home.[8]

For rural girls and women, domestic service is still the traditional point of entry into the urban labor market. Modesta Quispe, who works a seventy-five-hour week for forty dollars a month as a live-in maid, says, "I started when I was sixteen when a family from the city came to my community and took me back with them." A common goal among these women is to become street vendors. "My friends are almost all domestic workers from the countryside," says Quispe. "We dream of saving enough money to be able to set up our own stalls."

Self-employment is one of the few options open to women who have small children and must organize their days around running their homes. These women earn only 60 percent of the average wages of men doing similar work, and they tend to have less schooling. Women's entry into the labor market is generally motivated by necessity, but once there they tend to appreciate the relative independence gained from having their own incomes. "I like earning my own money," says street vendor Margarita Laurente, who brings in about two dollars a day. "That way I can decide what we most need at home."

The number of child workers in the street is estimated to have increased 60 percent since 1985, although Bolivian law prohibits children under fourteen from entering the labor force. Starting as young as seven years old, they earn small amounts as shoeshine boys, domestic workers, and market and street vendors, working an average of fifteen hours a day. Leaving school may address immediate survival needs, but does not bode well for the country's future needs for a literate workforce from which to draw skilled labor.

Since the early 1990s, informal workers have become the rage among international aid and development experts, who often extol the entrepreneurial spirit they supposedly represent. But could such small-scale activities constitute an alternative development model? The government has traditionally ignored small businesses in favor of export-oriented industries and agribusiness. Could a shift in government priorities, advocated by these same development specialists, transform informals into a springboard for sustained economic growth?

As a development strategy, the informal sector offers certain advantages. The average investment required to create a formal-sector job has been estimated to be twenty-six times higher than that needed to create an informal one. In addition, most micro-enterprise manufacturing is almost exclusively based on the use of local resources rather than imports.

The widely circulated position of Peruvian economist Hernán de Soto, that the informal sector can provide a solution to the impact of structural-adjustment policies, finds little resonance in Bolivia. "De Soto's emphasis on the removal of legal barriers that the informal sector faces makes little sense here," says Silvia Escobar. "In Bolivia, the legal registration of businesses is a lot less complicated than the one he describes in Peru. And even if you remove the legal barriers, you still have not addressed the problems of lack of access to credit, low skill levels, low productivity, and so on."

Where the informal economy has become a motor for growth, as in central Italy, researchers have identified a series of factors in its success, such as the development of upscale market niches, strong internal integration and cohesion, and an entrepreneurial environment, all of which Bolivia lacks. And beyond all that, successful informal models in other countries have received considerable government support. If the informal sector is to maximize its potential, it will require innovative responses from the state rather than simple deregulation or rigid centralized planning.

Many policymakers, following de Soto's lead, have criticized government overinvolvement, promoting a vision of individual solutions to what are, in essence, structural problems. Following this trend, the previous La Paz city government, with World Bank support, developed a program for micro-enterprises which, among other things, reduced the number of steps needed to register with the municipality.

The sector of the informal economy with the greatest potential to contribute to solid economic development is the artisan sector, producing everything from Bolivian imitations of Calvin Klein jean jackets to cake pans. Though artisans make up a quarter of the urban informal economy, the flood of contraband has cut into their markets, while mushrooming unemployment and frozen wages have reduced demand. In addition, unemployed workers have increased competition by rushing to set up their own tiny workshops. Artisan producers are increasingly undercapitalized, purchasing smaller quantities of supplies at higher prices, thus cutting down the amounts they earn. "Another big problem we face," explains José María Herrera, a goldsmith belonging to the Confederation of Bolivian Artisans, "is getting raw materials produced in Bolivia. Most are shipped out of the country in bulk." The nongovernmental organization CEDLA has been working with the artisans' union to help them gain access to credit and technical assistance, some tax benefits, and market protection.

The most serious problem experienced by all small businesses, both commercial and artisan, is their lack of access to credit. Banks provide credit to those with collateral such as cars or houses, not to the urban poor. The informal credit services which have sprung up to fill this vacuum often charge as much as 7 percent interest a month. In the absence of government policy and support, PRODEM, a nongovernmental organization set up in 1986 and funded by the U.S. Agency for International Development, began making loans averaging $150 each.

The demand for these services outstripped the group's capacity so rapidly that they set up a bank to exclusively service the sector. BancoSol now loans over $1 million a month in amounts which average $275 each. Half the loans go to commercial activities and half to artisans, and 75 percent of the bank's clients are women. Interest rates are the same as those charged by commercial banks, and each loan is guaranteed by a solidarity group, made up of participants who agree to back each other's loans. "Our default rate is very low—about 0.22 percent," explains credit manager Bernardo Santa Maria. "These people may be poor, but they fulfill their obligations."

Another nongovernmental organization working with the informal sector is the Center for the Promotion of Economic Initiatives (FIE) which began by providing 1,800 loans exclusively to the artisan sector in 1988, almost all backed only by personal guarantees. They too are moving towards becoming a bank. FIE also offers basic training in administration and bookkeeping. Defaults are rare. "Word contract is still very strong in Bolivian society, stemming from a culture which places a high value on personal honesty," says former director Pilar Velasco. "We never have people asking for more money than they need. The producers we work with are incredibly flexible and innovative, always finding new ways to adapt products to facilitate their sale in a highly competitive market."

These projects are in some sense formalizing the informal economy, according to sociologist José Blanes. But "the informal sector does not represent an alternative development model for the country," says Blanes. "It is a transitional model only, towards what, we are not sure, but it is clear that the old models are now broken. The problem is that the tendency towards informality provides a very poor base for the country's future."

In the meantime, traditional community values continue to help low-income Bolivians survive the austerity policies which have fallen disproportionately on their shoulders. Among them are the apparently contradictory elements of fierce competition and cooperation. I witnessed a dramatic example of this early one morning in the mining town of Llallagua. The buses were on strike, so the train was packed.

Hundreds of people fought tooth and nail to get into the few carriages available. Finally, station personnel added on a box car and those of us left on the platform pushed and shoved our way in, elbows and curses flying. At the last moment, one more woman squeezed on. She was in tears, and explained she had been robbed on the platform. The people in the box car immediately reached into their pockets and passed around a hat for her.

Such spontaneous sharing is inspiring, and it allows thousands to feed themselves and their families each day. The community values by which Bolivians weather the daily struggle may not constitute an alternative model for national development, but they do point the way towards the formulation of an indigenous model of development based on values significantly different than those of the Western models imposed on them to date.

Notes

The author would like to thank José Blanes for his comments on this article.

1. La Paz micro-enterprises paid over $500,000 in municipal taxes in 1989. About half are also registered with the national government taxation system, but only about 10 percent actually pay. See Antonio Pérez Velasco, Roberto Casanova Sainz, Silvia Escobar de Pabón, and Hernando Larrazábal Córdova, *Informalidad e ilegalidad: una falsa identidad* (La Paz: CEDLA, 1989).
2. Hans Buechler, "Doña Flora's Network: Work Relations in Small Industries in La Paz, Bolivia," in George Gmelch and Walter P. Zenner, eds., *Urban Life: Readings in Urban Anthropology,* 2d ed. (Prospect Heights, IL: Waveland Press, 1988).
3. The word is said to come from *pasa,* Spanish for pass, and *naku,* a Quechua suffix denoting reciprocity.
4. The links between contraband and the cocaine economy are particularly hard to specify because of the illegality involved. For a discussion of how they affect Bolivia, see José Blanes Jiménez, "Cocaine, Informality, and the Urban Economy in La Paz, Bolivia," in Alejandro Portes, Manuel Castells, and Lauren A. Benton, eds., *The Informal Economy: Studies in Advanced and Less Developed Countries* (Baltimore: Johns Hopkins University Press, 1989).
5. Roberto Casanova Sainz, *El sector informal urbano en Bolivia: elementos para un diagnóstico y lineamientos generales de políticas* (La Paz: CEDLA, 1989).
6. Silvia Escobar de Pabón, "Small-Scale Commerce in La Paz, Bolivia," in Narguerite Berger and Mayra Buvinic, eds., *Women's Ventures: Assistance to the Informal Sector in Latin America* (West Hartford, CT: Kumarian Press, 1989).
7. Vivian Arteaga and Noemi Larrazábal, *La Mujer pobre en la crisis económica: las vendedoras ambulantes de La Paz* (La Paz: FLACSO/Centro de Promoción de la Mujer "Gregoria Apaza," 1988).
8. Ibid.

14

Chile:
The Underside of the Miracle

Cathy Schneider

The Chilean economic miracle has received a great deal of press over the past decade. Governments as far away as Prague and Moscow have sought the advice of Chilean economists on matters ranging from privatization and economic restructuring, to unemployment and poverty. The Chileans point proudly to almost a decade of the highest growth rates in South America (averaging over 5 percent yearly), low inflation rates (averaging about 20 percent a year), and unemployment rates that are lower than those of the United States (unemployment fell below 5 percent in 1993). The ability of the Chilean economy to yield consistently high rates of economic growth has helped forge a new consensus among Chile's formerly antagonistic political parties. But for most of Chile's working poor, the economic model has been anything but miraculous.

Poverty and income inequality which grew by colossal proportions during the years of the Pinochet dictatorship have scarcely been addressed by the new democratic regime. In 1969, four years before the military coup, 28.5 percent of Chileans lived in poverty.[1] Urban poverty was a major campaign issue in the 1970 election of the socialist Salvador Allende. In 1979, however, six years of military rule had increased poverty levels to 36 percent. By 1989, 42 percent of Chileans were living in poverty, and over 12 percent, compared to 8 percent in 1969, were destitute (unable to pay even rent).[2] Caloric intake for those Chileans in the bottom 20 percent had dropped by more than 23 percent since 1969 (from an average of 1,925 calories to 1,474 in 1989).[3]

The situation is even more dramatic in the capital city of Santiago, home to almost half of Chile's population. In 1969, 28 percent of

Santiago residents lived in poverty. By 1976, a year and a half after the coup, poverty in Santiago had increased to 57 percent. Despite the current government's large increases in spending on health care, education, and social services, over 49 percent of Santiago's residents still live in poverty.[4]

The relative inequality of income between the top and bottom fifths of the population has also increased dramatically since the implementation of the new economic model. In 1969 the income share of the wealthiest fifth of the population was 44.5 percent as compared with 7.6 percent for the poorest fifth. By 1988 that ratio was 54.6 percent to 4.4 percent.[5]

Although unemployment rates have fallen, underemployment and casual employment rates have swelled. The rapid growth of raw material exports in areas such as fruit, seafood, and lumber has coincided with the collapse of large industry in sectors such as textiles and construction. The number of unionized workers, as a percentage of the overall labor force, has fallen from 41 percent in 1972 to less than 13 percent today.[6] At the same time, the number of Chileans who are self-employed—who work alone or own firms with less than four employees—has rapidly grown. The ratio of workers to employers is half what it was in 1960. The growth in self-employment is reflected in the explosive development of *microempresas* (microenterprises) which contract out to large conglomerates, or service the industrial sector in areas such as information, publicity, marketing, security systems, and repairs and maintenance. These now employ over 45 percent of the current work force.[7] The sharp drop in the size of the average firm has severely weakened labor's clout.

The owners of such small enterprises often live on the verge of poverty, dependent on temporary contracts from large conglomerates called AFPs (*Asociaciones de Fondos Provisionales*, or Mutual Funds). They are thus neither willing nor able to give permanent contracts to their employees. Current labor legislation encourages this "flexible" use of labor. While the ten richest families in Chile control the AFPs, workers in *microempresas* are paid salaries barely above subsistence, without fringe benefits or job security. Irregular hours, unstable employment, and low caloric intake have increased levels of physical and mental exhaustion. The number of serious injuries in the workplace tripled between 1980 and 1990.[8]

The change in work patterns has had a significant impact on social relations. Economist Alvaro Díaz notes: "There has been a displacement from the neighborhood and the street to the workplace; from relationships with neighbors to relationships with clients; from a relationship with the administrator of the emergency employment program to one with a private entrepreneur. Work hours have been changed, family relations modified, and the quantity of social interactions has multiplied."[9] The fragmentation of the social relations of the work place has obscured the sense of collective fate and identity among Chile's working class.

Poor salaries have also forced women to enter the labor force in large numbers. Women made up 34.6 percent of the labor force in 1985, up from 27.6 percent in 1976. Most working women toil in the lowest-wage, least-organized, sectors of the economy. Over 25 percent are employed in domestic service alone.[10] New employment opportunities in seasonal agriculture, for instance, have been filled largely by women, who work for minimal wage, and have no organizational representation and no history or familiarity with labor organizing.

The transformation of the workplace has been complemented by the transformation of the political system. Chile's multiparty system based on proportional representation has been supplanted by a two-party system in which the governing coalition includes seventeen political parties, ranging from left to center. The current government's concern with economic stability and political cooperation from the military and the political right has dissuaded all seventeen governing parties from organizing among the urban poor. The powerful right-wing Renovación Nacional party is regularly consulted on policymaking, due to its control of the Senate (a consequence of Pinochet's new electoral law, and his nine "designated" senators), while the once powerful Chilean Communist Party has virtually disappeared. The Socialist Party, the second largest in the governing coalition after the Christian Democrats, has embraced the free market, leaving, ironically, only the neofascist Independent Democratic Union (UDI) with an incentive— which it vociferously pursues—to mobilize from below.

The church has also withdrawn from political activity, hoping to reestablish spiritual unity within its ranks and to defuse some of the more radical Marxist and feminist organizations nurtured on its doorstep. Foreign governments and nongovernmental organizations have cut funding to popular organizations, while the Chilean government provides funds only to those popular organizations willing to convert into small businesses. Many soup kitchens, for example, have become private bakeries, groceries, or restaurants with government support. The entrepreneur is encouraged, the political organizer is repressed.

The transformation of the economic and political system has had a profound impact on the world view of the typical Chilean. Most Chileans today, whether they own a small, precarious business or subcontract their labor on a temporary basis, work alone. They are dependent on their own initiative and the expansion of the economy. They have little contact with other workers or with neighbors, and only limited time with their family. Their exposure to political or labor organizers is minimal, and with the exception of some important public service sectors such as health care, they lack either the resources or the disposition to confront the state.

The fragmentation of opposition communities has accomplished what brute military repression could not. It has transformed Chile, both culturally and politically, from a country of active, participatory grassroots communities, to a land of disconnected, apolitical individuals. The cumulative impact of this change is such that we are unlikely to see any concerted challenge to the current ideology in the near future.

Notes

1. National Institute of Statistics (INE), cited by Jaime Ruiz-Tagle, "Las Políticas Sociales en 1990-91," in Gonzalez Riva, ed., *Economía y Trabajo en Chile* (Santiago: Programa de Empleo del Trabajo, 1991), 46. It has been common since the 1960s, and in the work on poverty of the Economic Commission on Latin America and the Caribbean (ECLAC) to define poverty by comparing household income to the cost of a minimum food consumption basket, one that would meet the caloric and protein requirements of the household. A household is defined as poor if the income of the household is equal or less than two minimum food consumption baskets, and as indigent if it is lower than one.
2. INE, cited by Ruiz-Tagle, "Las Políticas Sociales en 1990-91," 46.
3. Elaborated by PET (Programa de Economia del Trabajo), and based on surveys conducted by INE in 1969, 1978, and 1988 in Gonzalez Riva, ed., *Economía y Trabajo en Chile*, 196.
4. Ricardo French-Davis and Dagmar Raczynski, *The Impact of Global Recession and National Policies on Living Standards: Chile, 1973-1989* (Santiago: CIEPLAN, 1990), 37.
5. INE, cited by Ruiz-Tagle, "Las Políticas Sociales en 1990-91," 46.
6. Jaime Ruiz-Tagle, *El Sindicalismo Chileno despues el plan laboral* (Santiago: PET, 1985).

7. Librecht Van Hemelyryck, "El Desarollo de la pequeña y microempresa en Chile: Un Desafío para el futuro," 143-77, in Eduardo Valenzuela, *Proposiciones 20* (Santiago: SUR, 1992), 154.

8. Alvaro Diaz, "Nuevas Tendencias en la Estructura Social Chilena. Asalaración Informal y Pobreza en los Ochenta," in Valenzuela, *Proposiciones 20*, 88-119.

9. Alvaro Diaz, "Nuevas Tendencias en la Estructura Social Chilena," 117.

10. Maria Elena Valenzuela, "The Evolving Role of Women," in Paul W. Drake and Ivan Jaksic, *The Struggle for Democracy in Chile* (Lincoln: University of Nebraska Press, 1991), 161-87.

15

Haiti: A Sweatshop Model of Development

Barbara Briggs
and Charles Kernaghan

In the memorable NAFTA debate on "Larry King Live" between Vice President Al Gore and Ross Perot, there was a particularly lively exchange about the threat of jobs moving south to where wages are cheapest. If U.S. companies are only interested in a low-wage labor force, Al Gore asked, why aren't U.S. companies flocking to Bangladesh and Haiti? The question caught Ross Perot off-guard; in typical fashion, he turned defensive and scoffed that the answer was obvious. Neither man seemed to know that Haiti has indeed caught the U.S. government's eye. Over the last decade, the U.S. Agency for International Development (USAID) has worked hard to promote Haiti as a low-wage site for U.S. companies fleeing offshore. This is more than just talk. USAID poured over $100 million into Haiti's corrupt and tiny business elite to enlist their support in this effort.

The United States has a significant economic presence in Haiti. Prior to the 1991 military coup, U.S. investment was estimated to represent over 90 percent of total foreign investment in the country; 95 percent of Haiti's light-manufacturing exports are destined for the U.S. market. According to the U.S. Commerce Department, the United States had "an estimated $120 million [$90 million excluding inventory] invested in Haiti as of early 1991. With the exception of several oil companies and banks (Texaco, Exxon, Bank of Boston, Citibank), U.S. investment is almost entirely in the assembly sector."[1]

In 1986, USAID put $7.7 million into an Export and Investment Promotion Project "to recruit assembly contracts and attract overseas investors" to Haiti. USAID felt that "medium and smaller sized American compan[ies]..., which often do not have overseas offices, have to be reached through aggressive outreach efforts." Haiti's "large pool of productive, competitive, labor-seeking employment" would be one of the "factors enhancing" this promotional effort.[2]

According to USAID, one of its primary objectives is to help Haitian women. In a 1986 report, the agency observed that "assembly industries in Haiti have a tendency to create a relatively greater demand for female workers who are believed to be better qualified for work which requires detail, dexterity, and patience. This carries a particular advantage in that increased employment for women in urban areas provides additional income which will more directly bear on the welfare of infants and children."[3] USAID took this position despite their caveat that "the conditions under which [women] work are not generally conducive to realizing their productive capacities nor adequately safeguarding their children's welfare."[4]

The agency's public stance is that its real goal has always been to create decent paying jobs that would allow Haitian families to live in dignity and health. In a 1991 report, the agency noted that "most of these jobs will be for low-income citizens, with a large proportion of these going to women. As citizens enjoy employment opportunities, they can then secure their shelter, provide necessary nutrition for their families, place their children in schools and provide adequate health care for their families. With improvement in the social status of its citizens, Haiti's new democracy will be strengthened and the participation of its population assured."[5]

Despite this professed concern, USAID has no empirical studies documenting the number of jobs created in Haiti's assembly-export sector, nor has it conducted any studies on what percentage of these jobs went to women, whether or not the minimum wage was paid, how many hours were worked, whether overtime and benefits were paid, what working conditions were, how people traveled to and from work, what transportation cost and how long it took, and how families could afford to live on the wages paid. In 1984, the agency observed, "Haiti has no reliable workforce data."[6] In 1992, the U.S. Commerce Department again noted, "no reliable data exists" on wages, and "reliable data on employment are non-existent in Haiti."[7] USAID never documented the most basic working and living conditions of the very people whom they were supposed to be assisting. What little information exists has to be culled from between the lines, or sought in places other than USAID reports.

On the other hand, there is no shortage of USAID-sponsored studies about the advantages that Haiti offers U.S. business interests. As early as 1980, USAID was funding studies that showed that it was far cheaper for U.S. companies to produce goods in Haiti than in the United States, even taking into account the costs of relocation, setting up production, freight, and customs. A survey of Haitian and U.S. electronic assembly plants operating in Haiti established that 38 percent of the companies enjoyed savings of between 20 and 40 percent over U.S. production, while 20 percent enjoyed savings of between 40 and 60 percent.

This study may also have pinpointed the real interest in women assembly workers: "Women workers tend to be quieter." The study went on to state that "traditional management prerogatives such as the right to hire and fire are respected by the government. There are no profit-sharing schemes or featherbedding requirements." Only quiet women, who "are young and highly motivated" and "who adapt easily to industrial discipline," are strong candidates for employment.[8]

Concerned about working conditions in plants closely linked to the U.S. economy, a delegation of U.S. trade union leaders visited Haiti in 1991, just after the military coup. Their business sector hosts took the delegation to a "model" apparel factory in Haiti's export assembly sector. At the factory, where fabric is sewn into clothing to be exported to the United States, the highest paid workers receive the equivalent of U.S.$1.48 a day. These workers' average transportation cost to and from work is 44 cents a day. A meager breakfast and lunch comes to 33 cents. This leaves 71 cents to bring home at the end of the day. Multiply this by six days, and working people have $4.26 to meet their family's expenses for a week. Since a working family needs about a third of this to cover rent and other expenses, family members have approximately $2.75 a week with which to feed themselves.[9]

Not one single collective-bargaining agreement is in effect in Haiti's export-assembly sector. According to the U.S. Labor Department, "it appears that many employers of the export industry are not in fact willing to bargain with trade unions." Further, "many employers, domestic and foreign, still question the legitimacy of unions."[10] While freedom of association, the right to strike, and the right to organize are legally provided to all workers in Haiti, few workers actually enjoy such rights whether employed in export-processing operations or local firms.[11]

Aristide's unexpected victory in the 1990 elections threw a wrench in USAID's well-laid plans. Under the Aristide government, observed USAID, "businesses are postponing investment and reducing inventory while waiting to see the future directions of the new government before making significant business growth decisions."[12] USAID, which had spent tens of millions of U.S. tax dollars since 1980 to foster offshore investment in Haiti's low-wage assembly sector, stopped promoting investment when Aristide took office in 1991.

A USAID/Haiti Mission internal staff assessment concluded that the incoming government "could benefit from position papers staking out the issues" in order to suggest "possible policy solutions" for economic development. "However," continued the study, "in view of legitimate political sensitivities, greater policy ownership by various Haitian interest groups may be more important than more donor-produced studies and reports." The "donor"—USAID—was supposed to go backstage. "Enhancing indigenous policy dialogue capacities within the private sector," the study concluded, "may be the most productive course of action...."[13]

In country after country throughout Central America and the Caribbean, USAID's development strategy is based on working with local business elites in order to help them to more efficiently utilize their large pools of low-wage labor. Accordingly, USAID's next move was to quickly allocate $26 million to the "ad hoc committee of business organizations" under USAID's control in order to help keep "Haitian production competitive in world markets."[14] An internal working paper recommended that the ad hoc committee be organized and placed "under the umbrella of USAID's export and investment promotion project (Prominex)." Prominex, which after a series of scandals changed its name to PROBE (Promotion of Business and Exports), receives 99 percent of its funding from USAID, and is in fact a USAID front group. USAID allocated $7.7 million to Prominex, $12 million in loans to business, and $7 million to foster democracy "from a business perspective." After 67.5 percent of the Haitian people had voted for change, USAID worked with the Haitian business elite to keep things the same.

The refurbished Prominex/PROBE operation was supposed to work with local business organizations to develop internationally competitive local production, build constituencies for open-market policies, and move Haiti toward becoming a full partner in the hemispheric free trade block (*sic*)." Of course, it was Haiti's "highly productive, low-cost labor" which was to be the engine for integrating Haiti into this bloc.

By the middle of Aristide's short pre-coup presidency, USAID was declaring that "signals" from the constitutional government "to the business community have been mixed." USAID went on the attack saying that, "decisions have been made which could be highly detrimental to economic growth, for example in the areas of labor and foreign exchange controls."[15] The agency was displeased with the fact that Aristide wanted to place temporary price controls on basic foodstuffs so the people could afford to eat.

But USAID's real wrath was targeted at labor-reform efforts. They opposed the Aristide government's attempt to raise the pitifully low minimum wage in Haiti's export-assembly industry. According to the agency, the proposed minimum-wage increase would price Haiti right out of the low-wage assembly market. "Wage systems," USAID said, "should not be the forum for welfare and social programs." It warned that "high distortion in labor costs"—the fifty-cent hourly wage proposed by the constitutional government—"can lead to capital-intensive, rather than labor-intensive responses to opening of markets."[16] Haiti, the agency seemed to fear, might turn into Switzerland or Denmark.

Three months before the coup, the agency mused: "If Haiti's investment climate can be returned to that which existed during the CNG [the National Council of Government headed by Lieutenant General Henri Namphy, a Duvalier loyalist, who took power after Duvalier fled] or improved beyond that, and the negative attitude toward Haiti appropriately countered, Haiti stands to experience significant growth."[17]

In April 1992, as the military regime that ousted Aristide became increasingly intransigent, the U.S. Commerce Department calmly noted:

> After an internationally recognized government is reestablished, the best long-term prospect for U.S. business will continue to be investment in export-assembly operations. Haiti's proximity to the United States, its access to Generalized System of Preferences (GSP), Caribbean Basin Initiative (CBI), and Section 807 U.S. Customs benefits, as well as its abundance of low-wage, productive labor should make it a good location for assembly operations when the country achieves some level of political stability.[18]

While USAID's projects may be a boon for U.S. and Haitian business interests, they have done little to alleviate the devastating poverty of residents of Port-au-Prince. The poor continue to live in miles and miles of broken-down shacks made of rough concrete, mud, straw, cardboard, and scrap sheet metal. When the wind blows in off the ocean, the metal roofs strain and rattle. It's like being inside a tin can. Open sewers flow down the dirt streets, which are deeply rutted by erosion. When it rains, the sewage overflows into people's homes. There are no bathrooms, no running water. Thousands depend upon a public faucet, or a broken water main where the people scoop up water. Children can be seen playing and washing in the open sewers. Under the military government, the government didn't collect garbage. It piled up everywhere in great mounds that the people burned to reduce the volume and to check the spread of disease.

The most common meals for working families are cornmeal with onions or some boiled plaintains with beans—when families can afford beans. Almost everyone eats only one meal a day. Many working families have only bread to eat, and rely on sugarcane water to fill themselves up.

The poor are barely surviving, and they are getting sicker. While the restoration of Haiti's elected government was an urgent and necessary first step, the economic development strategy that Haiti will pursue has great significance for the growth—and sustainability—of democracy. USAID and other "donors" might consider that the foundation for a viable development strategy must be more than the comparative advantage afforded by "cheap labor."

Notes

1. U.S. Department of State, American Embassy in Port-Au-Prince and U.S. Department of Commerce, International Trade Administration, "Haiti," *Foreign Economic Trends and Their Implications for the United States,* 6 April 1992.
2. USAID, "Haiti," *Project Paper/Export and Investment Promotion* (Project No. 521-0186), 8 August 1986.
3. Ibid.
4. USAID, *Country Development Strategy Statement: FY 1986: Haiti,* January 1984.
5. USAID, "Haiti," *Project Paper/Promotion of Business and Export Project* (Amendment No. 1: Project No. 521-0186), 29 June 1991.
6. USAID, *Country Development Strategy Statement.*
7. U.S. Department of Commerce, "Haiti," *Foreign Economic Trends and Their Implications.*
8. Haiti, Ministry of Economy, Finance, and Industry; Investment Promotion Division, *The Electrotechnical Industry in Haiti,* 1981 (estimated).
9. M. Catherine Maternowska, Ph.D. candidate in anthropology, Columbia University, New York. See also USAID/Haiti, *Concept Paper Economic Recovery Assistance II,* November 1986.

10. U.S. Department of Labor, Bureau of International Labor Affairs, *Worker Rights in Export Processing Zones*, August 1990.
11. Ibid.
12. USAID, "Haiti," *Project Paper/Promotion of Business and Export Project*, 29 June 1991.
13. USAID, "Haiti Macroeconomic Assessment," *Staff Working Papers*, February 1991.
14. USAID, "Haiti," *Project Paper/Promotion of Business and Export Project*.
15. USAID, "Haiti Macroeconomic Assessment."
16. USAID, "Haiti," *Project Paper/Promotion of Business and Export Project*.
17. Ibid.
18. U.S. Department of Commerce, "Haiti," *Foreign Economic Trends and Their Implications for the United States*.

16

Trade Unionism Across the Border

Robin Alexander
and Peter Gilmore

For six years Fernando Castro had responsibility for the management of chemicals at a motor plant owned by General Electric (GE) in the Mexican border city of Juárez. In November 1993 he was fired for union organizing, a relatively common occurrence in Mexico. But this time, things were different. In the shadow of the NAFTA debate, a spotlight was cast on the dismissals at this GE plant. By the following February, the soft-spoken technician was on tour in the United States, stressing to North American audiences the importance of the assistance that the Mexican workers and their union had received from trade unionists north of the border.

"I want to tell workers here," Castro said, "that some of us who have been fired are continuing to organize from the outside, together with workers on the inside. I am here to make a commitment to those who are supporting our efforts that we will not stop until we have succeeded in organizing the plant."

The GE motor plant, Compañía Armadora or CASA, employs approximately 950 workers and one hundred supervisory staff. It produced 35,000 small motors in 1993—up from 24,000 the previous year. Work at the plant largely came here from a Decatur, Indiana plant closed in 1989, which had been represented by the United Electrical, Radio, and Machine Workers of America (UE). The hourly wage of GE workers in Decatur—approximately $13.50—was more than twice the *daily* wage of their Mexican counterparts in Juárez.

"Workers in the United States and Canada share a common interest in ensuring that Mexican workers are successful in organizing democratic unions and improving wages and benefits," UE Secretary-

Treasurer Amy Newell asserted. "If they fail, we share a future of common misery. I prefer to think of a future where we sit together at the bargaining table with trade unionists from Mexico and Canada, and together take on transnational corporations such as General Electric and Honeywell."

For these reasons, explains Newell, UE and Mexico's only independent labor federation, the Authentic Labor Front (FAT), created a Strategic Organizing Alliance two years ago. "We believe it is imperative that we develop a new kind of international solidarity—one which is focused on organizing."

In this alliance, FAT agreed to target transnational companies in the *maquiladora* zone that have a bargaining relationship with UE in the United States. Since last summer, UE and STIMAHCS, the metal workers' union affiliated with FAT, have targeted the Juárez plant. UE has also established a solidarity fund, and recently launched a sponsor-an-organizer campaign to encourage unions, individuals, and other concerned organizations to contribute a fixed amount each month for a year. This will enable FAT to finance its budget and to put some of the fired workers back to work as organizers.

From November 4 to 7, 1993, a delegation composed of General Electric workers from UE Locals 506, 731, and 1010 met with workers from Compañía Armadora engaged in organizing. The U.S. delegation toured the neighborhood where the majority of Mexican GE workers live, and discussed ways in which GE workers in the United States could support the efforts of the Mexican workers to organize a union. A "MacNeil/Lehrer" news team filming a story on cross-border organizing accompanied the delegation during part of its trip.[1]

Revelations that GE management had actively obstructed union-organizing efforts outraged (but did not surprise) the UE members. They learned, for example, that the company now requires buses to drop workers off inside company property, so as to prevent them from receiving union literature. In other instances, managers snatched union literature out of workers' hands.

In a more serious instance, last fall GE terminated or pressured into "voluntary" resignations more than one hundred Mexican workers, including a woman who attended the UE convention last August in Cleveland. This was widely perceived as an effort by GE to rid itself of senior workers, of workers who speak up or complain about shop conditions, and of union activists. Because the economic pressure on workers to accept indemnification (legally mandated severance pay) is so extreme, most of them leave quietly and do not challenge the company's actions.

The Mexican GE workers revealed that the company uses chemicals which have been banned at U.S. GE facilities. They described a variety of other violations, including failure to: pay overtime properly; give light work to pregnant women; provide adequate protective equipment and properly ventilated work areas; comply with health and safety requirements; and properly test workers who may have been exposed to chemicals or inform them of the results of these exams. The U.S. and Mexican workers also discovered that they were subject to the same unacceptable company practices—such as providing pizza, in lieu of compensation, to workers who meet major production goals. Out of these conversations, the workers began to develop plans for future communication and support.

Upon their return to the United States, two UE Locals immediately shipped a typewriter and health and safety information to STIMAHCS in Juárez. On November 22, UE leader Amy Newell wrote to the U.S. headquarters of General Electric outlining the types of labor law violations described by the Mexican GE workers, and requested a company investigation and corrective action. An article about the trip was published in the November 19 edition of the *UE News*.

Then the reprisals began. Over the course of the next two weeks, GE fired ten Mexican workers, all for spurious reasons related to union activity and what the company called "insubordination." Most had attended the meeting with the UE delegation. Among those fired were the man who hosted the gathering with UE, and a worker interviewed on "Mac-Neil/Lehrer."

As news reached UE's Pittsburgh headquarters, Newell wrote a series of letters to General Electric. She gave the company until December 10, the date of a previously scheduled conference board meeting of UE leaders from GE plants, to correct the situation. When the board convened, delegates instructed Newell to inform President Clinton about the firings. They stressed the need for prompt action in light of the promises to protect labor rights made during the NAFTA debate.

On December 22, General Electric advised UE that it had offered to reinstate six of the ten fired workers. GE sent form letters to those people who inquired about the Juárez firings, declaring that all of the workers in question had accepted statutory severance pay. In fact several of the fired workers—one of them Fernando Castro—have refused all deals, and are demanding their jobs back.

Meanwhile, at Honeywell's Chihuahua plant, a second factory targeted by the Strategic Organizing Alliance, low pay, lack of protective equipment, and poor treatment by management had convinced workers to organize as a local of STIMAHCS, the metal workers' union. The company responded viciously, coercing twenty women into signing statements that said they were voluntarily resigning. Management interrogated the women individually for up to four hours, in some cases offering them money if they revealed the names of those responsible for the organizing effort.

The Honeywell management offered in-shop organizer Ofelia Medrano a deal: if she signed a statement assuming responsibility for the organizing campaign and pledging to abandon the campaign, the company would guarantee her continued employment at the plant. After hours of harassment, Medrano eventually signed the statement, but was fired anyway. The Teamsters union, which represents many organized Honeywell workers in the United States, took the initiative in developing the U.S. support effort for the Mexican workers. The Teamsters encouraged concerned trade unionists to write protest letters to the company and President Clinton.

Dissatisfied with the responses of GE and Honeywell, and with the failure of President Clinton to even answer their correspondence, UE and the Teamsters took further action. On February 14, the two U.S. unions—with the full support of FAT—filed the first two complaints under the labor side agreement of NAFTA, with the U.S. National Administrative Office (USNAO), a small agency housed in the U.S. Department of Labor.[2] The unions requested that the USNAO initiate an investigation, and hold hearings on the mass firings and numerous labor-rights violations committed by GE and Honeywell in response to organizing campaigns at their Juárez and Chihuahua plants. UE and the Teamsters also asked the USNAO to examine the failure of the Mexican authorities to enforce Mexican and international laws protecting organizational and labor rights.

The two unions also organized a thirteen-city tour by fired GE worker Fernando Castro, fired Honeywell worker Ofelia Medrano Sánchez, and STIMAHCS General Secretary Benedicto Martínez, to publicize the violation of workers' rights in Mexico. The tour included rallies, press conferences, and meetings with members of Congress and a wide variety of groups. The tour was supported at the local level by various unions, Jobs with Justice chapters, and fair trade campaigns.

The efforts of UE, the Teamsters, and FAT, through STIMAHCS, to organize GE's Juárez plant and Honeywell's Chihuahua plant are two examples of what has become known as cross-border labor organizing. The global reach of this type of organizing mirrors the rapid globalization of the world economy and the increasing mobility of international capital.

The Mexican government under President Carlos Salinas has enthusiastically implemented a neoliberal "modernization" program which has decimated real wages, cut social services, privatized much of the state, and opened the country to foreign investment. In the fire sale of state companies to private business overseen by Salinas, the government savaged collective-bargaining agreements, slashed wages, laid off thousands of workers, and destroyed job-security guarantees. The PRI's development strategy culminated with the implementation of NAFTA on New Year's Day.

A centerpiece of the drive to attract foreign investment is the *maquiladora* program. The *maquiladoras*, with foreign ownership, produce goods for export, largely to the United States. Today, half a million workers toil in some 2,000 *maquiladora* factories. While once restricted to Mexico's northern border, *maquiladoras* are now appearing in the interior as well. The *maquiladora* work force is overwhelmingly women and poorly paid.

Over 8 million Mexican workers are unionized. The vast majority, however, belong to unions tied directly to the "official" or government-dominated federations. It is extremely difficult to organize independent, democratic unions. "When we begin an organizing campaign," says Benedicto Martínez, one of FAT's national officers, "it is with the knowledge that we are taking on not only the company, but the government and official unions as well."

In general, unions within the AFL-CIO have been both reluctant and unable to establish meaningful relationships with independent unionists in Mexico. In part this is because the AFL-CIO has a historic relationship with the corrupt, government-dominated Confederation of Mexican Workers (CTM). The reluctance is also, in part, a consequence of protectionist and xenophobic cultural traditions within the United States and the trade union movement. The changing economic reality—reflected in the loss of thousands of high-wage jobs in the

United States as U.S. corporations move to Mexico to take advantage of low-wage labor and slack environmental controls—is prompting U.S. unions to change their tune.[3] The debate around NAFTA has caused many in the U.S. union movement to question the AFL-CIO's exclusive relationship with the CTM and to explore the meaning of international labor solidarity.

Some U.S. unionists have begun to envision a future that includes not only cross-border organizing, but coordinated bargaining, strikes, and political action. Progressives see similarities in the struggles that U.S. and Mexican workers face. The labor laws in Mexico are, ironically, much better than those in the United States, but enforcement of these laws is a major problem in both countries. Organizing is tough in Mexico, but is hardly easy in the United States. Trade unionists generally agree that U.S. unions should not organize in Mexico; rather, they argue, U.S. unions should help provide resources and create the conditions—through pressure on the U.S. government and U.S.-based transnationals—to enable Mexican trade unionists to organize in Mexico.

"We need an organizing response, not a political response," says Baldemar Velásquez, the president of the U.S. Farm Labor Organizing Committee. "We must fashion a union with workers in alliance, state by state, country by country. We must insist that workers' rights to wages and benefits such as health, education, and environmental safety be protected everywhere. As Americans and Mexicans alike, we are now less citizens of the nation in which we are born, and more citizens of the company for whom we work. This makes us equal. We must insist that this equality be reflected in our paychecks, our work conditions, our living conditions, our environmental conditions—for which the common company is responsible. This should impact the security of our jobs here and in Mexico."

U.S. progressives within the labor movement have responded to the crisis of labor rights in Mexico with a wide range of solidarity actions. These efforts have taken four forms: worker-to-worker interchanges, ranging from exchanges of information to financial or other kinds of aid; general support for independent organizing efforts; relationships between unions, ranging from exchanges of information to joint organizing projects; and efforts to spotlight poor environmental and working conditions, especially in the *maquiladora* sector.

One of the most interesting relationships was spearheaded by members of the United Auto Workers (UAW) Local 879, where Ford workers from Minneapolis joined with Canadian Auto Workers (CAW) members to provide support for Ford workers in Cuaútitlan.[4] Unionists from all three countries have met on several occasions. In a symbolic gesture of solidarity, they have worn black arm bands to commemorate the death of Cleto Nigmo, a Ford worker killed by CTM goons. The UAW local has also initiated several innovative campaigns to provide financial assistance, among them an adopt-an-organizer campaign in which the local has pledged $300 a month for the Ford Democratic Movement.[5] Workers who contribute receive an international organizers' jacket patch.

Other efforts have focused on unorganized workers. *Mujer a Mujer*, an organization based in San Antonio, Mexico City, and Toronto, facilitates contacts among women workers in Mexico, the United States, and Canada. It has organized tours, enabling rank-and-file and unorganized women—especially garment workers from Mexico and the southern United States—to begin a dialogue.

Labor Notes, a monthly publication of the Labor Education and Research Project, and the Transnational Information Exchange (TIE) have also organized conferences and delegations in an effort to foster a dialogue between both unionized and rank-and-file workers, generally on an industry-wide basis. TIE has helped organize several trinational auto workers' conferences in Mexico, which were attended by both union leaders and rank-and-file members. It also helped coordinate a telecommunication workers' conference in Mexico in February, which was attended by members of CAW, the Canadian Communication, Energy and Paperworkers' Union, and three Mexican telephone workers' unions. This conference focused on changes in technology in the telecommunications industry, and the unions' response. Participants agreed to exchange information on a continuing basis via electronic mail, to summarize collective bargaining agreements, and to create a bilingual compilation of telecommunications terms.

The North American Worker to Worker Network, a newer coalition based in North Carolina, serves as an informational clearinghouse. It sponsors tours of activists, and is developing an emergency-response network for labor rights violations in Mexico.

The American Friends Service Committee (AFSC) has also brought workers and union officials together in a variety of forums. It places greater emphasis on dealing with representatives of Mexico's official unions. AFSC also provides financial and other support to the Border

Committee of Workers (CFO), an independent organization of women workers in the *maquiladora* industry. CFO is composed of women workers from a variety of plants, who meet together in their neighborhoods to learn about their rights under Mexican labor law, and to develop tactics to enable them to assert these rights without jeopardizing their jobs. CFO representatives have attended two annual Zenith shareholders' meetings to talk about low wages, long shifts, and exposure to hazardous substances at the Reynosa plant.

Cooperative efforts have also been made to provide training and technical assistance to Mexican workers, especially in the areas of health and safety. Last October, AFSC and the American Public Health Association sponsored the creation of a binational network of health and safety experts to provide free counsel for *maquiladora* workers. In a more problematic example given this union's reputation and top-down organizing approach, the Laborers' International Union of North America recently announced that it intends to begin training Mexican workers in environmental clean-up; the union hopes to receive funding earmarked by the EPA and USAID for this purpose. *Labor Notes* also recently conducted a cross-border organizers' school which focused on the nuts and bolts of "successful mutual solidarity efforts."

Other efforts have focused on highlighting labor and environmental problems, especially in the *maquiladora* sector. During the anti-NAFTA campaign, the International Labor Rights Education and Research Fund submitted a petition to the U.S. government seeking to expel Mexico from the Generalized System of Preferences. The petition, drawn up with the assistance of the Mexican National Democratic Lawyers' Association, detailed systematic labor-rights violations in Mexico.

The Coalition for Justice in the Maquiladoras (CJM), a coalition of labor, religious, and community groups, initially focused on environmental contamination by U.S.-based transnational corporations. CJM was responsible for much of the media attention during the NAFTA debate on environmental pollution along the Mexico-U.S. border, including reports of the high rate of anencephalic births in the Brownsville/Matamoros area. In coordination with community leaders, CJM targeted specific polluters on "chemical row" in Matamoros. These campaigns led to the closure of two plants, which significantly reduced pollution in the neighboring *colonias*. More recently, CJM has supported community and worker organizing efforts, both directly and through activity by shareholders. It has begun an initiative to draw attention to the problem of the inadequate translation of warning labels on chemical containers, and has been instrumental in publicizing the recent firings of and police brutality against Sony workers in Nuevo Laredo.

Relationships between unions—generally either industry- or company-specific—also have been developing for some time. One of the first company-specific relationships was developed by the Farm Labor Organizing Committee (FLOC) with its counterpart SNTOAC, an official farm workers' union which represents Campbell's workers in Mexico. FLOC president Baldemar Velásquez credits the exchange of information and mutual support with helping SNTOAC get a 17 percent increase in wages and benefits in its contract at a time when a 10 percent ceiling was in place. The International Ladies' Garment Workers Union also views work with Mexican workers and unions as a "key strategic front for the American labor movement," according to Jeff Hermanson, the union's director of organizing. It meets with Mexican unionists to provide them with encouragement and assistance in organizing.

Others, such as Eduardo Diaz of the U.S. Postal, Telegraph, and Telephone International, views the international secretariats of trade union federations as promising vehicles for furthering international solidarity efforts. Historically, the international labor secretariats functioned primarily to promote their respective capitalist or socialist political programs. With the end of the Cold War, however, some trade secretariats are turning their attention to supporting organizing work by member unions. "It is important to refocus the secretariats away from meetings and resolutions," says Diaz, "and to provide concrete assistance to those who are trying to organize."

The Mexican trade unionists who toured the United States in February received a warm welcome at various union meetings, clearly signaling a greater openness on the part of the AFL-CIO and affiliated unions to expand their support beyond the CTM. This is an important and welcome change which has been developing over time.[6]

"I give credit to UE for being in the vanguard of efforts to raise living standards in both Mexico and United States," says Rosemary Trump, international vice-president of the Service Employees International Union. "We are working through our international department to encourage the AFL-CIO to follow UE's lead in supporting independent trade unions in Mexico."

With respect to internationalization, multinationals have been way ahead of the unions. The debate over NAFTA had one silver lining: it forced U.S. unions to reconsider international solidarity. Unionists will encounter innumerable obstacles in their efforts to forge linkages with their counterparts in Mexico, among them differences in language and culture, limited resources, the historical relationship between the AFL-CIO and the CTM, and a strongly ingrained sense of rivalry between U.S. and Mexican workers. It is imperative, however, that unions move forward to establish strategic international alliances. Ultimate success, of course, will require political change, not only in Mexico, but in the United States and Canada as well. But nothing will happen unless workers begin taking what at this point appear to be impossibly small steps.

Notes

1. The "MacNeil/Lehrer" report aired on 11 January 1994.
2. The structure of the North American Agreement on Labor Cooperation (NAALC) can be thought of as a pyramid. At the foundation, the national administrative offices can accept complaints about a wide variety of labor violations. The local USNAO can initiate an investigation, hold public hearings, and consult with other national administrative offices; it has, however, no authority to resolve complaints. At the next step, the parties can request ministerial consultations. If those do not resolve the problem, they can convene an evaluation committee of experts. If still unsuccessful, the parties can initiate a multi-step process culminating in sanctions. There are a number of major problems with this system. First, the only type of violations which are subject to sanctions are occupational health and safety, child labor, and minimum-wage technical labor standards. Sanctions cannot be invoked for the following types of violations: the violation of rights to organize or associate including collective bargaining and the right to strike; disputes concerning forced labor, over-time, employment discrimination, workers' compensation, and equal pay; or the violation of the rights of migrant workers. Second, the complainant must not only demonstrate that a company has engaged in massive violations of workers rights, but must show evidence of a persistent pattern of failure to enforce the laws. Third, although a private party may file a complaint, private parties have no standing within the process, and absolutely no control over the proceedings. In fact, it appears that they do not even have basic due process rights of participation. Fourth, although NAFTA took effect on January 1, 1994, procedures and permanent personnel are not yet in place. Fifth, even if all of the government entities were operational, most of the steps include no time frame, appear extremely bureaucratic, and may take years to complete—even assuming that relief were available at the end of the process. Nevertheless, if the NAO is willing to investigate aggressively, cast

a major spotlight on violations, and use diplomatic pressure to encourage resolution, the process will be valuable. Only time will tell.

3. A 1993 study by the Inter-Hemispheric Resource Center estimated that U.S. corporations moved as many as 180,000 U.S. jobs to Mexico during the last twelve years. It is significant that all of the top one hundred U.S. corporations have at least one plant in Mexico, and that General Motors is the largest private-sector employer in the country. Moreover, the *Wall Street Journal* reports that almost one half of U.S. companies surveyed have initiated or plan to initiate alliances with Mexican companies, open offices, or establish production facilities in Mexico. See *Wall Street Journal*, 25 May 1994.

4. On December 22, 1989, Ford announced it would not pay the Christmas bonus (a significant part of Mexican workers' yearly wages) and profit-sharing as required by the contract. The workers protested; some fired workers erected a *plantón*—an encampment with banners publicizing their protest—outside the factory, demanding the right to elect their union leaders. On January 5, 1990, CTM thugs attacked the *plantón*. The workers responded with a work stoppage. On January 8, dozens of armed CTM goons, clad in Ford uniforms, were allowed into the factory where they shot and killed one worker and wounded eight others. The workers captured three of them, who admitted they had been hired by the CTM. The workers occupied the factory for fifteen days until evicted by the police. As a result of the occupation, the company fired more than 750 of the most active trade unionists. Subsequently, Ford workers democratically elected new leadership for the local. Once again, however, the CTM intervened to oust the new leadership.

5. Although it never really got off the ground, the Dime-a-Month campaign was designed to provide both significant financial support to Mexican workers as well as an opportunity for those initiating the campaign to speak about both the situation in Cuautitlán, and the differences in wages and standards of living in the United States and Mexico.

6. See, for example, *Steelabor*, March/April 1993, for criticism of the official unions, and the *AFL-CIO News*, 21 February 1994, for a report on the GE and Honeywell firings and on the February tour sponsored by UE and the Teamsters. In addition, AFL-CIO unions at the local, regional, and national levels have met with the leadership of the FAT, in some cases simply to get acquainted, but in other instances to develop deeper relationships and provide financial support.

17

Brazil's New Unionism

Iram Jácome Rodrigues

Brazil is no exception to the global restructuring of production and the fragmentation of labor which that restructuring has brought about. These processes are posing new challenges to union power everywhere. Unlike the situation in many other countries, however, the trade union movement in Brazil has been able to grow in influence and expand despite an economic environment that is unfriendly to labor. Indeed the Brazilian experience runs counter to an international trend of labor union decline, reflected in the widespread drop in unionization rates.

The strength of unionism in Brazil is inextricably linked to the wider role that unions have taken on in Brazilian society. Because of the country's ongoing political crisis and the consequent weakness of the party system, trade unions have gone beyond their own specific interests to become effective social and political actors and, in one case, to form a major political party. Brazilian unions have not confined themselves to wage demands or other narrowly defined labor matters. Rather, they have become involved in a broad spectrum of issues including industrial policy, company competitiveness, productivity, the effects on workers of the shift to services, social policy, and regional integration.

The broad mass movement of the late 1970s and early 1980s against the military dictatorship created two major tools for labor organizing: the Unified Workers' Central (CUT) and the Workers Party (PT), both of which went on to have a great impact on public life in Brazil. Workers' calls for labor union freedom, and their protests against declining wages and workplace authoritarianism became a struggle not only for new workplace rights, but for a more genuine citizenship.

Founded in 1983, the CUT—one of three labor federations in Brazil—was a product of the mass trade unionism that had developed in the industrial region of greater São Paulo since 1978, especially among the metalworkers of São Bernardo do Campo. While its main bases of support have remained there over the past twelve years the CUT has managed to grow very rapidly, greatly expanding its social and political influence in the process. Today, the CUT is emblematic of the country's "new unionism."

Union activity in São Bernardo do Campo was also the cradle of the Workers Party, the CUT's sister organization. After 1978, opposition to the existing authoritarian union structure merged with broad-based resistance to the military regime. This opposition began to appear in fits and starts as early as the late 1960s among such groups as the Metalworkers Opposition Movement in São Paulo (MOSMSP). Luis Inácio "Lula" da Silva was elected president of the Metalworkers Union in São Bernardo do Campo in 1975. He was soon to become the labor movement's most effective spokesperson. In November 1989, he ran for president of Brazil, receiving 39 percent of the vote in a runoff against Fernando Collor de Mello, the eventual victor. Although Lula once again lost in the October general elections last year, the PT elected two governors, Vitor Buaiz in Espírito Santo and Cristovam Buarque in Brasília, along with a significant number of state and federal deputies.

Prior to 1978, trade unionism in Brazil, though not entirely paralyzed, was confined to small-scale, largely invisible, local activity in certain sectors of the labor movement. Between 1974 and 1978, slow-downs and stoppages occurred, but were usually confined to a single shop. The iron boot of the military dictatorship prevented mass resistance. The traditional trade union structure was corporatist and authoritarian; union leaders—the so-called *pelegos* (collaborators)—had close ties to government and management.[1]

Starting in the mid-1970s, workers awakened from a long political dormancy and began to express opposition to the military regime's economic policies, which were squeezing the wages of the poor and the middle class. Workers began to retake the initiative in relations with the state and management. A wave of strikes broke out in 1978, first in São Bernardo do Campo, then spreading throughout the country. That same year, the São Bernardo metalworkers held their first congress where they defined the main programmatic principles for union activity: collective bargaining, freedom for unions, and a basic labor law containing their fundamental rights.[2]

Proponents of the "new unionism" denounced the existing labor union structure, advocating free negotiations between management and labor without government interference. All the while, they continued to construct a different model of trade unionism by doing on-the-ground grassroots organizing in an effort to strengthen unions at the factory level.

In the Brazilian transition to democracy, the labor movement thus emerged as a key political actor. The large corporatist labor unions were run like businesses, and besides their labor and political muscle, had considerable fiscal resources. Thus when they began to reorganize, unions were able to finance congresses, seminars, leadership training courses, trips around the country to build contacts between labor union members, and so forth.[3] This social movement, which over time became a political movement, gave the working class a way to become involved in public affairs. This is the context out of which the CUT emerged to take such a prominent role on the Brazilian labor scene.

Three currents came together in the formation of the CUT: the traditional left, "independent" unionism, and Church-based activism.[3] The first current was made up of trade union activists who belonged to socialist political parties. In the early 1970s, these leftist activists took stock of their militant past and tried to reach out to the "masses"—either through organizing in poor neighborhoods, or by taking jobs in factories. By the early 1980s, these left-wing activists continued to work in the labor movement in small everyday battles both in factories in the country's major industrial centers—most notably in the South and Southeast—and in rural regions such as the North and Northeast. They were, however, scattered, often out of contact with their parties or at odds with them.

Those in the second major current of the new labor activity called themselves "independents." This current reflected the new profile of the working class, which was a product of the economic and social changes through which the country had passed during the dictatorship. It was led by young workers, many of them migrants from poorer areas, particularly the Northeast. They were first-generation industrial workers who shared neither ties to the traditional left nor the nationalistic ideological vision of the pre-1964 populist trade unionism. This strain of unionism was largely patterned on the metalworkers union in São Bernardo do Campo. Gradually throughout the country, these new "independent" leaders came to fill the vacuum in the traditional union apparatus.

Both of these currents maintained a close relationship with the progressive sector of the Catholic Church. The Church, closely woven into the country's social fabric, built a movement of Christian base communities (*comunidades eclesiais de base* or CEBs) throughout the country. In the early 1980s, there were about 80,000 base communities, involving approximately 2 million "believing and oppressed" people. These CEBs became a channel for the expression of a broad collective sentiment of social revolt and critique of the existing political order. The CEBs, rooted in the everyday practice of the people, organized groups of people who demanded their basic rights as citizens. As a catalyst of popular aspirations, these Catholic movements formed one of the pillars of the reorganization of the labor movement.[4] They influenced labor activism by speaking of the dignity of the worker—that is, seeing the worker not simply as a tool for creating wealth, but as a person endowed with certain rights.

Growing out of the reorganization of the labor movement in the late 1970s and early 1980s, the creation of the CUT represented the fulfillment of one of the Brazilian labor movement's long-held aspirations.[5] Since its founding in 1983, the CUT has grown significantly. In 1984, the CUT held its first congress with 5,000 delegates. The second congress, held two years later, was attended by 5,564 delegates whose organizations represented 12 million workers at the grassroots. (Unions in Brazil represent all of the workers in their jurisdiction, regardless of whether they are dues-paying members of the union.)

By April 1993, 1,878 unions (627 rural and 1,251 urban) were counted as CUT affiliates, representing 16.5 million workers. Of the 5.5 million rural workers, over 600,000 were union members. Of the 11 million urban workers, 3 million—about 25 percent—were union members.[6] By the fifth congress, in May 1994, the CUT had approximately 2,300 affiliates, which represented around 18 million workers at the grassroots.[7]

From the wave of strikes in 1978 up to the birth of the CUT in 1983, labor organizing proceeded feverishly. Between 1983 and the third national congress in 1988, the CUT successfully built an organized labor militancy. During those five years, the CUT built from within and asserted itself toward the outside. This movement-style, liberating, socialist, conflictive period—called the organization's "heroic" phase— ended with that congress.

The third congress marked the beginning of a shift in a vision of the CUT from a movement to an organization. From that point on, the organization began to adopt a vertical, administrative structure, which was complex and, in that sense, bureaucratic. This restructuring amounted to the construction of a rational "business-style" union. The fourth and fifth congresses, in 1991 and 1994 respectively, continued to reflect the shift within the CUT from a more confrontational stance toward a new willingness to negotiate.

The third congress formalized changes that were already underway within CUT trade unionism. Through amendments to the organization's bylaws, labor union council delegates were given priority over grassroots representatives, and the number of representatives elected to the CUT congress was changed to reflect the number of affiliated unions and not the categories of workers represented. This resulted in a decline in the proportion of congressional delegates who came out of the trade-union opposition of the 1970s—generally the more left-leaning part of the CUT. In addition, the congress decided that participants in future national congresses were to be elected in state congresses. This, in effect, was a "funnelling" process of the representation of the workers, since in practice it prevented a grassroots worker not represented in any of the CUT's internal tendencies from being elected to the national congress. Lastly, the third congress decided to hold congresses every three years instead of every two. The more leftist tendencies regarded these moves as a blow to the internal democracy within the CUT.

The upshot was the creation of what has been called a "democracy of tendencies," which has left many of those tendencies unhappy. Many leftists, for example, feel that the ordinary nonmilitant worker no longer has a role in the organization. This "democracy of tendencies," they argue, contradicts the democratic set of ideas championed by the new unionism. For others—primarily CUT moderates who are more narrowly focused on labor issues—the political skirmishing among the tendencies reflects an excessive politicization. They fear that this discord could eventually lead to the loss of the CUT's unique trade union identity.

At the fifth national CUT congress in May 1994, a twenty-five-member national executive board was elected. It was made up of one delegate from the rural sector, seven delegates from the industrial sector (three of them metalworkers), five bank workers (all from government banks), three officials from government-owned companies, and nine government employees. Seventeen of the board members are men, and eight are women. The most striking fact in the governing board's composition is the overwhelming presence of state employees, who make up practically 70 percent. This predominance may—aside from the merits of the case—have something to do with the labor federation's considerable resistance to the idea of privatization and the shrinking of the state apparatus. Even though rural workers constitute more than a third of workers at the CUT grassroots (approximately 6.5 million out of 18 million), this sector is practically absent from the CUT's executive board, and thus absent from the prism of internal democracy.

Nevertheless, the São Bernardo do Campo metalworkers continue to have the most authority and legitimacy within the CUT. They represent the majority tendency within the organization, called the "Labor Articulation." This tendency's dominance is reflected in the organization's presidency. From its foundation in 1983 until May 1994, the CUT president was Jair Meneguelli, a metalworker at the Ford Factory in São Bernardo do Campo, and former president of the Metal Workers Union in São Bernardo do Campo and Diadema. He resigned after being elected a congressional representative for São Paulo in the October 1994 general election. Meneguelli was replaced by Vicente Paulo "Vicentinho" da Silva, another leader from São Bernardo do Campo.

Equally notable, the CUT leadership is made up primarily of middle-class workers. Almost 60 percent of the delegates to the 1994 congress, for example, were university graduates, in a country where 32 million people—more than 20 percent of the Brazilian population—are illiterate. The current process is thus one of deep institutionalization, and hence of greater professionalization, impersonality, and bureaucratization within the CUT.[8] It also reflects the overrepresentation of middle sectors within the organization, and hence a growing gap between the grassroots and leadership.

The new trade unionism has thus come face to face with a basic paradox: at the very peak of its influence in the broader political process, it may be losing its effective workplace presence. If CUT unionism fails to become more broadly organized within companies, its more general representative bodies, the trade unions, and the CUT itself will weaken since they will be removed from the everyday activity of workers.

The only way to strengthen union activity is to maintain an organized broad base of support in workplaces. This requires a certain degree of militance. Despite the CUT's militance at various points in its history, the dominant forces within the organization today are increasingly seeking compromise and negotiation. The CUT has moved from a rather radical conception of trade unionism, starting with the strikes in 1978 and the harsh critique of the traditional labor union structure at the heart of the new unionism, to a more pragmatic conception.

The challenge faced by the Brazilian trade union movement is no different than that faced by its sister movements around the world: to maintain its strength in the face of the relentless attack from increasingly mobile international capital. From time to time, this may require a stance of compromise and accommodation, but no trade union movement can survive the abandonment of workers at the grassroots. The CUT still has the loyalty of those workers but, at the peak of its strength, dramatic tensions are present at the heart of the organization.

Notes

1. The corporative labor union model developed in the 1930s, which—despite some changes introduced in the 1988 constitution—still ties trade unions to the state, is based on the following elements: a) monopoly of representation granted by the state; b) the single union: in a particular territory, only one union from a particular category, such as metalworkers, may represent those workers; c) the so-called union tax: an obligatory fee collected from all workers, unionized and nonunionized, equivalent to one day of work a year; and d) the legal power of the labor court system.
2. Ricardo Antunes, *A Rebeldia do Trabalho* (São Paulo: Editora Unicamp/Ensaio, 1988), 17.
3. Leôncio Martins Rodrigues analyzes this process, its various stages, and the more general reasons for it in "As tendencias politicas na formaçao das centrais sindicais," in Armando Boito Júnior, *O Sindicalismo Brasileiro nos Anos 80* (São Paulo: Paz e Terra, 1991). See also Eder Sader, *Quando Novos Personagems Entraram em Cena* (São Paulo: Paz e Terra, 1988).
4. See Heloisa de Souza Martins, "Igreja e Movimento Operário no ABC (1954-1975)," (Ph.D. thesis, University of São Paulo, 1986).
5. See Leôncio Martins Rodrigues, *CUT: os militantes e a ideologia* (São Paulo: Paz e Terra, 1990), especially chap. 1, "A formacao da CUT," 5-30.
6. Data from the CUT general secretariat, 13 April 1993.
7. See Adriana Lopez and Alvaro Comin, "Delegados ao CONCUT: um perfil," *De Fato* (São Paulo), vol. 2, no. 4, July-September 1994.
8. Iram Jácome Rodrigues, "Perspectivas do sindicalismo no Brasil; o caso da CUT," in Eli Diniz, José Sérgio Leite Lopez, and Reginaldo Prandi, eds., *O Brasil no Rastro da Crise* (São Paulo: ANPOCS/HUCITEC/IPEA, 1994), 40.

18

Labor and Mercosur

Marcelo Montenegro

The Southern Common Market (Mercosur), a regional trade bloc comprised of Brazil, Argentina, Paraguay, and Uruguay, has been hailed by government and business leaders as a rousing success. Over a four-year transitional period that ended on December 31, 1994, negotiators dismantled 90 percent of tariffs and nontariff barriers between countries in the bloc. During that time, trade among the Mercosur nations has quadrupled. In 1993 alone, commercial transactions totaled $8 billion. In addition—unlike the North American Free Trade Agreement (NAFTA)—Mercosur is a true customs union with a common external tariff for goods coming from nations outside the bloc.

Outside this strictly commercial area, however, things have been much murkier. The Mercosur countries are home to almost 90 million workers, of whom 30 percent—according to the region's unions—are at best irregularly employed. Despite this, labor questions have been relegated to the sidelines in the negotiations. Workers, unions, and the issue of labor in general were excluded from Mercosur's founding Asunción Treaty of 1991 and its accompanying protocols and annexes. At a meeting in São Paulo in October 1994, Vicente Paulo "Vicentinho" da Silva, the president of Brazil's Unified Workers Central (CUT), called attention to the "deficit that Mercosur has had since its birth," alluding to this marginalization of workers.

Supporting the CUT president's assertion, labor lawyer Raimundo Teixeira Mendes, a participant in the negotiations and the author of a 1995 book on labor in the context of Mercosur, notes that not a single union initiative was incorporated in the documents issuing from the negotiations. On the contrary, discussions during the transitional period centered around the nuts-and-bolts problems of trade barriers and high tariffs blocking the customs union, while social and labor issues were put on the backburner.

Compared with other integration processes, such as the European Union and NAFTA, Mercosur may not be worse off from the point of view of enforcing labor rights and protections. But, as Teixeira Mendes points out, both NAFTA and the accords of the European Union at least have side agreements which address labor concerns. Mercosur has no such accompanying accords.

Eleven working subgroups were established in 1991 to discuss the harmonization of policies by sector. The subgroup on labor issues created eight commissions to study those topics considered fundamental to the well-being of workers, including collective bargaining, worker training, health and safety conditions, and rural labor. Their recommendations fell, however, on deaf ears.

Mercosur's government negotiators assert that Mercosur is just a customs union and does not, for now, contemplate the free circulation of workers in the four member countries. As a consequence, the negotiators simply ignored that topic, which was excluded from the main agenda. The problem, sources in all four countries agree, is that even if the free circulation of labor does not formally exist on paper in Mercosur, it does exist in practice in certain sectors of the economy such as construction. In Buenos Aires, Argentina and Punta del Este, Uruguay, for example, construction companies have been accused of illegally "importing" workers from Brazil. Without work papers and outside the reach of any legislation, these workers toil in conditions of semislavery.

The South American unions recognize that the integration processes set in motion by Mercosur acutely affect the region's workers and are provoking drastic changes in the structures of production. Since the clock cannot be set back, the unions are clamoring for a seat at the negotiating table in order to wield as much influence as possible over future decisions.

At the annual summit of Mercosur presidents held in Ouro Preto, Minas Gerais, in December 1994, a new permanent governing body— the Consultative Economic and Social Forum—was created that might open the door to wider negotiations. The forum gives unions and chambers of commerce an institutional channel to make recommendations to the Common Market Group, one of Mercosur's executive bodies. Even though the forum is merely consultative, union and business representatives welcomed its inclusion in the Ouro Preto Protocol.

According to Celso Amorim, minister of foreign affairs in the administration of President Itamar Franco (1993-1994), Mercosur's delay in dealing with social issues was a result of the fast-track schedule of the Asunción Treaty which focused attention on meeting the deadlines for the implementation of the customs union. With these targets now met, Amorim concludes, attention can shift to social concerns. "This is not a definitive, closed process," he says. "It's not like we've built the house, and now no one can make any changes. The house is going to be renovated and improved."

At the São Paulo meeting, CUT President da Silva said that until very recently the Latin American unions were practically ghettoized in the negotiation process, making it impossible for them to pressure governments to adopt social and labor policies. With the transition period over, labor unions and other social actors are now turning up the heat.

At the Ouro Preto meeting, the unions persuaded the governments of the region to promise that the labor question would move to the top of Mercosur's agenda for 1995. They have redoubled their calls for a Charter of Fundamental Principles, a regional accord on basic health and safety work standards, recognition of the right to union affiliation, commissions of workers from multinational companies, a regional labor tribunal, and the formation of a support fund for "reconversion" and professional reclassification. If the unions' demands still go unheeded, Mercosur's "deficit from birth"—in the words of da Silva—has the potential to become a big headache for everyone in the region.

19

Guatemala: Labor's Transnational Showdown

Deborah Levenson-Estrada and Henry Frundt

Labor solidarity in the 1990s must move beyond fantasies. The exhortation, "Workers of the world, unite! You have nothing to lose but your chains," inspired socialist trade unionists over the last century toward an idealized vision of working class internationalism. Their hope was partially realized with the formation of international trade secretariats attached to various unions, but as protective national labor movements thrived and the left-wing labor impetus faded, the original notion of global worker unity grew distant, archaic, and dreamy.

Meanwhile, capitalists have become the internationalists for whom borders are an obstacle and nationalism a waning ideology. Capitalists have accelerated the globalization process with their own firms backed by powerful international organizations such as the World Bank, the International Monetary Fund (IMF), and now the new World Trade Organization which will oversee the General Agreement on Tariffs and Trade (GATT). Such organizations operate outside political regimes, command enormous resources, affect the daily lives of millions of people, and have no public accountability. Yet as capitalists pursue the internationalization of economic and financial policies, their agreements on trade and related issues—indirectly bolstered by the December 1994 heads-of-state summit in Miami—can mean life or death for millions of Latin Americans.

The new phase of capitalist expansion has weakened traditional accommodations with national unions which have long been declining in strength. Today, even with less than 12 percent of the private U.S. workforce unionized, companies look toward the available world pool of bargain-price labor. To counter the international clout of mighty corporations, cross-border cooperative struggles of workers and kindred groups have become a matter of survival.

Corporations increasingly have interconnected global operations. Take the world's largest shirtmaker headquartered in New Jersey, Phillips Van Heusen (PVH). While it has mainland factories, PVH subcontracts all over the map, with direct production facilities in Honduras, Guatemala, Costa Rica, and Puerto Rico. All of these plants can be visualized as "departments" of a single global factory. In the U.S. "department," for example, after a particular garment is designed, workers size the model, then mark and cut the cloth into component parts of the shirt. These parts are shipped to another "department," a *maquiladora* finishing or assembly plant in Honduras or Guatemala. There, the "lower-skilled" tasks are completed—the stitching together of components, pressing, folding, and packaging. The garment is then shipped back to the United States where it is marketed.

The PVH example represents a step beyond the process Lenin wrote about when imperialism meant the internationalization of capital. Now, it involves the internationalization of production and distribution. Class solidarity now demands the confrontation of common employers like PVH. Ultimately, this necessitates organizing the various departments. Many workers, however, have no means of communicating with workers in other countries, even if their hands touch the same cloth. This must change. Working class internationalism is not a utopian vision, but a bread-and-margarine, rice-and-beans issue. Without it, employers will freely maneuver within their global operations to maximize profit with little regard for the impact this has on the workers they hire and fire around the world. If production and ownership is global, workers' organization must be as well.

A clear cross-border organizing strategy must first shift from nationalism as the primary trade union response to the loss of jobs when U.S. factories move abroad. It must combat the xenophobia of U.S. workers who protest the "giving" of "American" jobs to nonunion "foreigners"—whether the reference is to workers in a Central American city, or to a seedy sub-contracting workshop in a U.S. Chinatown.

Many labor activists realize that a new sort of internationalism must be created. During the Cold War, U.S. unions often organized abroad under U.S. government auspices. The AFL-CIO-sponsored American Institute of Free Labor Development (AIFLD), which sought to undermine the appeal of Communist-led labor organizations, also organized under the patronage of the U.S. government. With the end of the Cold War, the importance of these anticommunist groups is diminishing. Today, a number of U.S. unions, influenced by the example of European international trade secretariats, are expanding pragmatically, not to undercut the left, but to maintain bargaining power with employers. Mexico has been the site of lively organizing drives by the United Electrical Workers (UE) working with the Authentic Workers Front (FAT) at General Electric, the Teamsters at Honeywell, and the United Auto Workers (UAW) at Mexican Ford and Volkswagen plants. The Amalgamated Clothing and Textile Workers Union (ACTWU) and the International Ladies Garment Workers Union (ILGWU) are also following factories across borders to organize textile workers in the Dominican Republic, Guatemala, Honduras, and elsewhere.

Building a new labor internationalism is a task fraught with difficulties. There are numerous economic, political, and cultural differences to be worked through, as well as mutual suspicions flowing from ideological divergences and past allegiances. Many Latin American trade unionists, for example, believe their Northern counterparts may still have links to the CIA, while some U.S. activists worry that the Latin Americans' leftist orientation may compromise shop-floor organizing. Despite these difficulties, a fresh internationalism has been developing on the unlikely terrain of Guatemalan labor struggles. Because it is neither highly industrialized nor highly unionized, Guatemala may appear an unlikely birthplace for a new internationalism, but workers in this "peripheral" nation have stimulated innovative approaches to cross-border organizing.

In mid-1975, 150 workers organized a union at a Coca-Cola bottling plant in Guatemala City. The franchise owner, a U.S. national, was notoriously anti-union, and was pleased to be living in a country where trade unionists were—and are—routinely disappeared and tortured to death. After considerable anti-union violence, workers at Coke and their supporters contacted the American Friends Service Committee staff working in Central America, and the New York-based Interfaith Center on Corporate Responsibility (ICCR), which took up their cause. International pressure from these religious groups, combined with continuous shop-floor agitation inside the plant, led to union recognition and a contract in 1978. Subsequently, the company did everything it could to destroy the union, constantly violating the contract, and beating and jailing union leaders. Several workers were killed, and trade union membership declined.

In 1979, the Geneva-based International Food and Allied Workers Secretariat (IUF) joined religious and human rights groups in an enormous global campaign, bringing a class perspective to what had been largely a human rights issue. From late 1979 to mid-1980, the IUF combined a successful letter-writing campaign to the Guatemalan Presidential Palace with support strikes in Venezuela, France, and Mexico, along with union endorsements of a Coca-Cola boycott in over twenty countries including Canada, Germany, Italy, and Israel. It convened meetings between the representatives of the parent company in Atlanta, Georgia, and the Guatemala City union. It inspired hundreds of newspaper and magazine articles in dozens of languages about the violence against Guatemalan Coca-Cola workers. It also encouraged the world's largest trade union body, the International Confederation of Free Trade Unions (ICFTU), to support a tourist boycott of Guatemala. In the plant, sixty besieged unionists kept on with the struggle. In August 1980, shortly after another five Coca-Cola workers were killed, the pressure on the company's Atlanta headquarters became unbearable. It transferred the franchise to new owners on condition that they respect the union—a tremendous victory for the workers and their international supporters.

By this time, Guatemala was engulfed in a civil war, and most of the nation's unions had been destroyed by state-corporate violence. Yet, protected by international support in this adverse situation, the Coca-Cola union, an exceptional survivor, grew. Over the next few years, it developed a profound sense of historical mission, a David overcoming Goliath, a symbol of the capacity to accomplish what seemed impossible. In February 1984, the new owners—experienced soft-drink businessmen in Latin America—closed the company due to "bankruptcy." In fact, Coca-Cola had sold them the franchise so they could milk it dry. Even though the country was under military rule, over 400 workers occupied the plant for one year. With the support of the IUF and a remobilized international movement, the workers won their third major battle in ten years. In 1985, Atlanta officials sold the franchise to yet another set of owners who, to date, have kept their agreement to respect the union, which remains one of the strongest in the country.

The Coca-Cola example contains many of the ingredients required for the international labor solidarity of the future. The union's survival in the face of repeated and grotesque attacks depended on the initiative of a small number of individuals: the minority of workers at Coke who kept the union going in the worst of times; the few religious/human rights workers in Central America and elsewhere who promoted their cause; and the dedicated individuals at the IUF who decided to make an international case out of Coca-Cola. The Coca-Cola union's perseverance was also the result of large-scale collective actions: mobilizations by the majority of workers; letter-writing by thousands of people; and beverage boycotts and solidarity strikes by thousands of consumers and workers around the world.

The reciprocal interrelation of individual actions, which often appear to be idealistic uphill battles, and the large institutional efforts that ultimately sheltered the union, were key: international secretariats, even social democratic ones like the IUF, cannot singlehandedly build a large and expansive global campaign. In this instance, the campaign politics were simple enough: opposition to state and company violence, and support of workers' right to a living wage and decent conditions. It was, however, the interplay of individual initiative and collective action that kept the union firm, relatively democratic, and effective. Without the strong local, the international campaign would have been meaningless, and without the international support, the union would have been destroyed. A future international labor movement must emulate the Coca-Cola model by maintaining both local and international strength. The model must, however, be modified to fit patterns of international production and distribution that involve subcontracting, legal restructuring, and intercompany trade.

In the ten years following the success at Coca-Cola, Guatemalan workers have attempted this adaptation in fits and starts through cooperation with the Guatemala Labor Education Project (GLEP) and related groups. After Guatemala was returned—by the military—to a shaky civilian rule in 1986, rural and urban workers began to organize into a number of confederations such as the independent Union of Guatemalan Workers (UNSITRAGUA), and the Confederation of Guatemalan Unions (CUSG) which was largely funded by AIFLD. In 1987, U.S. activists, Guatemalan exiles, and staff members of ACTWU inaugurated GLEP to build on the solidarity generated by the Coca-Cola strike.

The GLEP was premised on the understanding that the intensity of Guatemalan state violence made it very difficult for workers to win anything without international solidarity. The need for a special mediating group like GLEP—as opposed to a committee within an existing U.S. union—was clear. Without having to wade through the bureaucracy of a U.S. union, GLEP could act directly and quickly to support Guatemalan labor unions, look for ways to educate U.S. workers, and encourage U.S. unions to join in these efforts. But GLEP, in common with the IUF and the post-1986 labor movement in Guatemala, faced additional, unforeseen challenges due to transformations in the Guatemalan economy and workforce.

By the mid-1980s, with the labor movement small and plagued with the traumas state terror constantly reproduces, existing Guatemalan industry had slithered into crisis due to lower revenues and increased debt payments. Factory after factory—including many in the food and beverage sector where the IUF sought to organize—shut their doors. As the existing industrial working class stagnated, workers moved into the informal economy where they enjoyed even fewer legal protections. By 1995, Guatemala City's informal sector employed two-thirds of its economically active population. In the formal sector, many workers had moved from larger companies to smaller ones where working conditions remained harsh, and organizing was particularly difficult.

New industries, largely composed of *maquiladoras*, arrived during this period of growing urban and rural poverty, when capitalist restructuring called for privatization, a sharp decrease in social spending, and the lowering of labor costs through the lowering of wages and the downgrading of labor conditions. Since 1986, *maquiladora* plants, located either in the city or on the outskirts of nearby towns whose residents usually work in agriculture, have increased from six to nearly 500. They are owned by citizens from Guatemala and other countries, notably Korea. Guatemalan *maquiladoras* generally are finishing plants, assembling garments cut in the United States. The approximately 100,000 workers they employ are primarily young women—some as young as eleven years of age. As elsewhere in the hemisphere, they have now replaced men in a new "re-gendering" of Guatemala's industrial workforce. Organizing the *maquiladora* sector and allying with workers in the informal economy posed problems that extended international solidarity beyond the Coca-Cola model. In the 1980s and 1990s, GLEP,

Guatemalan unions, and their U.S. union supporters have employed new means to respond to these new issues.

Several union-busting actions at *maquiladora* plants in the late 1980s led to local-international labor cooperation. At the Lunafil thread plant in 1987, and the U.S.-owned Inexport *maquiladora* in 1988, the owners locked out all union members. In 1988 the Playknits *maquiladora*, a subcontractor for Liz Claiborne, suddenly shut its Guatemalan facility, without even covering workers' back-pay. Following the Coca-Cola example, the UNSITRAGUA-affiliated workers occupied the premises of all three companies until they were ejected by police, at which point they camped out in front of the facilities. In all these cases, GLEP rallied with protests and publicity about U.S. corporate behavior and, on behalf of Playknits' union, GLEP was able to arrange negotiations in New York between union representatives and the company. Negotiations won monetary compensation for laid-off workers. At Lunafil and Inexport, GLEP helped the workers gain reinstatement and maintain union recognition.

Between 1991 and 1993, GLEP generated a huge U.S. campaign to force Phillips Van Heusen to recognize the CUSG-affiliated union in its Guatemalan plants where intimidation was rampant. GLEP circulated information about the PVH *maquiladora* inside U.S. textile unions, and organized demonstrations at scores of PVH outlets in at least fifteen states. Although bargaining has yet to occur, the company improved wages and working conditions, and acknowledged the union. Accelerating pressure on contract purchasers Sears, J.C. Penney, and Wal-Mart, GLEP also supported a reinstatement of women workers at a *maquiladora* called *Confecciones Unidas*. Even though the incipient *maquila* unions remain fragile, GLEP, Guatemalan labor organizers, and a representative of the ILGWU have been working to approach other *maquiladora* workers. To increase rank-and-file solidarity in the United States, GLEP even brought some ILGWU members from the Leslie Fay plant in Pennsylvania to Guatemala. The Leslie Fay workers, who had mounted protests to prevent the company from shifting operations to Guatemala, left the United States thinking Guatemalan workers were the problem. They returned thinking they shared problems with their Guatemalan counterparts.

Labor activists in both countries have also pressed employers to enforce labor codes that incorporate employee protections. They have successfully elicited such codes from PVH, Coca-Cola, and various U.S.

purchasers of *maquiladora* products. Working with ACTWU, Levi-Strauss has authored its own worldwide code, and contracts have been terminated for noncompliance. Recently, GLEP supporters have extended the call for codes to the rural sectors. In the United States, they are leafleting Starbucks, a popular gourmet coffee company, demanding adoption of a code of conduct that would require Guatemalan plantation owners from whom they purchase to respect basic rights, pay a living wage, and honor safety and health standards.

GLEP, U.S. supporters such as the International Labor Rights Education and Research Fund (ILRERF) and the Central American Working Group (CAWG), and Guatemalan trade unionists have also successfully employed U.S. trade law to call attention to labor abuses in Guatemala. This involves pressuring the U.S. Trade Representative (USTR) to penalize Guatemala under the provisions of the 1984 General System of Preferences (GSP). The GSP allows for penalties against countries which do not make progress in eliminating five types of labor violations: interference with free association; obstruction of union organizing/bargaining; use of child labor; slave labor; and subminimum working conditions. Because *maquiladora* owners regularly commit four of these abuses—there is no slave labor in the *maquiladora*—there were ample grounds for action. In 1992, Guatemala was placed on GSP probation.

Between 1991 and 1994, GLEP-ILRERF missions visited Guatemalan factories, spoke to corporate leaders and public officials, and met with union groups from all the major confederations. All this pressure had an effect. In late 1992, Guatemala revised its labor code to speed union recognition and improve rights for women. For the first time, it punished several corporate violators in the *maquiladora* sector. In mid-1993, when President Jorge Serrano Elías attempted to assume dictatorial powers, unions participated in the battle to restore constitutional rule. The private sector, and eventually the military, refused to support Serrano because they feared the loss of U.S. trade privileges, forcing him to flee the country.

By 1994, facing insistent demands from the U.S. Embassy to support Guatemala's new president, Ramiro de León Carpio, the U.S. Trade Representative was poised to drop its review but twice backed down, first because of ILGWU mobilization over Leslie Fay, and then after 500 police attacked protesting workers at the Empresa Exacta cattle ranch in the western highlands who were demanding union recognition to assure their legally required minimum wages of two dollars a day. The police wounded thirteen workers, killed two, and abducted one, later dropping his tortured body from a helicopter.

Guatemala remains a difficult country for union activity. Workers may win union recognition, but since 25 percent of the workforce must join before negotiations are mandatory, they often gain no contracts. *Maquiladoras* are especially problematic because they can close quickly, move out machinery, and reopen elsewhere in the same country or a nearby country whenever an organizing drive begins. One innovative approach proposed by Guatemalan trade unionists has been to organize in the neighborhoods where *maquiladoras* tend to be concentrated, not only inside the factory. Then, should the factory leave, the workers have some organization, and they can better discuss and confront their problems. Workers' neighborhood committees facilitate self-defense in many arenas, and link informal- and formal-economy workers.

In thinking out a fresh approach to organizing, Guatemalan unions are debating what tactics are most useful under varying conditions of repression. At issue is the extent to which repression has changed from being officially sanctioned (as under the regimes of Romeo Lucas García and Efraín Ríos Montt, from 1978 to 1983) to being controlled by specific owners or landholders who have certain military connections. Even under officially sanctioned repression, as in the case of Coca-Cola, organizers could sometimes achieve victory through noisy public demonstrations in conjunction with international support. However, as repression has become more selective and less official, some argue that *maquiladora* and other organizing should be more systematic and clandestine to assure the 25 percent union membership necessary for bargaining. "The army really doesn't care what happens to Korean or North American firms, and we should take advantage of this to quietly build union strength," stated one labor activist. Others remain willing to hold a well-publicized demonstration in front of a plant, but are less convinced that the clandestine door-to-door work can be done safely, even though it would increase union membership.

A fresh approach requires examining the old issue of gender practices and beliefs. The trade union movement on both sides of the border conceives itself as male and is male-led, although both men and women belong to unions. Even the ILGWU, which has a long tradition of organizing women workers in the United States, has not yet overturned sexism and male domination within its union. To assist in, and not undermine the organization of *maquiladoras*, male trade unionists have been challenged to alter their perceptions of women as primarily housewives, not workers, who are fragile and need protection by male trade unionists, and who in a short time will be out of the factory and back "where they belong," in the home.

Within the Guatemalan labor movement, this understanding is one most men share with the many women who see their factory work as temporary and their *maquiladora* wage as supplementary to male wages—even absent ones. The identification of women *maquiladora* workers as moonlighting housewives and not as workers makes organizing difficult. Despite the female leadership of *maquiladora* sit-ins, male trade unionists have been hesitant to organize the *maquiladoras* in part because they see the workers there as less "real." Since they are not men, they are thought to be incapable of the militancy that trade unionism requires. While some women workers hold this view, many, in increasing numbers, reject it. In the Guatemalan labor movement, women are inventing a grassroots working class feminism.

The Guatemalan case has shown that corporate campaigns and code demands, combined with strong local organizing, can be an important antidote to the unrestricted corporate expansion promoted by NAFTA and GATT. The advantage of corporate codes is that they offer the U.S. public a chance to apply consumer pressure as a sign of labor solidarity abroad. It should be axiomatic that if a worker at a cattle ranch which exports beef to the United States is dumped out of an army helicopter to prevent him from organizing a union, as happened at Empresa Exacta, or if a labor leader at a banana plantation that sells to Chiquita is shot dead by anti-union thugs, as just happened at the Chinnok Finca in the eastern part of the country, we do not buy Empresa Exacta beef or Chiquita bananas. Labor solidarity must determine how to generate a larger, more analytical, creative, and activist "we."

The labor rights strategy is also an essential political approach that requires the collaboration of unions on both sides of any border. While other groups have effectively documented cases of rights abuses, what makes GLEP-Guatemalan labor solidarity worthy of imitation is its cultivation of a two-way process in developing a labor-rights strategy using U.S. trade law. Given the loss of any meaningful labor rights provisions in NAFTA, cross-border trade union supporters are evoking trade provisions to emphasize the upholding of local labor laws.

Quiet, systematic organizing is a third requirement, but the battle will be a long one. After a number of apparent successes, unionized workers have been isolated and prevented from any meaningful ability to negotiate a contract, and companies have often closed. As the PVH and other Guatemalan examples suggest, success will eventually require organizing all of the company's "departments" around the world. This begins when a strong and strategic local organizing effort is combined with international worker and consumer support. It demands both sophisticated international coordination and on-site individual involvement.

Finally, an effective challenge to male domination and "normative" gender roles and ideologies is yet ahead. The decades-old "imagining" of class militancy as male really backfires in the new global economy—even if it hadn't before. A new internationalism must "demasculinize" conceptions of class, militancy, and leadership. U.S. unions are not significantly less male chauvinist than their Latin counterparts, but many of the U.S. men and women who work in Latin American labor solidarity tend to be more conscious of the discourse of feminism. If they are not self-critical, however, they risk being patronizing and condescending toward Latin American workers—male and female. The problem of sexist ideology and practice, like many others, is international, and the solution must come from the women and men who suffer because of it.

Drawing on the Coca-Cola model, these strategies offer the beginnings of a program for labor solidarity. They enable unions and supporters across borders to effectively fight the elimination of wage equity, health and safety protections, and union rights. The strategies protect the hard-fought-for rights recognized by the International Labor Organization, now encoded in the labor legislation of most nations. The labor solidarity movement is demanding its own codes of accountability and trade-based labor standards and is pursuing basic organizing principles and gender sensitivity. Only in this way will it break the chains forged by corporate power, and allow working people to build their own new and vital international bond.

Part III

THE BROADER
SOCIAL AND CULTURAL
CONTEXT

20

Mexico's Disappearing Countryside

David Barkin

While the crisis in Mexico is not new, until the dawn of 1994 it had been extremely well hidden. A heavily financed campaign had proclaimed the country ready to join the ranks of the advanced industrial nations, and the official criers were not only Mexican. Pundits in Washington were joined by colleagues in Paris and Geneva to usher the nation into the hallowed circle of respectable and wealthy nations, the GATT, NAFTA, and most recently the OECD.[1] But in Mexico, the claims that global integration will bring prosperity ring hollow for a large and growing segment of people whose struggle to survive is becoming more desperate—and perhaps even more hopeless—as the well-publicized recovery of recent years produced a cornucopia that only fed a few Mexicans and their designated foreign partners. This polarized reality encompasses all parts of the country and all dimensions of society: local cultures and fiefdoms, regional marketplaces, national culture, and internationalized consumption. The accelerating process of international economic integration is weaving urban and rural differences into a single battleground of conflicting interests, thrusting modern systems into traditional backwaters, and leaving important parts of Mexican society unprepared to compete in an economic and social environment that offers fewer, though more attractive, rewards to a small elite.

In rural Mexico, the battle lines, now so sharply drawn, can probably be traced to the mid-1960s. This was the period when the country finally proclaimed itself self-sufficient in basic foodstuffs, a historic achievement made possible by the successful application of the agrarian reform program put in place in the 1930s. This land reform, based on the breaking up of the colonial hacienda system, was the result of one of the most important demands of the Mexican Revolution of 1910 to 1917. The redistribution of land—written into Article 27 of the 1917 Constitution was only effectively implemented, however, during the presidency of Lázaro Cárdenas, from 1934 to 1940. The land reform redistributed hacienda land by creating rural communities—*ejidos*—whose members could work the land individually or collectively, depending on political circumstances. Although the community members—*ejidatarios*—did not have the right to sell, rent, or mortgage the land, their parcels were considered to be private property, to work as they pleased within the guidelines established by the community itself.

Post-Cárdenas administrations accorded less attention to this program and did not finance any significant technical assistance for these communities. The stimulus of having their own land to work was sufficient, however, to encourage most farmers to dramatically improve their productive conditions. Contrary to what many experts predicted, these poor, unschooled peasants were able to increase the productivity of their lands at an average annual rate of more than 3 percent following the redistribution of the 1930s, doubling their meager yields to more than 1.2 tons per hectare by 1960.[2] The system, put in place by *Cardenismo*, encouraged the peasants to achieve substantial improvements in productivity by the backbreaking application of inherited cultivation practices, together with the fruits of local experimentation with seeds, fertilizers, and soil and water conservation techniques. Despite this encouragement, however, the peasants were condemned to poverty by a rigid system of state control of credit and by the prices of agricultural inputs and products.

The import-substitution industrialization scheme of the post-Cárdenas period was also part of the development strategy. By producing consumer goods for the elite and more popular items for the masses, it contributed to general welfare by creating a rapidly growing demand for labor at a time when migration from the countryside was just beginning. The gains were real, as the purchasing power of minimum wages increased almost fivefold from a postwar low in 1946 to its apogee in 1976, while workers and peasants were able to claim an increasing share of national income, rising from 25 percent to 37 percent in the same period. Further improving the lot of workers and peasants, the populist state was offering important educational opportunities and medical care to virtually every segment of society.

Agricultural development over the half century following Cárdenas's reforms created a highly polarized rural society. Most *ejidatarios* were relegated to their traditional cultivation systems, producing maize and beans and a variety of other products for domestic consumption. They were highly constrained by an inefficient and corrupt federal bureaucracy, and unable to introduce modern farming systems or new crops for lack of credit or capital. Meanwhile, a highly capitalized commercial agricultural sector emerged as a result of substantial public investments in irrigation, rural road networks, agricultural research, production of high-yielding varieties of seed, and new cropping systems. Financed by generous agricultural credit-subsidy programs, and encouraged through a broad array of private and public incentives, these commercial farmers forged a new economy in the areas in which they operated, quickly transforming Mexico into an important participant in the international market for fruits and vegetables as well as for cattle.

In most of the country, the rural bourgeoisie channeled its struggle to control the countryside through the public investment program. Multipurpose river-basin development schemes, strategically placed throughout the country, opened up vast territories for commercial cultivation of crops destined for a new animal-feed industry and nascent fruit and vegetable markets in the United States, and later in Europe and Japan. With their new products and markets, the neo-latifundistas, as they were labeled by Mexican academics, began a cumulative process of investment and social differentiation that facilitated new forms of social control in the countryside. Social control was now imposed by the marketplace and enforced by a racist caste structure that made it more difficult for an indigenous and mestizo peasantry to participate in the modernization of rural Mexico.

Nowhere were these obstacles to progress more imposing than in the regions inhabited by the nation's many indigenous peoples. Whether in the colorful and well-known communities in the tourist centers among the Pure'hpecha of Michoacán, the Mayas of Yucatán, the Mixtecs and Zapotecs of Oaxaca, the Tzotziles and Tzetzales of Chiapas, or in the less accessible territories of dozens of other ethnic groups, the local pattern of *cacique* control was reinforced by draconian systems of official "justice" and police repression, supplemented where necessary by the arbitrary exercise of military force, sometimes camouflaged by a real or invented search for drugs. Official programs for local development, together with private concessions for the exploitation of natural resources, combined to threaten the traditional systems of resource management with a logic and pattern of extraction frequently incompatible with the social needs and ecological possibilities of the area. These outside pressures on resources were exacerbated by tensions created by growing population and poverty that often forced the communities to violate their own norms of resource conservation. As a result, indigenous communities and their regions were commonly even more devastated than other regions of the country in the name of economic progress and survival.

By 1990, rural development had left more than half the country's total rural area and its cultivated land to *ejidatarios*, colonists, and indigenous communities. The more than 3 million people in these communities, who make up the "social sector" in Mexican agriculture, were a major factor contributing to the country's political stability. As recently as 1990, they accounted for more than one half (55 percent) of the total domestic maize production, and controlled 20 million hectares (49 million acres) of arable land—more than half the total, though much of it was of marginal quality.[3] They are now engaged in an increasingly difficult struggle to survive, as the neoliberal policies of modernization through international economic integration threaten their very existence. With the uprising in Chiapas, Mexico was rudely reminded that many groups in rural society had been permitted to participate neither in the fruits of the revolution nor in the benefits of more recent material progress.

The Mexican government has for half a century channeled resources into the physical and institutional infrastructure necessary to consolidate the development of a modern rural sector. This deliberate role began as early as 1943, when the government joined with international groups to facilitate the development of what would become an imposing global structure of research institutions creating and encouraging the "green revolution." Behind this seemingly benign label, "naive" foreign scientists decided that traditional research institutions in Mexico were a brake to progress. So they collaborated with others, with more venal motives, to terminate programs that were helping dry-land beneficiaries of land distribution programs.

In the ensuing decades, rural policies became more complex but their objectives remained the same: to promote newer, higher-valued crops cultivated by a group of better-schooled farmers. The original program to develop dwarf wheat varieties, cultivated under irrigated conditions in the northwest, was acclaimed a success by 1960 and its group leader, Norman Borlaug, was awarded the 1970 Nobel Peace Prize for feeding the hungry. Little concern, however, was expressed for the traditional wheat farmers who groped for new ways to eke out a living as their traditional seeds, sown in rainfed lands in the central plateau, could not compete. These displaced farmers were the forerunners of large contingents of small-scale landowners who became contract producers and day laborers for a new agroindustrial complex serving domestic and transnational interests. With declining real incomes and fewer job opportunities, internal and international migration became a significant feature of Mexican life. As the men left in search of wage incomes, women were obliged to join the wage-labor force in increasing numbers, exposing themselves and their children to heretofore unknown health risks associated with the use of pesticides and sewage water in irrigation and a wide variety of hazards in other occupations.

The new production systems, requiring the intensive use of irrigation and agrochemicals, have had environmental effects that are still being sorted out. Overirrigation has initiated a destructive cycle of salinization, while the use of petrochemical fertilizers and pesticides has produced a good deal of water and land contamination.

The impoverishment of the peasantry heightened with the imposition—beginning in 1984—of neoliberal programs of economic stabilization. At first, the administration of President Miguel de la Madrid channeled resources to producers of export crops, abandoning its commitment to food self-sufficiency. Although it modified this policy later in the 1980s, when annual food imports rose to an alarming $5 billion and the popular outcry for change became widespread, supports for maize and beans were channeled mainly to the nation's richer farmers, working in the irrigation districts and the fertile plains of the north, rather than to the peasant farmers who traditionally sowed these crops on rainfed lands. By the time the administration announced the decision to negotiate NAFTA, however, there was an explicit commitment to eradicate the traditional forms of cultivation of basic food crops in rainfed areas. In fact, the present undersecretary of agriculture, Luis Téllez, has stated unequivocally that it is the government's intention to encourage the emigration of more than 13 million people from the rural areas during the remaining years of this decade, people who not only were "redundant," but were actually preventing progress in rural Mexico. In the meantime, however, in 1993 a transitional income-support program, Procampo, was substituted for the traditional price supports as a way of accommodating popular demands for assistance with international pressures against subsidies.

In early 1992, a constitutional reform of Article 27 was promulgated that paved the way for a reorganization of land tenure and the introduction of corporate capital into farming. Its goal was to modernize rural production in a way that a corrupt and underfinanced bureaucracy could not. By permitting *ejidal* titleholders to enter into a wide variety of commercial contracts, the private sector is expected to finance land improvements and cultivation. The new program probably will be very effective in pushing a select group of farmers into export production and facilitating urban expansion. The remaining millions of farmers, whose plots are too small and/or whose land is of marginal quality, will be isolated from the institutional and financial supports that allowed them to continue to farm in the face of unfavorable market conditions. To many thoughtful critics, the country can ill afford the effects of a narrowly defined program like the one presently being implemented.[4] The environmental, political, and social problems that another massive rural-urban migration would occasion are beyond the capabilities of the system to manage.

Yet the present economic program of modernization and integration offers the prospect of a bright future for a small but significant segment of the population.[5] Foreign investment will flow into the country to create numerous new enterprises, both in agriculture and industry. This new investment will install the most modern work processes and produce high-valued products for the international markets. We might even anticipate that part of this production will be directed to local markets where it will drive out less modern producers unable to compete, either because of low productivity, inadequate capitalization, or the inability to survive the intense marketing battles. Local producers throughout the country are already beginning to enter into various kinds of production agreements with Mexican and foreign interests to produce under contract for export and local specialty markets, accelerating a process that was evident thirty years ago.

The winning groups will be dispersed throughout rural Mexico. They will be concentrated in the northern irrigation districts, but many investors will choose to improve productive infrastructure in other parts of the country in order to get around the labor bottlenecks that frequently occur in the North. Furthermore, technological advances will offer opportunities for other farmers to take advantage of special programs to increase productivity in basic food-producing sectors. Recent advances in the achievement of food self-sufficiency, for example, are based on important advances in yields, resulting from the use of new seed varieties and agrochemicals. This is evidence of the official decision to promote domestic food production without tying it to the traditional producing groups who, in the official view, would hold back the pace of modernization.

Similarly, for those organized groups of *ejidos* willing to accept production agreements with the private sector, generous flows of resources will be available to promote technological change in which members of the "social sector" can participate. It is evident, however, that these joint ventures are less attractive to investors and more difficult to manage than originally imagined; the showcase collaboration between an *ejido* and the transnational food conglomerate GAMESA in the northeastern part of the country was recently dismantled because of disagreements about the way to account for investments and to distribute profits.[6] Past experience also suggests that private investors are generally unwilling to sustain long-term commitments as market, production, and technological conditions change. Because of the lack of such a commitment, most foreign investors are unwilling to contribute to the conservation activities that—for local farmers everywhere—are normally a part of the production process. This lack of long-term commitment has ominous consequences for the preservation of natural resources.

There is no doubt that the new, more flexible institutional structure will offer profitable opportunities for important groups of farmers. The most significant development in this regard is the increase in organizing efforts by the many regional peasant groups who, in turn, are members of national and provincial coalitions. The new negotiating strategy of the agriculture ministry clearly demonstrates its preference for dealing directly with the coalitions, rather than with individual producer groups. Although the producers' groups are presently experiencing substantial difficulties in obtaining financing, it seems obvious that these obstacles will be reduced through the complex political negotiations that the NAFTA process stimulated.[7] This expansion of the arena for negotiation, and the active participation of local groups in complex discussions about the way in which they will be included in the modernization-integration process, offers an important new channel for well-organized regional coalitions to attempt to obtain privileged access to new productive opportunities in the neoliberal environment.[8]

A few years ago, I proposed a "war economy" as a complementary strategy for rural development.[9] Building on the experience of Great Britain during World War II, this strategy suggests that a concerted effort to mobilize idle domestic capacity for food production among small-scale producers in Mexico would contribute to stimulating the growth of the domestic market for consumer goods by the country's workers and peasants. The simulation exercises conducted in conjunction with this proposal demonstrated the substantial linkage effects of this approach in generating income and new employment opportunities throughout the economy.[10] The peasant-based food self-sufficiency strategy offered by this proposal, however, now seems insufficient, in light of the further intensification of the official assault against peasants in rainfed agricultural areas. Because of important shifts in the world market, occasioned by the competition to subsidize food exports among the advanced industrial countries, basic food production itself has been devalued; it no longer can offer a viable option for economic advancement for most people in rural Mexico. In the face of the narrowly focused model of industrial modernization, there is a critical need for a more diversified productive base, taking advantage of abundant and varied natural resources and the enormous reserve of inherited knowledge stemming from Mexico's cultural diversity. Such an approach requires programs to productively employ a significant part of Mexico's population that still struggles to remain in the countryside.[11]

This approach must offer a new development strategy that explicitly redresses the inherited imbalance between rural and urban areas. In one way or another, this requires a recognition of the importance of rural society for national—and urban—welfare. The historical pattern of discrimination against rural producers imposes an unacceptably heavy burden on society as a whole. To reverse this pattern, ways must be found to help rural communities diversify their economies, and to rebuild their patterns of diversified production which have long been an integral part of their survival strategies. In this new context, traditional food production will become one of a number of enterprises in which peasant communities engage as part of their overall strategy to survive, to improve their standard of living, and to defend their social and cultural integrity. In the new world process of economic integration, they must find additional productive activities as well as forms of paid employment that offer greater income, because food production alone will no longer allow them to live.

In Mexico, one way to begin this process is to identify small projects that might help individual communities and regional groups use the resources they have, in as creative and productive a way as possible. Small-scale projects, for instance, are underway involving groups who can contribute to the essential task of protecting endangered species as a way of generating additional incomes in traditional food-producing communities. The incomes generated by using conservation funds to employ local people and to construct appropriate tourist facilities to stimulate visitors will allow rural communities to strengthen important environmental programs while at the same time diversifying their traditional productive activities as a means of defending their communities. Two examples of communities working to protect endangered species are in nesting areas of the monarch butterfly and the marine turtle.

A similar approach involves an abandoned geyser that is spewing brine over the lands of a Michoacán commercial farming community. The community is thinking about how to transform this nuisance into something productive. The geyser was created by the Federal Electricity Commission (CFE) in its search for exploitable geothermal resources, but the engineers did not consider it important enough to harness for power generation. So, for more than a quarter century it has simply been cordoned off and left to contaminate the land. A proposal is being developed to enable the community to participate directly in the transformation of the site into a tourist attraction, a spa, a training area for sporting activities, and even a showplace for alternative energy sources. This is a complex activity, because the community requires outside assistance to develop a proposal and to determine its feasibility, and the CFE must acknowledge that it has abandoned the geyser and give the land back to the community. Another example, also in Michoacán, involves a group attempting to create an agroindustrial park powered with geothermal energy, as part of a plan to diversify rural production and reduce losses from spoilage and inadequate marketing channels.

These are examples of the way in which people are attempting to confront the growing imbalance between rural and urban development, and the resulting polarization in the countryside. They offer ways in which people can begin to use the natural resources at hand to protect not only the resources themselves but the very economic viability and social integrity of communities whose existence is in question. The three cases cited above are only examples of approaches that might encourage others to look for different projects with the same goals: to diversify the productive base so that rural communities can continue to exist, even to thrive, and to continue to produce food as part of a broader strategy for rural development. This strategy draws part of its inspiration from the need to protect the rich heritage of natural diversity that is so important in Mexico, using strategies that also encourage the preservation of the extraordinary reserve of cultural diversity that has managed to survive in spite of the systematic attack to which it has been subjected during the past centuries.[12]

Clearly, the economies of North America are integrating. For Mexico, this integration will mean more trade and some new jobs; production will continue to increase in certain privileged sectors, like automobiles and consumer products for export. Traditional industries, if left to themselves, will continue to wither with a further weakening of the labor market, increasing social polarization. At the same time, with the "shrinking" of the public sector, there are fewer institutions prepared to deal with the problems that the neoliberal strategy is creating and with the people that it is leaving behind. The *salinista* modernization strategy is based on the presumption that foreign investors will bring sufficient resources to Mexico to pay to correct the problems, but this seems like a major gamble.

Policymakers today are unwilling to "*darle tiempo al tiempo*"—give time a chance, as the popular Mexican expression has it—to allow society to adjust to the process of international integration that is linking nations and cultures. They forget the lesson of another popular saying: "simply by waking up earlier, the sun won't rise sooner" ("*No por mucho madrugar, amanece más temprano*"). That is, Mexico—the country, its people, its culture—will not magically change its course, its very essence, simply because the president orders its industrial structure modified, its resources sold or leased, or foreign goods imported on a massive scale. The country is beginning to realize the nature of the changes underway, though it is still too soon to predict the modifications that people will demand. It is likely, however, that the neoliberal dreams of today's ruling elites will not survive the vigorous rejection of Mexico's diverse but impoverished peoples.

Notes

1. GATT is the General Agreement on Tariffs and Trade, to which Mexico acceded in 1986; NAFTA is the North American Free Trade Agreement, signed with Canada and the United States in 1993, after a protracted legislative battle in the U.S. Congress; and OECD is the Organization for Economic Cooperation and Development, a consultative body of the world's richest nations which admitted Mexico as a full member in 1994.

2. To put this achievement into perspective, the 3 percent increase in productivity might be compared with the goal of an annual average of about 1.5 percent for the economy as a whole in advanced countries over long periods of time. Maize yields on rainfed lands in Mexico are still extremely low by international standards. The average for farmers in the United States is about 3.5 tons per hectare, similar to what is obtained, on average, in irrigation districts in Mexico. Once the lack of capital to pay even for the living expenses of the farmers, and to finance the purchase of fertilizers and other inputs is taken into consideration, many analysts believe that peasant agriculture is Mexico is quite efficient; that is, it uses its very scarce resources quite effectively.

3. A note on data sources is in order. It is extremely difficult to obtain a systematic series of economic data in Mexico on any particular subject over a long period of time. This is the result of changing criteria for data collection, official dissatisfaction with initial results, corruption at various levels in the chain of command, or simple inefficiency. Detailed census material for 1980, for example, was never published because of the unacceptable quality of the data. Throughout the country, the systems for data collection are sufficiently informal that different departments within the same ministry often publish differing data about the same phenomena, even when they receive their information from the same originating source! Another frequent problem is access to the information. In general, reliable information is not readily available, even for a price, although contacts and informal arrangements can release materials that money cannot buy. Rather than present a detailed discussion of these problems or the data sources, I am limiting myself to a general qualitative picture of the rural crisis, and refer the interested reader to a new survey that offers a quantitative examination of the current state of the countryside: Ministry of Agriculture-Economic Commission for Latin America and the Caribbean (SARH-CEPAL), *Productores del Sector Social Rural en México* (La Jolla, CA: Center for U.S.-Mexican Studies, University of California at San Diego, 1994).

4. For an informed discussion of this policy direction, see the articles in Cynthia Hewitt de Alcántara, ed., *Economic Restructuring and Rural Subsistence* (La Jolla, CA: Center for U.S.-Mexican Studies, University of California at San Diego, 1994).

5. This discussion does not consider the entrepreneurial and financial beneficiaries who are in a class by themselves. It goes without saying that the benefits will also be unequally distributed among the members of this

group, and that, as a result, there are likely to be important internal struggles among them.

6. From its inception, the project had been the target of widespread criticism because it was unable to absorb as much as half the local population in the new productive system, forcing many "partners" to migrate in search of work.

7. It is interesting that some of these negotiations are taking place in unusual circumstances. Not only are the regional coalitions actively participating in the various events organized to express concern about and even opposition to NAFTA (where they are clearly using these platforms as another forum for negotiating their claims), but they also have begun to find ways of expressing their opinions through the analyses of many younger scholars who are voicing their positions in international fora. Because some peasant leaders are themselves academics, some have also gained direct access to these fora, such as the Latin American Studies Association, where a number of the organizers of panels on problems of rural Mexico invited important actors or spokespeople in rural Mexico to participate as speakers.

8. It is important to note that this process, in which local producer groups and their regional or national coalitions participate in the domestic and international negotiations to create new opportunities for their members, is being actively supported by international foundations and foreign-based NGOs which have assumed an effective advocacy role in the domestic political system. The World Bank and other international agencies are being pushed to finance these initiatives.

9. David Barkin, *Distorted Development: Mexico in the World Economy* (Boulder, CO: Westview, 1990).

10. David Barkin and J. Edward Taylor, "Agriculture to the Rescue," in Daniel G. Aldrich and Lorenzo Meyer (eds.), *Mexico and the United States: Neighbors in Crisis* (San Bernardino, CA: The Borgo Press, 1993), 7-39.

11. This short paragraph owes a great deal to Guillermo Bonfil's insightful argument that a recognition of the vitality of Mexico's indigenous past is essential to any solution to the country's present problems. See his seminal book, *México Profundo: Una civilización negada* (Mexico City: Grijalbo/CON-ACULT, n.d.). The search for these solutions is the basis for the present research agenda of the author and several colleagues. In one of Bonfil's last articles (in *Ojarasca*, no. 7, April 1992), he vividly details the problems created by the confrontation between the trend towards neoliberal globalization and the possibility, indeed the necessity, of a different, more pluralistic world, if humanity and the earth itself are to survive. This current of thought has become increasingly influential in Mexico and elsewhere in the third world, where people of many different persuasions and approaches have adopted this approach in social analysis, action programs, and political platforms.

12. See Bonfil, *México Profundo*, with regard to Mexico, and Eric Wolf's different approach [*Europe and the People Without History* (Berkeley: University of California, 1982)] to the problem of understanding the role of cultural diversity in world development, and the threats that the internationalization of the economy represent for both nature and people.

21

Salinas's Failed War on Poverty

Julio Moguel

When Carlos Salinas de Gortari became president in 1988, he announced a plan for a new war on poverty, one that would reach out to the 48 percent of the Mexican population then classified as poor, and especially to the 19 percent classified as extremely poor, or indigent. Salinas's plan became the National Solidarity Program (Pronasol). The Solidarity program captured the imagination of many Mexican progressives because it was also meant to respect and encourage community initiative, participation, and responsibility in the planning and administration of the program. It was meant, in short, to transform Mexico's authoritarian state-society relations. Six years later, as Salinas prepared—he hoped—to transfer power to his designated successor, it was clear that the program had fallen far short of its goals.

At his inauguration, Salinas promised that Pronasol would confront poverty and eradicate it. While the program's budget grew from $547 million in 1989 to $2.54 billion in 1993, we are not speaking here of extraordinary amounts of money. The amount spent between 1989 and 1991 was less than the amount spent between 1980 and 1982 in antipoverty activity. If we divide the total investment in Pronasol into the official number of the Mexican poor (40.3 million people), it works out to $53 per year, or 15 cents per day, per person. In the case of Chiapas—the poorest state in the republic—where around 70 percent of the population, or 2,247,347 *chiapanecos* fall below the official poverty line, Pronasol funds amount to 13 cents a day for each one of them. This represents about one eighth of what the World Bank considers to be the line of absolute poverty in Mexico—about three new pesos (one dollar) a day—and about one seventieth of what the country's National Population Council (Conapo) considers necessary to satisfy the basic needs of a family.

In Mexico, the reality of poverty is impressive. Official statistics reveal that 40.3 million Mexicans (about half the population) can be classified as poor, and that 17.3 million of these live in indigency. And the problem is approaching disastrous dimensions. In 1989, the Consultative Council of Pronasol calculated that without a program of income redistribution, a sustained 3 percent rate of economic growth would lift the poorest 10 percent of the population out of poverty in sixty-four years; the next poorest 10 percent would have to wait thirty-three years to satisfy their basic needs; the following 10 percent would have to wait twenty-one years, and the next 10 percent, ten years.

The rural drama, even as reflected by official sources, is particularly eloquent, especially in the face of Salinas's inauguration pledge to "eradicate extreme poverty." Between 1984 and 1989, extreme poverty in urban areas grew in absolute numbers from 4.3 to 6.5 million people, and then declined to 4.8 million by 1992. No such decline occurred in the Mexican countryside, where extreme poverty grew in absolute numbers before and after the existence of Pronasol. Between 1984 and 1989, the number of indigents grew by 1.7 million. Between 1989 and 1992, yet another 400,000 joined the ranks of the extreme poor. In sum, neoliberal policy applied during the 1984-1992 cycle produced more than 2 million new poor people in the countryside.

Other data show a process of growing impoverishment among the social sectors to which most Mexicans belong, within a framework of growing polarization. Between 1982 and 1991, salaries paid to laborers in manufacturing industries lost 36 percent of their purchasing power. The real wages of white-collar workers in those same industries fell 22 percent, and the value of social services fell 23 percent. But the hardest hit lived in the countryside. Average real wages paid to agricultural workers fell 51 percent over that same period. At the same time, the gap between rich and poor is colossal. In 1990, just over 2 percent of the Mexican population received 78.55 percent of the national income.

On the first of January 1994, Mexico awakened to the news that a group of heavily armed indigenous rebels in the state of Chiapas had assaulted and seized half a dozen district capitals, among them the prominent plaza of San Cristóbal de las Casas. Two days later, the country's astonishment was replaced by the general conviction that in a few short hours, something truly significant had happened. In a small corner of southeastern Mexico, all the certainties and values of a long phase of social peace and political stability crumbled.

The terrain on which this process of indigenous struggle had been cultivated over the past ten years was nothing more complex than poverty, or to be more precise, an extreme poverty which neoliberal policies were incapable of mitigating. The Chiapas insurrection was thus converted into an "armed critique" of the social programs of the Salinas administration, particularly Pronasol. The program was not only incapable of reducing the abysmal social situation of the least well-off, but it also proved unable to achieve its genuine—though never explicit—objective of neutralizing and containing the discontent generated by the application of structural-adjustment policies.

Most of the state's more than 3 million people suffer dramatic inadequacies in their living conditions. Of all the dwellings in the state, 43 percent have no indoor plumbing, 35 percent lack electricity, 50 percent have dirt floors, and 74 percent are classified as overcrowded. Eighty percent of the employed population earns an income of less than two minimum wages—placing them below the official poverty line. Of the population over the age of fifteen, 30 percent is illiterate and 62 percent never completed primary school. Using these indicators to construct an index of marginalization, Conapo ranks Chiapas the poorest state in Mexico, followed by five other states with "very high" indices of marginalization: Oaxaca, Guerrero, Hidalgo, Vera Cruz, and Puebla.

Chiapaneca society is not only the most backward in the country, it also has the highest levels of inequality and discrimination. In the area of the peasant insurrection, only 667 individuals own 817,400 acres, which means on the average each one holds about 12,251 acres. In contrast, the region's communally held property amounts to only 1.5 million acres.

The Chiapas "armed critique" of Salinas's social policy is not exclusively—nor even fundamentally—about the amount of resources provided. As in sandy soil, the waters of Pronasol were lost the moment that they were poured. Neither does the "critique" question the lack of intelligence and insight brought to bear in this war on poverty. The problem lies with the strategy itself. Antipoverty policies akin to Pronasol have been developed and promoted by important international organisms—particularly the World Bank—throughout Latin America over the past eight years. Applied simultaneously with the neoliberal policies of adjustment, they constitute an indispensible component of that process. The first program of this type was Bolivia's Social Emergency Fund (FSE), which was created at the beginning of the 1980s with the firm support of the World Bank. Since then, similar funds have been formed in at least ten countries in Latin America, among them Pronasol.

These new programs are different from the older forms of state intervention. They were designed, to begin with, to neutralize or compensate for the most detrimental social effects of the policies of economic adjustment—particularly the sharp declines in real wages. They then became important instruments of long-term "structural change." In neither the short nor the long term were these programs intended to "eradicate poverty." Rather, they were holding actions, designed to make the bitter medicine of adjustment policies less painful. Neoliberal reforms were implemented solely to redynamize the economy, so that—perhaps—later on, the tasks of generating the conditions for equity and social justice could be undertaken.

These antipoverty programs tried to avoid any impact on the macro variables of policy—like salaries or relative prices—and, therefore, eliminated any elements of redistribution. They would not put the unfettered accumulation of capital—the neoliberal motor force of the economy—at risk by threatening any private riches. They were not evaluated according to their ability to eradicate poverty, but their ability to assuage the growing misery which was becoming unmanageable and politically dangerous.

The "design" or "format" of the antipoverty programs was therefore fundamentally defined from the beginning. Resources were not directed to major works of reconstruction, or social and economic rehabilitation; rather, they were used in small investments which would have local or regional impact. Without altering any of the macroeconomic conditions of adjustment or restructuring, these programs achieved—from the perspective of the model—high social and political returns from the investment.

In addition, resources were channelled according to local demand, thus reducing the heavy and clumsy planning bureaucracies, and lowering administrative costs. In many cases the government also decided to work with and through nongovernmental organizations in the administration of the projects, thus reducing costs even further, and giving greater responsibility to local organizations. This is, however, only one side of the coin. Responsibility, in this model, does not equal real power. The central government still exercises great political control over the antipoverty programs.

On the whole and in its parts, the Mexican antipoverty model represented by Pronasol reflects these components of strategy and format. Investment is a drop at a time, with a generally low ceiling for each project. This makes it difficult to achieve any real objectives of development. Its logic is basic short-term assistance, and it operates within a clientelistic framework.

Chiapas is the state in which the largest number of Solidarity committees were registered, which ought to suggest that it is the state in which the greatest changes were made in the "state-society" relationship. The peasant insurrection in the jungle demonstrates that this may be the case, but in a different sense from that assumed from the statistics and official declarations. Of the 8,824 registered Chiapas Solidarity committees, 1,229 operate in the area of coffee production. These committees correspond to the groups that have been receiving emergency aid in the areas terribly battered by the fall in international coffee prices and the disbanding of Imcafé, the state coffee company.

Of the remaining 7,595 Solidarity committees, the two biggest categories of investment are school improvement (the *escuela digna* program) and municipal funds. This distribution is clearly tied to an instrumental rather than a political-social logic. The *escuela digna* program is directed in almost all cases to the renovation of classrooms, and its committees are formed in almost all cases by teachers and parents of schoolchildren. The municipal funds are funnelled to bases of traditional political power—especially in Chiapas—among *caciques,* ranchers, and PRI officials. According to a recent survey conducted in Altos de Chiapas, most of the municipal funds are channelled into the construction of assembly halls, with no particular linkage to any type of educational or cultural agenda. Pronasol's investments in Chiapas show a pronounced tendency toward the categories of "welfare" and "basic infrastructural support." Pronasol moves clearly on the plane of social assistance, with resources—given the magnitude and extension of poverty in the area—that are quite limited. The program has a clear political-clientelistic character.

In Chiapas, more than anywhere else, the management of Pronasol went out of its way to refrain from altering the socioeconomic relations of power. The decentralization of authority and the management of programs simply meant that economic and political power were given to the local political bosses—*caciques*—and farm owners. Many resources were used to finance the construction of sumptuous public works. Other resources—when they arrived—were dropped in the extensive ocean of Chiapas poverty, proliferating in small works of limited impact. Important resources like those directed to the growing of coffee could not compensate for the fall in international prices over the last several years, nor for the consequences of the withdrawal of other governmental support programs.

Pronasol did not modify the state-society relationship in the locations with the greatest incidence of poverty either, despite the fact that some of its architects considered this to be its greatest contribution to strategies of social reorganizaton and efforts to end poverty. The transformation of state-society relations was to have been carried out by Pronasol through the creation of 150,000 Solidarity committees officially registered in 1993 at the national level. But such a huge figure simply corresponds to the sum total of the groups that received funding.

Many committees are so ephemeral or temporary that their life span is exactly as long as their funded project. Others limit the direct involvement of their "members" in work and activity. The formation of the committees mostly has to do with political-electoral necessities rather than any specific antipoverty requirements. No clear correlation exists between the locations with the highest indices of marginality and the organizational effort made by the promoters of Pronasol, if this is measured by the number of committees constituted.

The state of war that broke out on January 1, 1994 demonstrated that the Solidarity committees have very limited powers of social transformation. The regional forces that today are proposing policies of change and social, economic, and political rehabilitation are none other than the insurgents of the Zapatista National Liberation Army (EZLN), and the peasant and popular organizations with their own independent bases of development. Many of these independent groups were at some point catalogued by Pronasol as enemies of the pro-*salinista* strategy of development, because they lacked "democratic methods," reproduced "corporatist vices," and refused to be incorporated into the PRI-dominated chain of command. Today, these definitions and perspectives of the "change in the relations between the state and the people" seem part of ancient history. The "critique of Chiapas" has forced us to rethink all the old categories. The poor and indigent are demanding a *real* dialogue. The old discourse aged decades in the ten days that shook Mexico.

22

The Latin American Metropolis and the Growth of Inequality

Thomas Angotti

At the edge of Mexico City, east of the airport, lies Nezahualcóyotl, a sprawling shantytown of 2 million people located on the bed of what was once Lake Texcoco. It is one of the many self-built neighborhoods that house the majority of the metropolitan area's 20 million people—neighborhoods where it is hard to find decent housing, good jobs, clean water, or parks.

Living in Nezahualcóyotl can be exhausting. In "Neza," you may have to live with three generations of your family in a tiny two-room house that you built little by little over the years. Even if you have water piped into your house, you are never sure whether there is enough pressure, and chances are the water is loaded with bacteria. If you are lucky enough to have a regular factory or office job, you probably have to commute one or two hours in each direction on rickety buses through horrible traffic jams, with portions of your journey on unpaved roads.

The contrast between Neza and the wealthy neighborhood enclaves near the Paseo de la Reforma in the central city is dramatic. In the modern luxury districts you most likely have all the services of a North American suburb, even if you can't entirely escape the foul air, crime, and disease of the city as a whole. To one degree or another, all major Latin American cities have these extremes of wealth and poverty, but the conditions in Mexico City are most dramatic because the city is so immense. Mexico City's problems crystallize the urban question in Latin America, not so much because of its size, but because of its economic and social inequalities, and its declining quality of life. The Latin American metropolis is characterized by mass poverty and severe environmental pollution on a scale generally unparalleled in the North.

As poor as life may be in the major Latin American cities, however, they continue to attract large numbers of people. Cities are a product of economic development. As agriculture becomes mechanized and subsistence farming declines, urban industry and services grow. The surplus labor force in the countryside is drawn to the cities where people can find more employment, housing, and cultural opportunities. Urban life, though flawed by poverty, inequality, and lack of basic services, nonetheless marks an improvement over the oppressive living conditions in declining rural areas.

Latin America's urban growth has been driven by capital investment, mainly from North America, but also from Latin America's growing capitalist accumulation, and increasingly from Europe and Japan. The concentration of capital in cities results in the concentration of labor. Over the last century, Latin America has been transformed from a mostly rural to a largely urban region, with the urban population concentrated in very large metropolitan areas. Latin America is now the most urbanized of so-called third world regions, a fact that bears some relation to its economic dependency on North America, which is the most urbanized region in the world. The metropolis and not the *campo* now defines the Latin American landscape. Half of all Latin Americans now live in cities with a population of more than 100,000, and by the year 2000 half will probably live in large metropolitan areas with populations of more than 1 million.[1]

There are now forty-one cities with a population of more than a million in Latin America [see table 1]. The average size of these megacities is 3.6 million people. Mexico City, São Paulo, Buenos Aires, and Rio de Janeiro are among the twenty largest metropolitan areas in the world. Meanwhile, the fastest growing cities are the somewhat smaller ones like Monterrey, Mexico and Recife, Brazil.

An economic and urban gulf has opened between the more developed metropolitan countries and the less developed rural ones. In Latin America, the four wealthiest countries are also among the most urbanized. In Venezuela, 45 percent of the population lives in cities over one million, in Argentina 43 percent, in Brazil 39 percent, and in Mexico 34 percent. Columbia and Chile, which have recently undergone rapid economic growth, have 41 percent and 36 percent of their populations, respectively, in metropolitan areas. The less developed countries, such as Peru, Bolivia, and Guatemala, by contrast, tend to be less urban and have larger rural populations.

TABLE 1

Population in Cities, 1989 (in Thousands)

City	Thousands	City	Thousands
Mexico City (Mexico)	20,250	San Juan (Puerto Rico)	1,816
São Paulo (Brazil)	18,770	Goiânia (Brazil)	1,788
Buenos Aires (Argentina)	11,710	Barranquilla (Colombia)	1,775
Rio de Janeiro (Brazil)	11,370	Guayaquil (Ecuador)	1,638
Lima (Peru)	6,780	Cabo (Brazil)	1,577
Bogotá (Colombia)	5,270	Guatemala City (Guat.)	1,460
Santiago (Chile)	4,500	Belém (Brazil)	1,357
Caracas (Venezuela)	4,180	Asunción (Paraguay)	1,350
Belo Horizonte (Brazil)	3,890	Nova Iguaçu (Brazil)	1,325
Curitiba (Brazil)	3,772	Maracaibo (Venezuela)	1,295
Medellín (Colombia)	3,601	Cordoba (Argentina)	1,285
Guadalajara (Mexico)	3,200	Puebla (Mexico)	1,260
Pôrto Alegre (Brazil)	3,180	Montevideo (Uruguay)	1,248
Recife (Brazil)	3,040	Quito (Ecuador)	1,220
Monterrey (Mexico)	3,010	La Paz (Bolivia)	1,210
Salvador (Brazil)	2,650	Santos (Brazil)	1,139
Fortaleza (Brazil)	2,422	Valencia (Venezuela)	1,135
Cali (Colombia)	2,402	Rosario (Argentina)	1,122
Brasília (Brazil)	2,400	León (Mexico)	1,077
Santo Domingo (D.R.)	2,170	Ciudad Juárez (Mexico)	1,006
La Habana (Cuba)	2,040		

Sources: Adjusted figures based on *UN Demographic Yearbook,* 1989; and Habitat '87, *Global Report on Human Settlement* (London: Oxford University Press, 1989).

Inequalities between the metropolis, smaller cities, and rural towns of Latin American nations are also gaping. When most of a nation's production, goods, and surplus are funneled out of the country through a single urban gateway, that gateway tends to overshadow all other cities. Latin America's capital cities in particular tend to dwarf secondary cities in size, economic activity, and political power. For example, the Lima metropolitan area has a population of about 7 million, a third of Peru's population; the second largest city, Arequipa, has fewer than 700,000 inhabitants, not substantially greater than the next largest cities of Trujillo and Chiclayo. The secondary cities lack the economic diversity, urban services, and cultural life of Lima. Their products go to Lima, their budgets are drafted in Lima, and their futures are decided in Lima. While the old centralized structures of power are being challenged as many secondary cities undergo rapid economic growth, those smaller cities have not gained greater political power or improved government services.

The economic role of the Latin American metropolis has its basis in the structure of colonial administration. The colonial era established the conditions of extreme centralization conducive to metropolitan expansion. Almost all of Latin America's metropolitan regions developed around colonial seats of power. The early capital cities were modeled on their European counterparts and served as coastal gateways for export-based dependent economies. (The capital cities located in the interior are exceptions that prove the rule: Mexico City is the center of the only Latin American nation bordering the United States; Bogotá was for a long time the center of one of the most balanced Latin American economies; Asunción and La Paz are the capitals of land-locked nations and relatively small.) After independence, urbanization went hand in hand with economic growth, even when import-substitution strategies lessened the influence of exports, and sometimes moderated the influence of the capital cities.

It is often argued that recent revolutionary changes in technology, communications, and industrial production will make large metropolitan areas obsolete. If transnationals can now set up small shops anywhere in the world, some analysts predict a pattern of decentralized production which will slow urbanization and perhaps alter the pattern of inequality. Since the 1970s, capitalist production has begun to look more and more like a global assembly line. Deindustrialization in North America has led to the flight of the most labor-intensive and noxious industrial operations to the South. The South has seen a growth and dispersal of sweatshops and enclave industries—like Mexico's *maquiladoras*—once confined to isolated zones such as the U.S.-Mexican border. In addition, Northern transnationals are setting up factories in Latin America to produce cars, computers, and other goods aimed at the region's small but growing upper middle-class market. The North American Free Trade Agreement (NAFTA) seeks to institutionalize this new international division of labor.

Despite the globalization of production and consumption, however, the new international division of labor is not producing any major shifts in urbanization patterns. New industrial enclaves have emerged in Latin America, but they still do not account for more than a small proportion of capital investment on a global scale. Most new industrial plants, like the scores of auto assembly lines springing up in Mexico and Brazil, are within existing metropolitan areas, where investors expect to take advantage of the large, diverse, and low-cost labor pool.

The movement of manufacturing from North to South therefore contributes to the historic trends of metropolitan growth and centralism within the South. With NAFTA and other agreements for trade liberalization, the small border enclaves in free trade zones may become less significant as magnets for rural migration, but these enclaves were never among the largest metropolitan areas anyway.

Capital investments in the major cities of Latin America disproportionately favor export industries that are not closely linked with the national and regional economies. Since their closest links are with firms and services in the North, export industries seldom spin off the creation of large numbers of urban firms and services. Further, since most of the surplus produced in these industries leaves the country, an insufficient amount remains to build adequate housing, roads, water and sewer lines, and utilities for city dwellers.

The dramatic growth of Caracas, for example, was the result of Venezuela's oil boom, which began in the 1920s. As with most Latin American metropolitan areas, Caracas is now a center of consumption and lacks the range of productive activities that can be found, for example, in Houston, a Northern oil city of comparable size. About half the population in Caracas lives at the margin, in the humble *ranchos* that blanket the steep hills around the center. Much of the oil profits end up outside the country. The lion's share of the oil money that remains in Venezuela goes to lavish residential enclaves like Caracas's "Country Club" neighborhood, and to the privileged middle-class automobile owners who can burn the country's gas at a bargain price. Venezuela's elites are wed to Northern patterns of conspicuous consumption and rake off many of the benefits of the meager Venezuelan welfare state.

On the surface, Latin American cities appear to be sharply divided between a vast "informal" sector or "marginal" population, and a "formal" economy made up of regulated, tax-paying industries, wage-earners, and commercial establishments. A closer look reveals this divide to be far from sharp. The informal sector includes street vendors hawking everything from cigarettes to contraband radios, freelance plumbers and carpenters, garbage pickers, and women who make clothing at home. Many salaried workers in the formal sector hire domestics and handymen from the informal sector. Informal activities may be unregulated by government, but they engage practically the entire population in one way or another, and at one time or another. Many workers move in and out of formal work, and many families have both formal and informal workers.

Poverty and informality may not have been created by transnational corporations, but they serve their interests well. The majority of the population in Latin American cities survives at a level of subsistence far below North American standards. This allows for the suppression of wage levels in the North as well as the South. Latin American workers make up a ready labor reserve for transnationals, who encourage immigration only to the point that it lowers labor costs in the North, and make use of the pool of cheap labor when their industrial investments come South. Through the austere policies of the International Monetary Fund (IMF) and World Bank, Northern capital discourages national governments from making expenditures that would substantially improve the urban quality of life in Latin America, thereby sustaining the low level of subsistence that corresponds with low wages.[2] Indeed, urban consumption levels declined in the last decade as a result of austerity measures undertaken to meet debt obligations. This led to the "IMF riots" in Buenos Aires, Lima, Santo Domingo, Caracas, and elsewhere.[3]

Thus, the Latin American metropolis is an integral part of the global urban network dominated by the North. The *barriadas, favelas,* and *ranchos* are ready reserves for international capital to utilize in its global assembly line. The huge labor surplus in the Latin American metropolis is as necessary to transnationals as the small proportion of the population actually employed in commodity production for exchange on the international market.

Despite the widespread perception that the large cities of Latin America are unplanned and unmanageable, there has been considerable planning by government agencies as well as the private sector. This planning, however, has mostly benefited the wealthy and powerful. The first urban planning regulations in Latin America, promulgated by the Spanish Crown in the sixteenth century "Laws of the Indies," established rules for the organization of urban space around the central *plaza,* which became the seat of political and economic power. Located on the perimeter of the plaza were the representatives of the Crown, the Church, and civil authorities. Urbanization by other colonists near the plaza was regulated, but areas occupied by the indigenous masses were unaffected by planning.

In the twentieth century, the modernist downtown models of Europe and North America replaced the Laws of the Indies. The colonial neglect of the indigenous neighborhoods was supplanted by North America's laissez-faire approach to real estate development. The downtown skylines of the major metropolitan areas in Latin America offer stark images of the influence of the Manhattan model, where central real-estate values combine with official urban-renewal plans to produce monumental business districts. Downtown Caracas, for example, is now a collection of giant civic projects that dwarfs the colonial-era plazas and narrow streets. These megaprojects are connected by a network of intra-city highways that mimics the U.S. interstate-highway system. Residential areas for the elite are mostly private enclaves planned by developers anxious to cash in on the rampant land speculation unleashed by the oil rush. There are a few residential areas planned for the poor, like the 23 de Enero public-housing ghetto created during the Pérez Jiménez dictatorship, but for the most part, the poor live in neighborhoods without planned streets, potable water, sewage, utilities, and other services.

The planning of Latin American cities has thus reinforced many of the social problems of unequal development. The Latin American metropolis was planned in the image of the North, but without the resources and unique conditions of the North, which has flourished by importing capital and labor to build a diversified consumer economy. Unlike its Northern counterpart, the Latin American metropolis has grown unevenly by exporting its labor and resources. The North American metropolitan area is typically auto-oriented, sprawled over a large territory, and has sharp economic and social divisions between central city and suburbs. The real-estate market is loosely regulated, reinforcing the tendencies toward concentration in the central business district, displacement of low-rent activities, and expansion at the periphery.[4] This model has greatly influenced Latin American planners.

Many Latin American cities have strict master plans, and rent, subdivision, and zoning regulations that theoretically govern urban development. However, without the resources and institutions to implement these regulations, they are ignored or easily violated. Thus, an urban system designed to work with Northern wealth falls apart in Southern poverty. At the same time, indigenous forms of planning human settlements—such as traditional patios and plazas—are superseded by the real-estate market and ignored by government. As in the colonial era, the masses remain outside the orbit of planning.

Another key aspect of urban inequality in Latin America is displacement. The low-income community of Barra da Tijuca at the periphery of Rio de Janeiro, for example, has been the target of a concerted eviction campaign by land developers, supported by local government, who want to build luxury condominiums in this attractive mangrove forest area. The eviction campaign has included the assassination of community leaders by mysterious death squads, destruction of houses by military police, demolitions by local government, and forced evictions. Residents displaced from Barra da Tijuca, many of whom had already been evicted from other neighborhoods in Rio, are forced to move further out in the urban periphery or into increasingly overcrowded *favelas*.[5]

There is a direct link between displacement and the real-estate market. The market bids up the cost of land in central locations, and forces the eviction of low-income people in favor of office buildings, stores, and new housing for the professional and technocratic strata. Entire neighborhoods are often displaced to protect elite property rights. Shantytown dwellers who happen to be located on land that gains in real-estate value are among the major targets of eviction. Also, the uprooting of the many spontaneous communities that have sprung up on the outskirts of major cities serves to dampen demands for greater government expenditures for urban infrastructure—expenditures that might create further demands for wage increases.

Displacement and the generally poor living conditions in cities have given rise to perhaps the largest democratic movements in Latin America. In all major cities, large community-based movements arose in the 1970s to stop displacement and secure basic urban services. While the movements arose in separate neighborhoods, they have forged coalitions that play a significant role in local and national politics. For example, urban protest movements make up a large part of the popular base of the Brazilian Workers Party (PT), the largest leftist party in Latin America. In Mexico, the National Coordinating Committee of the Urban Popular Movement (CONAMUP) and the Assembly of Neighborhoods, led by folk hero Superbarrio, have assumed national importance. Women play a leading role and have become politically empowered in many of the community movements.[6]

Environmental contamination also plagues Latin American metropolises. Mexico City has perhaps the foulest air of any large city in the world. Carbon monoxide levels in the city far exceed these in the most polluted North American metropolises like Los Angeles and New York. Most of the pollution comes from motor vehicles, whose use is subsidized by the government; gasoline prices are kept low to promote and protect the national oil industry and solidify popular support for the government. Although the rate of vehicle ownership is lower than in the North, cars, trucks, and buses are older and have inadequate emission systems, and fuel is cruder and more polluting. Children living in the barrios are especially vulnerable to respiratory illnesses from the dust kicked up by vehicles on unpaved and poorly maintained roads. Attached to the dust particles are often fungus and bacteria from the open garbage dumps and burning refuse in outlying areas.

Following the lead of North America, many Latin American cities tore up their trolley lines to make room for cars, trucks, and buses. The few cities that have subways still have horrendous traffic congestion because auto use continues to increase. Inter-city freight moves mostly by truck, since the few railroads were built only to extract raw materials from specific locations by individual foreign corporations.

Mexico, like Venezuela and Brazil and a number of other Latin American countries, is locked into a regime of accumulation that forces it to rely on environmentally damaging petroleum energy. A large part of its national surplus and export earnings comes from petroleum, so any restrictions on this sector are looked at with disdain. Mexico emulates the model of sprawled, auto-based metropolitan growth of the United States, but lacks the resources to control its disastrous ecological consequences. Latin American economies crippled with foreign debt can barely afford the institutional infrastructure—urban planning and a coherent set of regulatory mechanisms—to enforce environmental standards, much less maintain physical infrastructure like highways and bridges.

The neoliberal craze for deregulation could further worsen air quality. In Santiago, air pollution got worse during the years of the Pinochet dictatorship, in large measure because deregulation of the bus system encouraged the importation of used buses. A huge squad of some 11,000 diesel buses now spews black fumes into the air.[7]

Contamination of water and soil are also critical environmental problems. In São Paulo, as in most other large cities, most sewage is discharged without treatment into rivers and streams, only a small fraction of solid waste is treated, and air quality is extremely poor.[8] The city is becoming even less sustainable as real-estate development favors new construction over preservation, and wasteful low-density sprawl over more compact forms of growth.

Urban strategies that have been favored throughout the region often target cities themselves as the problem, and seek to stop urban growth instead of improving the urban—and rural—quality of life. There has been much talk, for example, about "spatial deconcentration"—the dispersal of the urban population from megacities to small cities and towns. There is little admiration for the extreme centralism associated with the region's huge cities, and the destruction of popular, democratic, and communal structures of governance that has gone along with it. But despite decades of talk, no nation has been able to stop urban growth or reverse the centralizing trends except, perhaps, for Cuba, where a major shift of resources to the countryside led to negative growth in Havana. Brazil moved its capital to Brasília, but even though this contributed to urban growth in the interior of the country, the two megacities on the coast—Rio and São Paulo—continue to grow.

While a favorite strategy of the international aid establishment has been to promote local government and citizen participation, local government has traditionally been a means for legitimizing elite political power. David Collier's classic study of Lima's *barriadas* demonstrates how popular participation at the local level can be used to coopt potential opposition and reinforce central authority.[9] Local government is often an avenue to greater power for local property interests, who can become power brokers in league with the national government. When local government is able to generate its own revenues—a mostly unfulfilled goal of U.S. aid programs—it can strengthen local power brokers without benefiting the victims of inequality.

International donors favor supporting local self-help housing initiatives by giving financial aid, construction materials, and technical advice. This strategy is often seen as a substitute for government-sponsored programs in housing and urban services. Self-help is basically an acknowledgment that the state will take little or no responsibility for the planning and development of poor neighborhoods. Self-help actually describes the way most metropolises in Latin America have been built—spontaneously and without government assistance.[10]

At times, of course, spontaneous building has been very organized and sophisticated. In Chile, for example, under the Popular Unity government of Salvador Allende, and in Mexico since the 1970s, local associations for improving the urban environment played key political roles nationally as well as locally, and have successfully pressured for government financing of urban development. These groups have, however, relied on self-help out of necessity, not because they believed it to be a preferred national strategy. Indeed, a constant among the strongest and most influential self-help groups is the demand for a stronger government role and a more equitable economic and political system.

The only way to achieve a balanced urban system and urban equality is to have a balanced economic system, one that is not dependent on a bloated export sector. In a balanced economy, a significant proportion of the national surplus can be used to improve the quality of urban life, and to provide a national social safety net so that large numbers of people are no longer forced out of rural areas. These resources can support the growing network of grassroots community organizations, and responsive local governments. They can foster sustainable forms of urban development and transportation based on indigenous traditions and appropriate technology. These resources can also supplement the enormous reservoir of self-help with socially responsible urban strategies. In the last analysis, the city is anchored in the regional economy. There is no way around the fact that livable cities require sustainable economic development.

Notes

1. Thomas Angotti, *Metropolis 2000: Planning, Poverty & Politics* (London: Routledge, 1993), chap. 1.
2. See Michael Peter Smith, *City, State and Market: The Political Economy of Urban Society* (Oxford: Basil Blackwell, 1988).
3. John Walton, "Urban Protest and the Global Political Economy: The IMF Riots," in Michael Peter Smith and Joel R. Feagin, eds., *The Capitalist City* (Oxford: Basil Blackwell, 1987), 364-86.
4. John R. Logan and Harvey L. Molotch, *Urban Fortunes: The Political Economy of Place* (Berkeley: University of California Press, 1983).
5. Miloon Kothari, "Tijuca Lagoon: Evictions and Human Rights in Rio de Janeiro," *Environment and Urbanization*, vol. 6, no.1 (April 1994).
6. See Manuel Castells, *The City and the Grassroots (Berkeley: University of California Press, 1983),* 190-209; and Geoffrey Fox, ed., "The Homeless Organize," *NACLA Report on the Americas,* vol. 23, no. 4 (November/December 1989).
7. Nathaniel C. Nash, "Scrubbing the Skies Over Chile," *New York Times,* 6 July 1992.
8. Vilmar E. Faria, "Metropolitan São Paulo: Problems and Perspectives," in Matthew Edel and Ronald G. Hellman, eds., *Cities in Crisis: The Urban Challenge in the Americas* (New York: Bildner Center for Western Hemisphere Studies, City University of New York, 1989).
9. David Collier, *Barriadas y Elites: De Odria a Velasco* (Lima: Instituto de Estudios Peruanos, 1981).
10. See Jorge Hardoy, "The Building of Latin American Cities," in Alan Gilbert, ed., *Urbanization in Contemporary Latin America* (New York: Wiley, 1982), 19-34.

23

Kids Out of Place

Nancy Scheper-Hughes
and Daniel Hoffman

Por esse pão pra comer	*For this good bread to eat*
Por esse chão pra dormir	*For this hard ground on*
	which to sleep
Por me deixar respirar	*For letting me breathe*
Por me deixar existir	*For letting me exist*
Deus lhe pague!	*God reward you!*

—Chico Buarque

On Friday, July 23, 1993, eight young "street children"—or *meninos de rua*—were gunned down as they slept near the Candelária Church in downtown Rio de Janeiro. The Candelária massacre brought renewed attention to the plight of street children, their "elimination" at the hand of death squads, and the wrenching poverty that has come to characterize life for vast numbers of urban residents in Brazil.

The pattern of violence reflected in the Candelária killings, though remarkable in its degree, is in no way new. In 1981 Hector Babenco's film *Pixote* stunned audiences with its brutal portrayal of the institutional and street life of marginalized children in Brazil. Filmed during the final years of a waning military dictatorship, *Pixote* focused on the generation forgotten by the Brazilian "economic miracle" of the 1970s.

In the ensuing decade the situation of marginalized children seems, if anything, to have gotten worse. Indeed, the contemporary plight and the problem of thousands of loose and "dangerous" street children has become the center of attention both within and beyond Brazil. Underlying the current formulation of the street children's crisis is a deep preoccupation with the future of Brazil, and with the increase in public violence that seems to have accompanied the economic crisis and transition to democracy. With the demise of the former police state, the structures that had kept the social classes safely apart and the "hordes" of disenfranchised, hungry, and "dangerous" *favela*—shantytown—children at bay also disintegrated. Suddenly, street children seemed to be everywhere.

Urban violence itself may not have actually increased with democratization. What has changed significantly is both the official discourse and the popular representations of marginalized children in Brazil over the past three decades. In the 1960s in the Northeast of Brazil, street urchins were a fairly familiar feature of urban life. They were commonly referred to with a blend of annoyance and affection as "*moleques*"—that is, ragamuffins, scamps, or rascals. *Moleques* were "streetwise" kids, who were cute and cunning, sometimes sexually precocious, and invariably economically enterprising. They tried to make themselves useful in a myriad of ways, some of these bordering on the criminal and deviant. Think of Fagin's "boys" from *Oliver Twist*, especially the Artful Dodger, and you have it. Many *moleques* survived by "adopting" an affluent or middle-class household for whom they did odd jobs in exchange for the right to sleep in a courtyard or patio.

Today, despite new and in many respects model legislation asserting the rights of children, street children in Brazil are viewed as a public scandal and a nuisance. They are now referred to either as "abandoned" children or, alternatively, as "marginals." The first denotes pity for the child (and blame for the neglectful mother), while the second denotes fear. Both labels justify radical interventions and the forced removal of these public "pests" from the urban landscape.

During a brief season of field research two years ago in Recife, the capital city of Pernambuco, and in Bom Jesus da Mata, a small market town in the interior of the same state, we made a point of asking ordinary townspeople the naïve question: "What is a *menino de rua* (street kid)?" While driving with a friend down a wide avenue in Recife, one of us, spying some scruffy boys walking in the grass along the road, asked: "Are those street kids?" "Of course," the friend replied. "How can you tell?" "Why, there's no parent with them." Pushing further: "Is any kid on the street without an adult a street kid?" In exasperation, the friend replied, "Look, they steal and sniff glue. That's why they're street kids."

What is rarely articulated but nonetheless quite clear is that street kids are poor children in the wrong place. A street child is, like our definition of dirt, soil that is out of place. Soil in the ground is clean, a potential garden; soil under the fingernails is filth. Likewise, a poor, ragged kid running along an unpaved road in a *favela* or playing in a field of sugar cane is just a kid. That same child, transposed to the main streets and plazas of town, is a threat, a potentially dangerous "street kid."

The very notion of a "street child" reflects the preoccupation of one class or segment of society with the "proper place" of another.[1] The term is a manifestation, albeit a semi-conscious one, of a kind of symbolic or psychological apartheid. Safely confined to the *favela*, the poor child or adolescent is invisible to the better-off city dwellers, and therefore of little interest or concern. Only when the child steps outside of his or her area is that child perceived as a problem about which "something must be done."

From the point of view of the *favela*, however, there is nothing inherently problematic about a child, especially a male child, flowing over into the main streets of the town. The street—especially the city center—is, after all, the primary site of employment and economic survival. As long as he or she doesn't get "in trouble" with the law in the process of trying to survive, the child that can successfully negotiate the realm of the street is seen as resourceful and self-reliant.

In the context of his own environment, the street child is nothing more than a "kid." The very term "street child" has no meaning in the shantytown. Indeed, it is almost never used as a term of reference or identification, although *favela* mothers will sometimes lament having permanently "lost" one or more boys "to the streets."[2] Here, the term "lost" and "street" are used to describe a poor child's declaration of independence from his home and his parents. But under ordinary conditions, to be a *favela* boy is to spend the better part of the day—and often enough the night as well—"*na rua*," in the street. Homes are overcrowded and mother's "*amigo*" or current boyfriend may make demands for privacy that preclude older kids sleeping at home. "Home" for many male *favela* kids is not so much a place to eat and sleep as an emotional space—the place where one comes from and where one returns, periodically.

For *favela* girls, the alternation between home and street is more vexed and problematic. The same home conditions that propel their brothers into the street affect them as well, but a *favela* girl must always declare a fixed assignment and a fixed destination in the "street." Surveillance of the immediate whereabouts of daughters is a perennial preoccupation of *favela* women who themselves must often be out working in the street for long periods of the day. From the age of seven or eight, *favela* girls are assigned child-tending and other domestic tasks that keep them close to home. But girls who are quick and savvy are often extremely useful to their mothers in dealings with the "somebodies" of the street, including shopkeepers, coffin makers, clinic doctors, patrons, political leaders, and clergy.

Most "street children" are today, as they were in the 1960s, "supernumerary" or "excess" kids, the children of impoverished and often single or abandoned women. While they may be quite economically independent, street kids remain deeply emotionally dependent and attached to the idea of "family." When nine-year-old "Chico" was asked if his mother loved him, he looked back incredulously. "She's my mother; she has to love me," Chico said, although both Chico and the questioner knew that his mother had tried to give him away several times to distant relatives.

Street kids in Bom Jesus da Mata—most of them boys—tended to be sentimental on the topic of mothers, their own in particular. When asked why they beg or steal, or why they live in the streets, poor children often replied that they were doing it to help their mother. Most share a percentage of their earnings with their mothers whom they visit each evening. "Fifty-fifty," said Giomar proudly with his raspy, boy-man voice. "Oh, *ché!*" his nine-year-old friend Aldimar corrected him. "Since when did you ever give your mother more than a third!"

A band of street children, who had attached themselves to Nancy Scheper-Hughes's household in the 1980s, liked nothing better than to be invited inside to use her flush toilet, to wash with soap and hot water, and, afterwards, to flop down on the cool floor and draw with Magic Marker pens. Their sketches were curious. Most drew self-portraits or conventional intact nuclear family scenes even when there was no "papa" living in the house or when the child himself had long since "left home" for the streets. These homeless children also favored religious themes—the crucifixion in particular—colored in with lots of bright red wounds. Cemeteries and violent death were also a frequent theme. But, despite all, their self-portraits were often surprisingly smiling and upbeat.

The street offers both opportunity and danger. There are many ways to be a child of the streets. Most work selling candy or popsicles, guarding cars, carrying groceries and other parcels, or shining shoes. While most street kids return home at night to sleep, some alternate nights of sleeping outdoors with sleeping at home. A very small number of children actually live full-time in the streets, rarely if ever going home to visit.[3] This minority is, however, very visible and greatly feared, fueling the stereotype of the "dangerous" and "uncontrollable" *menino de rua.*

These street children do not so much "run away" or "choose the streets" as they are thrown out of homes where hunger, abuse, poverty, and neglect make life under bridges and in bus station restrooms seem more "peaceful" (a term that more than one street child used to describe his life in an abandoned building in Recife) than life at home. Such children "of the street" are predictably more associated with theft, gangs, and drugs, and are the most common target of adult exploitation, violence, and death squads.

While most of those who actually *live* in the street are boys, young girls may also enter the anonymous space of the street, often escaping exploitative work as junior domestic servants or abusive homes. The vehicle of their "escape" is generally prostitution.[4] Domestic work in the context of semi-feudal Northeast Brazil is not infrequently described by *favela* girls and older women as "slavery," so that a flight to the "streets" and even to "prostitution" can be seen as acts of self-liberation. "The first time I sold my body was the first time I felt that it belonged to me," said one young "runaway" from the rural Northeast who chose "the streets" of São Paulo and prostitution over domestic servitude in Pernambuco.[5] Because these girls frequently live in brothels, prostitution may remove them somewhat from the dangers of life on the street. They suffer, however, increased risks of exposure to HIV infection, pregnancy, and sexual abuse.

Indeed, food and affection exchanged for sex is common among Brazilian street kids, the majority of whom are initiated into sex by nine or ten years of age in the big cities. Both street girls and street boys are often used for passive anal intercourse. Street girls in Recife are frequently raped by men, including policemen, and younger street boys as well as street girls are vulnerable to rape by older street boys.[6]

Street children—typically barefoot, shirtless, and seemingly untied to a home or a family—are separated from all the statuses and roles that confer propriety, rights, and citizenship. In the context of family-driven Brazil, the street child is barely a "person," and is vulnerable to the worst forms of exploitation, abuse, and manipulation. This is revealed in the proliferation of derogatory names for poor street children: *pivete* (thief), *trombadinha* (pickpocket), *maloqueiro* (street delinquent), *menor* (juvenile delinquent), and *marginal* (criminal).[7] Each term denies the validity and personhood of the child or adolescent and transforms him or her into a dangerous and disgusting object, one to be removed or erased with violence and impunity.

Bolstering and justifying the persecution, indeed the open warfare on street kids in Brazil today are rumors, radio reports, and sensationalized news stories about crimes committed by street adolescents. The popular newsweekly *Veja* reported that in the central plaza of São Paulo, the Praca da Sé, street children commit over 32,000 thefts and robberies a year, each child allegedly committing three thefts a day.[8] Further fueling the panic among middle- and upper-class populations were news reports of the *arrastão*—or sweep—in which large roving gangs of poor adolescents allegedly streamed across the elite southern beaches of Rio de Janeiro robbing anyone within reach.

Of course, many street children do, in fact, live through petty crime. Almost all of the street children we interviewed in 1992 at a shelter in Bom Jesus volunteered that they stole things, or that they "used to" before they mended their ways. But stealing, they said, was "*um jeito*"—a way of getting by—an unfortunate means of survival, not something they were proud of. There is a natural evolution from begging to stealing as begging becomes both humiliating and more difficult for the older child. When street children begin to show signs of physical maturity, they are chased away from public spaces and rarely evoke compassion or a handout from people on the street. Stealing is the next phase in the life cycle of a street child. When a younger child was continually pushed away from us at the street shelter in Bom Jesus by older and more "expert" kids who denied that the child had ever really been a street kid, the little one vehemently protested, "*Eu pedia, eu pedia!*" ("but I begged, I begged!").

Brazilian street children live in daily fear of the police, state children's asylums, anonymous kidnappers, death squads, and (more fantastically) imagined child-and-organ stealers.[9] In all, their lives are characterized by a profound sense of insecurity. The seemingly far-fetched rumors of street kids kidnapped for overseas adoption or mutilated for their organs coexist with an active round-up of street urchins, thousands of whom "disappear" each year into state-run reform facilities that are viewed with suspicion and horror by shantytown residents. "You won't ever turn me in to FEBEM (the misnamed state institution for the well-being of minors), will you, Nancy?" Scheper-Hughes was made to answer many times over. "They kill children there," little Luiz insisted. The more she denied that this could be so, the more the children ticked off the names of friends who had been "roughed up" or hurt at one of the reform schools. "Why do you think that they built the FEBEM school so close to the cemetery of Bom Jesus?" asked José Roberto, age twelve, with a quiver of fear in his voice.

Until the enactment of the new Child and Adolescent Statute (1990) which recognized the legal rights of minors incarcerated without due process, almost 700,000 Brazilian children and adolescents were locked up in FEBEM or related reform schools.[10] The film *Pixote* recreated the life of children in a FEBEM facility, portraying conditions of everyday violence and vulnerability where criminalization, rather than reform or education, were the only possible outcomes. In spite of the new legislation, the disturbing conditions dramatized in *Pixote* have not changed. On October 22, 1992, in the FEBEM facility of Tatuapé in São Paulo, a twenty-four-hour rebellion resulted in one death, forty wounded, and over 500 escapes (350 of whom were recaptured). The daily *Folha de São Paulo* reported that those adolescents returned to the 1,200-inmate facility were beaten severely by state functionaries. In the investigation that followed, a state legislator claimed that the youths were "caged up like animals." "Not even in maximum security are prisoners treated this way," a prosecutor said, commenting about one hundred youths who were kept locked up twenty-four hours a day in cells without ventilation or bathrooms. A director of FEBEM confirmed that the adolescents were being kept naked in the buildings "for reasons of security."[11]

Reform of the FEBEM system—a central demand of child advocates and an implicit provision of the 1990 Child and Adolescent Statute—remains elusive. The primary function of these "correctional" institutes continues to be the removal of unwanted children from the public sphere.

In addition to the thousands of children who fill Brazil's special reform schools, significant numbers of children are illegally detained in prisons alongside adult offenders. This appears particularly true of smaller municipalities that lack specially designated facilities for minors. The practice is in flagrant disregard of the new Brazilian Constitution with its bill of rights for the child. The newly appointed Children's Judge of Bom Jesus allowed us to visit a few dozen minors being held without bail in the local prison. The children were incarcerated, the judge explained, for their own safety. Outside they were already "marked for extermination" by local hit squads, he said, and they had been rejected by family members as well as feared and hated by the local population for whom their deaths would be counted as a relief.

In one cell of the local jail we found "Caju" and "Junior," fifteen and sixteen-year-olds whom Scheper-Hughes remembered as cute street urchins attached to her household in 1987. "Caju" was elected to represent the street children of Bom Jesus at the first national convention of street children held in Brasília in 1986, when street children from all over Brazil converged on the capital to voice their grievances and demand their human rights. Now, five years later, both boys were accused of assault, and Junior, of the rape of another street child. Thus were they rapidly transformed into precocious "little men" incarcerated and held accountable for their chaotic street behavior.

As a guard at the jail in Bom Jesus reflected, "the life of a young *marginal* here is short.... It's like this: for a *menino de rua* to reach thirty years of age, it's a miracle." The Federal Police reported that close to 5,000 children were murdered in Brazil between 1988 and 1990.[12] Few of these deaths were considered worthy of investigation, which is hardly surprising given that police officers are themselves perpetrators of many of these crimes.[13] Most of the victims are adolescent males, like Caju and Junior, between the ages of fifteen and nineteen, a particularly "dangerous" time, especially for the children of black *favela* dwellers.

The specter of violent and sudden death looms alarmingly close for poor adolescents and for street children especially. This is no less true for the children of a relatively small municipality such as Bom Jesus (population 50,000) than for those of major cities. Street kids of Bom Jesus had no difficulty identifying the names of murdered friends and companions. The list we gathered from several street children one morning in Bom Jesus in 1992 carried no fewer than twenty-one names. We offer them here as a small act of resistance and as a way of honoring their short lives:

Pedrinho	Zeze	Misso	Rihgue
Deda	Joca	Docideiro	Beto Boca de Veia
Bebe	Taiga	Ze Pequeno	Pipio
Regi	Geronimo	Xunda	Gilvam
Bodinha	Biu	Nino	Biopiolho
Fro			

A few of these adolescents and young men lost their lives after having fled to Recife, the regional capital. Some were summarily murdered when caught in the act of petty theft, or were the victims of vigilante "street justice." Still others died at the hands of death squads, their murders unresolved and little investigated.

In 1991 *Veja* reported that the public morgue in Recife received approximately fifteen bodies of dead children and adolescents a month. Black and brown (mixed race) bodies outnumbered white bodies twelve to one, and boys outnumbered girls at a ratio of seven to one. In 80 percent of the cases, the bodies had been damaged or mutilated.[14] The local human rights organization GAJOP characterizes the routine assassinations of poor adolescents as an unofficial death penalty which is carried out "with chilling cruelty and without any chance of defense whatsoever."[15]

Brazilian journalist Gilberto Dimenstein, in his forceful denunciation of violence against children, *Brazil: War on Children*, emphasized the complicity of off-duty policemen, hired killers, and store owners (*lojistas*) in the death squads.[16] Typically, it is store owners who pay to have "undesirable" adolescents and children eliminated. A similar conclusion was reached in a report by the São Paulo chapter of the Brazilian Bar Association, which indicated that "the military police and death squads paid by shantytown shopkeepers killed most of the nearly 1,000 street children slain here in 1990."[17]

Dimenstein writes that support of human rights for children in Brazil is confined to a relatively small minority, and that to make a case for the rights of children is perceived by many as "an attack on decent people's rights to walk down the street in safety."[18] Underlying this sentiment is a perception that street adolescents are dangerous criminals with little chance of reform. Discourses regarding human rights, including rights for children, easily come into conflict with popular concerns for public safety, leading some to claim that human rights are the "privileges of bandits."[19]

Support for death squads, "private justice," lynchings, and lethal tactics by the police is related to widespread perceptions that the justice system does not work, and that police are inefficient, corrupt, and frequently themselves involved in crime.[20] Residents of poor neighborhoods are often the strongest supporters of violent, extrajudicial solutions to local crime, a phenomenon that has been, in part, attributed to the lack of security in these communities. As one observer writes, "people are usually asking the police, whom they fear and accuse of being violent, to be violent 'against the side that deserves it.'"[21] The poor, it appears, feel every bit as besieged by crime, if not more so, as the rich and middle class do. This is crucial to understanding their acceptance of extreme forms of private justice, even when they are most likely to become the targets of its abuses.

Thus, each time a troublesome young street child was swept up in a police raid or was physically attacked or "disappeared" in Bom Jesus, people said nothing. Some residents were even sympathetic to these violent attacks on other people's "bad" children, and would occasionally murmur under their breath, "Good job, nice work!"

The tolerance for violence is also a legacy of the dictatorship. Throughout Brazilian military rule (1964-1985), the civil and military police were heavily implicated in the disappearances, tortures, and deaths of suspected "subversives." Although the process of democratization has been fairly rapid since 1982, it has yet to check the extraordinary power of the civil and military police over the poorer populations. Today, the police are called upon to enforce, often violently, the apartheid-like codes that seek to keep the poor and the black—young as well as old—"in their proper place." Indeed "race" and race hatred have emerged today as popular discourses that justify violent and illegal police actions in shantytown communities. Death squad persecution is directed at a specific class and *shade* of shantytown resident. Consequently, young black males in Brazil are increasingly a threatened population.

In all, the problem of "street children" is emblematic of a larger dilemma in Brazil: a failed economic development model that has relegated a vast proportion of the population to misery. Out of this configuration arises the specter of the homeless and abandoned street child, perceived by the more affluent classes as a blemish on the urban landscape and a reminder that all is not well in the country. Unwanted and considered human waste, these ubiquitous tattered, mainly black children and adolescents evoke strong and contradictory emotions of fear, aversion, pity, and anger in those who view their neighborhood streets, boulevards, and squares as "private places" under siege. But unlike other forms of debris, street kids refuse to stay in the dump (the *favelas* of Brazil). Instead, they often stake out the most public and most elegant spaces of the city to live, to love, and to work, thus betraying the illusion of Brazilian "modernity."

By invading the city centers, frequenting the public parks and upper-class beaches of Rio de Janeiro and Recife, and engaging in petty crimes against the middle class, street children defy the segregated order of the modern city. Street children are, in a sense, poor kids in revolt, violating social space, disrespecting property, publicly intoxicating themselves, and otherwise refusing to conform or to disappear. The risks and hazards of this inchoate domestic rebellion are great: illiteracy, toxicity from inhalant drugs such as glue, chronic hunger and undernutrition, sexual exploitation, and AIDS. It is this overall configuration of risks that leads child advocates in Brazil to defend the right of the child to be in the street, while recognizing that a life of the streets can only be self-destructive in the long term.

The new Brazilian Constitution and the subsequent Child and Adolescent Statute recognize the rights of children and the obligation of the state, civil society, and parents to protect these rights and to provide for the needs of children as individuals in a special condition of dependency, and physical and social development. The National Movement of Street Children (MNMMR), an organization of street educators and children's advocates, is at the forefront of legislative reform and the movement to engage and empower street children in their own environment: in the parks and plazas of the city. The MNMMR helps street children to form their own organizations, to develop their own leadership, and to articulate their own demands, so that individual acts of survival can be translated into collective acts of political resistance. The Street Children's Movement activists recognize the anger and indignation of street adolescents as appropriate to their marginalized and precarious existence.

The outcome of the struggle for childhood in Brazil will weigh heavily on the success of activists in the MNMMR and other organizations that share its vision of a new society in which all children are valued. For all its power, however, the Brazilian street children's movement has been unable to strike at the source of the problem. Until the chaotic economic and social conditions that cause desperately poor parents to "lose" their children to the streets are reversed, childhood for the vast majority in Brazil will continue to signify a period of adversity to be survived and gotten over as quickly as possible, rather than a time of nurturance to be extended and savored.

Notes

1. This and related themes are further elaborated in D. Hoffman, "Street Children and the Geography of Exclusion in Brazil," in Nancy Scheper-Hughes and Carolyn Sargent, eds., *Child Survival*, 2d ed. (Berkeley: University of California, forthcoming).

2. See Nancy Scheper-Hughes, *Death Without Weeping* (Berkeley: University of California Press, 1992), 469.

3. For a useful discussion of street children and family life, see *Childhood and Urban Poverty in Brazil: Street and Working Children and Their Families*, Innocenti Occasional Papers, The Urban Child Series (UNICEF, 1992).

4. See Gilberto Dimenstein's *Meninas da Noite* (São Paulo: Editora Atica,

1992) concerning prostitution rings and the near-enslavement of adolescent girls in the North of Brazil.

5. The young woman gave this testimony at a consciousness-raising meeting for young (mostly migrant) sex workers in São Paulo organized by a grassroots AIDS awareness group.

6. The rape of street girls by policemen has been reported by Ana Vasconcelos, founder of the Casa de Passagem, a support and shelter project for street girls in the northeast city of Recife.

7. *Menor* literally means "minor" in Portuguese. In the context of Brazil, it is stigmatizing, and specifically applied to poor adolescents who are assumed to be criminally inclined.

8. Maria Simas Filho, Eliane Azevedo, and Lula Costa Pinto, "Infância de raiva, dor de sangue," *Veja*, 29 May 1991, 34-35.

9. See Nancy Scheper-Hughes, "Theft of Life," *Society* 27, no. 6, (September-October 1990): 58-63.

10. See Anthony Swift, *Brazil: The Fight for Childhood in the City* (Florence: UNICEF International Child Development Center, 1991).

11. Agência Ecumênica de Notícias (AGEN), through the computer network Peacenet, 19 November 1992.

12. *Journal de Comércio*, 19 June 1991. See Ben Penglase, *Final Justice: Police and Death Squad Homicides of Adolescents in Brazil* (New York: Human Rights Watch/Americas Watch, 1994) for an excellent analysis of extrajudicial violence and murder against poor adolescents, including street children, in Brazil. Available from Human Rights Watch, 485 Fifth Avenue, New York, NY 10017-6104.

13. Penglase's *Final Justice* describes the many obstacles to achieving convictions in death-squad killings, particularly when cases involve the military police and the military justice system. See also Gilberto Dimenstein, *Brazil: War on Children* (London: Latin America Bureau/Monthly Review Press, 1991); and MNMMR et al., *Vidas em Risco: Assassinatos de Crianças e Adolescentes no Brasil* (Rio de Janeiro, 1991).

14. Maria Simas Filho, Eliane Azevedo, and Lula Costa Pinto, "Infância de raiva, dor de sangue," *Veja*, 29 May 1991, 34-45.

15. Gabinete de Assessoria Jurídica às Organizações Populares/Centro Luiz Freire (GAJOP), *Grupos de Extermínio: A Banalização da Vida e da Morte em Pernambuco* (Olinda: GAJOP, 1991).

16. Dimenstein, *Brazil: War on Children*.

17. Quoted in "Brazil's Police Enforce Popular Punishment: Death," *New York Times*, 4 November 1992.

18. Dimenstein, *Brazil: War on Children*, 63-67.

19. Teresa Caldeira describes these transformations in public life in contemporary São Paulo in her dissertation *City of Walls: Crime, Segregation, and citizenship in São Paulo* (University of California at Berkeley, 1992).

20. Caldeira, *City of Walls*, 179.

21. Ibid., 187.

24

The Struggles of a Self-Built Community in Peru

Jo-Marie Burt and César Espejo

On April 28, 1971, some 200 families invaded a small piece of state-owned land in Pamplona Alta, a peripheral area to the south of Lima. This invasion, like others before it, was carefully organized by leaders who had mapped out the land to be invaded, organized the interested families from slum areas of Lima, obtained construction materials, arranged for transportation, and set the hour and date of the invasion. Within days, some 9,000 families had joined the invasion, which had spilled over onto privately owned land. The military regime of General Juan Velasco Alvarado (1968 to 1975) faced an important test of its commitment to the poor Peruvians that its "revolutionary" experiment promised to benefit.

After a brief but tense period of confrontation, the Velasco government announced a plan to relocate the squatters to an extensive terrain of 7,800 acres of barren desert located eighteen miles to the south of Lima. The following day, 3,000 families were transported without incident to form a new settlement or *barriada*, Villa El Salvador.[1]

After receiving their plots of land from the Housing Ministry, the families began erecting *chozas*, makeshift housing constructions of cane matting, on the dusty sand dunes. Teresa, one of Villa's first settlers, recalls the precarious living conditions. "First I argued with my husband to build my *choza*," she remembers, "But then I realized that there was no water, no electricity, no schools for my children. I had only been thinking about getting my plot of land to build my house. I wasn't thinking of anything else. I cried for days, but I was determined to stay." It was this determination that helped Villa's new inhabitants "conquer the desert," and made Villa a common reference point for virtually any discussion of grassroots organizing in Peru.[2]

While Villa El Salvador enjoyed certain benefits from its special relationship with the Velasco regime, those privileges ended with Velasco's ouster in 1975 and the hardening of the military regime's posture towards Peru's popular sectors. Like other shantytowns, Villa had to organize to demand basic services from the government, and when government assistance was not forthcoming, they had to come up with their own solutions. This led to the formation of a vast network of grassroots organizations based on reciprocity and self-help. While such networks have operated in a context of sharp constraints, community organizing has allowed Villa to evolve from a shantytown made up of precarious *chozas*, to a bustling town of nearly 300,000 inhabitants. Today, Villa has paved roads and access to public transportation. The homes of over half of its residents have piped water, sewerage, and electricity. Villa is equipped with schools and health clinics, many built by the residents themselves as well as local businesses, active marketplaces, radio stations, and a municipal government. The desert is now filled with gardens and trees, each cared for by local residents despite the scarcity of water. The concrete achievements of grassroots organizing have created a strong sense of identity among Villa's residents, whose rallying cry was: "Because we have nothing, we shall do everything."

Villa El Salvador's evolution from a bare-bones shantytown to one of Lima's largest districts reflects the remarkable changes in Peru's capital city, especially in its *barriada* districts, over the past two decades. Villa's internal structure has changed significantly during this time. Some of its older areas have become consolidated both in terms of housing construction and access to basic services. Other areas remain underdeveloped, and new invasions confront the same problems that the older areas confronted in the beginning. In this sense, Villa also reflects the changing cycles of grassroots organization, and suggests the potentials and problems of community development in Latin America's cities and *barriadas*.

Fifty years ago, Peru was a predominantly agrarian society. The process of modernization and import-substitution industrialization, coupled with the decline of rural society, induced a long-term pattern of rural-to-urban migration that has converted Peru into an urban society, and Lima into an immense metropolis.[3] In 1940, Lima had slighty more than 500,000 inhabitants; by 1961, it had 1,846,000 inhabitants; and today, the city is home to 6.5 million people.

This explosive growth rate meant an increased demand for housing. Initially, migrants were absorbed into existing poor districts in the central parts of Lima. These areas, however, quickly became overpopulated. Massive land invasions have taken place since the mid-1940s. These invasions have dramatically changed Lima's topography, expanding the city's limits to the unoccupied deserts to the north and south, and to the rocky foothills of the Andes to the east.

The first wave of land invasions in the late 1940s occurred mostly in the eastern industrial part of Lima, which quickly became urbanized.[4] Within a short time, families were having to double up in the same homes in these areas, which became known as *tugurios*, or inner-city slums.

A true demographic explosion occurred between 1955 and 1971. With housing in the central areas no longer able to meet growing demand, land invasions began to spill over the traditional demarcations of Lima into the deserts, the "Northern and Southern Cones," far from any locus of economic activity. City slumdwellers, including migrants from the countryside and *Limeños*, led these massive and organized invasions, which usually took place on state-owned land, since invasions of private land were violently repressed. Because of the great number of people who participated in these invasions, and the government's lack of an alternative solution to the rapidly increasing housing demands, the state often had little choice but to allow the squatters to stay.[5] They were then left on their own to build their homes, and had to fight hard to obtain basic services like water and electricity. This laissez-faire policy of the Peruvian state allowed it to channel popular discontent for housing, and at the same time limit its own responsibilities in forging an urban housing policy. In 1956, the Northern and Southern Cones of Lima housed 6 percent of the city's population; by 1970, these areas composed largely of *barriadas* housed nearly half of the city's population.

The formation of Villa El Salvador represented a new attitude on the part of the state to land invasion. While the Velasco regime had prohibited uncontrolled land invasions since 1968, the Pamplona Alta invasion in 1971 presented the government with a fait accompli: a land invasion too massive to ignore. In response, state planners created a large planned *barriada* to deal with the pent-up housing needs of the urban poor. Villa became Velasco's model of urban development and part of his larger corporatist experiment of social change. By harnessing popular initiative to resolve urban problems, Velasco sought to create a bastion of popular support for his "revolution" and to undercut more radical initiatives.

What was particularly novel about the state's involvement in Villa was the organizing principle of *autogestión*, or self-management, which guided the entire project. The state encouraged the growth of grassroots organizations which would take responsibility for self-help housing and community improvement.[6] Through the *autogestión* model, the state assisted Villa in setting up community-owned enterprises that were intended to lay the foundation for Villa's autonomous and socialist development. This was part of Velasco's larger reformist experiment in social property, designed to increase worker participation and benefits in local enterprises.[7]

State planners mapped out Villa's urban structure with precision. It was laid out block by block, in grid fashion. Every block was composed of twenty-four family lots, thirty-by-fifty feet each; sixteen blocks constituted a residential group. Each residential group demarcated an area as communal land, which the residents developed according to their desires and needs. Small chapels, soccer fields, and community meeting halls, which in many cases doubled as nursery schools, were the most common uses of this communal land. Planners also set aside large areas for an industrial park and an agricultural zone. Today, Villa is comprised of approximately 126 residential groups, which are assembled together in seven large sectors.[8]

This territorial division was designed not only to ease the urbanization process, but to facilitate community organizing as well as state control over grassroots mobilization. Each block elected three representatives, and of the forty-eight chosen from each residential group, eight were selected as the main group leaders. State planners created a centralized governing body called the Self-Managed Urban Community of Villa El Salvador (CUAVES), which would oversee the development of the community and represent it before governmental and other outside agencies. The rank and file of the CUAVES was made up of the leaders of the residential groups, from which a ten-member executive council was selected.[9]

The first convention of the CUAVES was held in 1973. The following year, the Velasco government financed the formation of several community enterprises—including a credit union *(caja comunal)*, a cooperative bakery, a hardware store, and a kerosene store—which were to be administered by the CUAVES. The credit union was supposed to provide government-assisted financing for these other community enterprises. The CUAVES was to oversee community participation in the enterprises, and negotiate and plan with the appropriate government agencies. Housing construction, however, was to be undertaken by individual families, though neighbors often helped each other construct their homes.

Villa's initial years were marked by intensive organizing by the newly settled inhabitants. Today, Villa's first residents recall the enthusiasm and commitment with which they participated in different community-improvement projects. Some of these collective efforts were initiated by state agencies and planners, including organizing volunteer manual labor to build infrastructure projects—from installing water and sewage pipes, to leveling the sand dunes for road construction. Other activities evolved from the community's own initiatives. Perhaps the first true community effort was the construction of several classrooms, which were built and financed by donations from the residents themselves. At the block level, women organized "clean-up committees" to deal with the lack of garbage collection, and "tree committees" to beautify Villa with trees and gardens. Nursery-school teachers, called *animadores*, were chosen by the members of each community block to work with pre-school children. Local neighborhood-watch groups were formed to help prevent crime and punish wrongdoers. A wooden cross still stands in one of Villa's residential groups with a sign that reads: "On this cross, the community punishes thieves."

The state's presence in the early years of Villa El Salvador's development was important. Velasco created the National System to Support Social Mobilization (SINAMOS), a government agency in charge of guiding Villa's development and mobilizing local support for the regime. SINAMOS was to oversee the CUAVES and work with it to implement the government's vision of social property and self-management. Velasco visited the *barriada* frequently, and army trucks distributed loaves of bread and blankets to the settlers. His government also installed public lighting at the entrance of Villa, and provided large cisterns for water.

The Velasco regime did not, however, carry out all the promises that it made to the new settlement. Electricity, for example, was provided in 1975, but water and sewage were only installed in 1979. The agricultural zone and the industrial park, so touted by state planners as key to Villa's autonomous development, were never launched. Dissatisfaction with the scope and pace of government support coupled with conflicts with SINAMOS over the issue of autonomy led the CUAVES to assume an increasingly critical attitude toward the regime.

With Velasco's ouster in 1975, state investment in local development projects waned. Villa's special status as government showcase was revoked, and it became seen more as a political problem for the new regime. While Velasco had sought to prevent the development of autonomous organizations through cooptation, the newly installed Morales Bermúdez regime (from 1975 to 1980) attempted the same through repression. Hikes in gasoline and food prices in early 1976 led to a series of strikes and violent government reponses. The CUAVES, with a new leadership that was explicitly antigovernment, led a series of protest marches to demand local services, but also to protest antilabor measures and austerity programs. One protest, called by the CUAVES in coordination with the teacher's union (SUTEP) and local parent-teacher associations in March 1976, brought 30,000 Villa residents together to demand water, sewerage, school rooms, and job stability for teachers.[10] The government responded with fierce repression.

With the pullback of government support, community members worked hard to fill in the gaps. Women, for example, began organizing after 1979 in response to the economic crisis and their growing incapacity to meet their families' basic nutrition needs. Communal soup kitchens were organized in many residential groups throughout Villa, often with the support of the Catholic Church and development agencies. While foodstuffs and cooking equipment were often donated, the women themselves contributed their resources and time to shopping and cooking collectively to reduce food costs.

At the same time, the entire *autogestión* project was seriously weakened by the withdrawal of government support. Although the CUAVES was able to mobilize Villa residents in political marches against the government, its ability to carry out local development projects declined as official support dried up. The community enterprises, including the credit union, collapsed without government assistance. Charges of corruption in the management of these enterprises further undermined confidence in the CUAVES and its leaders, especially since many poor families lost their savings in the credit union's failure.[11] At the same time, national party politics, centered around the government's call for a Constituent Assembly and a return to democratic rule, increasingly distracted the CUAVES, which further weakened its link to the local community. A general period of disorientation and demobilization followed at the level of the block organizations, though the soup kitchens and other "survival organizations" flourished in a context of sustained economic crisis.

Villa El Salvador was at that point formally part of the neighboring municipal district of Villa María del Triunfo.[12] After Velasco's departure in 1975, Villa El Salvador was forced to turn to Villa María for its basic services. Despite the fact that Villa was the largest *barriada* in the Villa María district, it was largely neglected by municipal authorities, who could be counted upon to collect taxes, but little else.

By the early 1980s, municipal neglect combined with the crisis of the CUAVES left Villa El Salvador adrift. Demographic growth and new invasions presented new problems that were not easily resolved by local organizing. This was the backdrop to a surge of left-wing organizing in Villa under the leadership of Michel Azcueta, a Spanish-born professor who was co-founder of Fe y Alegría, Villa's first school, and an active and well-respected member of the community. Azcueta led the formation of the Multisectoral Commission, which brought together residential group leaders as well as other associations in Villa to take stock of the situation. Among its first actions, the commission won local support for its proposal to make Villa an independent municipal district, which was approved by the Peruvian Congress in June 1983.

Michel Azcueta was elected mayor of Villa El Salvador on the ticket of the United Left (IU) in the municipal elections of November 1983. He proposed an ambitious project of promoting grassroots participation and community development through local government. Despite the fact that he started out with no official budget, Azcueta rallied participation in the new local government, and in the first few months of his administration many people volunteered their labor in the municipality.

In his first act as mayor, Azceuta formally recognized the CUAVES as the central representative organization of Villa, and promised to respect its organizational autonomy. The Multisectoral Commission had helped reactivate and reorganize the block-level organizations, and new elections were called for the executive council of the CUAVES.[13] Azcueta later formally worked out an agreement between the municipal government and the CUAVES, which delineated their respective spheres of responsibility in the community.

Azcueta hoped to encourage the reorganization and renovation of the CUAVES, and then, in partnership with it, to put together a development project that would guide Villa into the next decade.[14] In a letter to the IU, Azcueta laid out his vision: "Our presence in the municipal government is a way of strengthening the popular organizations, using to the maximum the legality of the municipality, delegating to the [organizations] the power we have, and transforming the municipality into the mobilizing axis that, with the masses, solves some problems and works as an interlocutor with the central government."[15]

Azcueta also sought to incorporate new social actors into the development process and to increase grassroots participation in local decision-making. He supported the activities of existing organizations in Villa, such as youth groups, cultural groups, and soup kitchens, and sought to mobilize new organizations, such as market cooperatives and the Association of Small Business Owners of Villa El Salvador (APEMIVES). This latter organization became the central actor in the Industrial Park, which was resurrected by Azcueta's negotiations with the central governm ent and through donations by foreign governments and local nongovernmental organizations (NGOs).[16]

One interesting example of the municipal government's commitment to devolving power to community organizations concerns the Popular Federation of Women of Villa El Salvador (FEPOMUVES). The FEPOMUVES was formed in 1983 to centralize the various women's organizations operating in Villa, including the clean-up committees, the tree committees, the women's clubs, the popular soup kitchens, and the preschool *animadores*.[17] That same year, the municipality of Lima, under the left-wing administration of Mayor Alfonso Barrantes, developed a program to combat infant malnutrition through the provision of one glass of milk a day to children up to six years old.[18] Thousands of "Glass of Milk" committees, composed almost entirely of women, were organized throughout Lima to distribute the donated milk. To demonstrate his support for grassroots participation and decentralized decision-making, Azcueta transferred administrative control of the municipal milk program to the FEPOMUVES, which has managed the program ever since.

Villa grew from 105,000 residents in 1973 to 168,000 in 1984, and in the mid-1990s numbers 265,000, representing an annual growth rate of nearly 5 percent. This tremendous expansion and the consequent rising demands soon overwhelmed the limited resources of the municipal government. While the older areas of Villa El Salvador had progressed in terms of housing construction and the provision of basic services, the new invasions, which in 1984 made up 27 percent of Villa's overall population, often lacked piped water, sewerage, and electricity.[19] These poorer areas were composed largely of young couples with smaller families and lower incomes, who lived in housing made primarily of cane matting. Reflecting the poorer health conditions, these areas had a higher percentage of malnourished children than the more consolidated parts of Villa.

The internal diversification of Villa has presented new problems and challenges that are not easily resolved, and that community organizing may in fact be incapable of resolving. Villa is no longer a homogeneous *barriada*. The wide range of living conditions and socioeconomic prospects points to one dilemma of community organizing in a more complex environment. As some families advanced economically, the common living conditions and needs that were the basis of community organizing in Villa's early years broke down, making united action more difficult. There has been a general demobilization of block and neighborhood organizations over the past decade in the more consolidated areas, where basic services have already been obtained. The principle of solidarity rarely reaches beyond the local neighborhood unit. Residents of the better-off areas, for example, rarely mobilize to demand water and electricity for the more recent invasions.

The inhabitants of Villa's new invasions have increasingly looked to the municipal government to resolve their pressing basic needs—water and sewer systems, garbage collection, and paved roads. The heavily centralized nature of Peru's political system has meant, however, that the municipality must often depend on the central government to provide resources and services. While Azcueta, who was reelected to a second term in 1986, was able to muster international financial support for some community improvement projects, he could not make up the shortfall of an inadequate municipal budget. The municipal crisis grew worse after 1989 when hyperinflation cut into existing budgets, further reducing the capacity of local government to respond to growing demands. Because the left had promised so much, local residents' expectations were probably higher, and their disappointment consequently greater.

By the end of the 1980s, a feeling of pessimism had set in in Villa. Concrete setbacks forced a reassessment of the meaning of grassroots organizing. Clientelistic practices by parties across the political spectrum permeated grassroots urban organizing and undercut the horizontal linkages among local groups. The Peruvian left considered the forging of links among grassroots groups and simultaneously with left-wing parties to be essential in allowing local experiences to inform the larger policy process. Yet in Villa as elsewhere, intense sectarian rivalries emerged among the coalition partners of the IU. The different left-wing parties vied for their quota of power within local organizations like the CUAVES and FEPOMUVES, which resulted not only in the politicization of these organizations, but in their becoming riven by political divisions.

Grassroots organizations were also plagued by the age-old problem of *caudillismo* and authoritarian leadership styles. The problem was accentuated by the rank and file, which often demanded a direct relationship with the leader, who was expected to resolve all problems. Still, sharing power and responsibilities has, of course, been widespread in local community organizations. Yet the legacy of an authoritarian political culture remains a challenge to the construction of more democratic styles of leadership and participation at the grassroots.

Linked to this is the deep mistrust of politics which is pervasive among Peru's popular sectors, especially among its young people. Years of unfulfilled promises by governments of all political stripes have fed this mistrust. Today anyone with access to power and resources is suspected of seeking personal gain, and the social contract has withered as a result.[20] The arrest and subsequent impeachment of Villa's newly elected mayor, Jorge Vásquez, on corruption charges last year only added fuel to these suspicions. This basic mistrust has spread to include even grassroots leaders, whose position is perceived as providing them access to some perks. Organizing is not easy when the rank and file are mistrustful of their leaders, and corruption is assumed to be par for the course.

The political violence unleashed by Shining Path's war against the Peruvian state has also taken its toll on community organizations. Shining Path moved into Lima in 1988, altering its traditional Maoist approach of encircling the city from the countryside in favor of more open political work in the cities. The weakening of the left, coupled with the economic crisis, gave Shining Path a window of opportunity in the city to organize at the local level. In 1990, Shining Path singled out Villa as an ideal place to challenge the legal left and its "revisionist" posture. On three different occasions, Shining Path tried to assassinate Mayor Michel Azcueta in a campaign to decapitate Villa of its leadership and demoralize the rank and file.

María Elena Moyano, co-founder of the FEPOMUVES and vice-mayor of Villa, was not so lucky. In 1992, she was brutally assassinated by Shining Path. Her position as a recognized grassroots leader who openly challenged ShiningAth and as a member of the legal left had made her a double target. Shining Path launched a smear campaign against her, accusing her of mishandling funds linked to the soup kitchens and the municipal milk program. Given the general dis-enchantment with politics, many of Villa's residents were far too willing to believe such rumors. "In these times," one of Moyano's close friends told me, "people believe that everyone steals—everyone, even grassroots leaders like María Elena."

Shining Path's threats coupled with government inaction caused many of Villa's grassroots activists to quit their leadership positions, while others were forced into exile. Today, two years after Shining Path leader Abimael Guzmán's capture, people are less fearful, and a number of local groups, including the FEPOMUVES, have attempted to reorganize. But many believe that Shining Path has not completely disappeared, and the demobilizing effects of violence and fear remain.

In the final analysis, economic austerity and continued poverty may have had an even more profound negative effect on community organiz-ing. Local self-help initiatives such as the soup kitchens and the milk committees are often coping mechanisms designed to deal with economic down-turns and emergency situations. While the initial impact of harsh economic conditions prompted grassroots groups to respond with self-help efforts, the drawn-out recession may actually have undercut grassroots organizing in Villa, pushing people into more individualistic survival strategies.

President Alberto Fujimori's structural-adjustment program has un-dermined the resource base of many communal soup kitchens, deepened their dependency on external donations, and exhausted their members. "The enthusiasm that existed before is no longer the same," says Teresa, who has been active in communal soup kitchens since 1979. "It is necessity that forces us to participate, but there is no longer the joy that existed before. It used to be like a service to the community. Now the faces in the soup kitchen are hardened. There is much sadness, resentment, and bitterness. It is as if the women feel that if they do not go to the soup kitchen, they can't feed themselves and their families.... There is much poverty within the soup kitchen."

The soup kitchens do not come close to meeting the vast need that exists in Lima's *barriadas*. Some families cannot even afford the twenty-five-cent daily ration. "We know that the women can't afford to pur-chase rations for all their family members," says Gregory Chisholm, a Canadian priest who heads up Villa's parish, "so they buy three or four rations and stretch it out for five or six people. That undermines any work we try to do to provide a balanced and nutritious meal in the soup kitchen." The hardship that has befallen so many Peruvians has forced relief organizations and developmental NGOs to fall back on handouts, which further undermine the organizing potential at the grassroots. The government is also perceived by many women as trying to destroy community organizations. Military "civic action" programs in the *barriadas* hand out food directly to people, bypassing local organizations which are seen as linked to opposition groups.

What participation in these survival organizations means for women's daily lives is the subject of lively debate. Critics point out that these self-help efforts often add to women's already heavy burden of unpaid domestic labor, resulting in their further exploitation. In the end, these critics argue, women remain relegated to issues located in the domestic sphere, such as child care, nutrition, and food preparation, while the system of class and gender domination goes unchallenged. Enthusiasts, on the other hand, claim that the popular soup kitchens and the glass-of-milk committees have brought women out of the home and into the public arena, giving them a chance to share common problems and to assert their independence from both husband and home. By participating in these self-help initiatives, thousands of women have gained valuable experience in adminstration and leadership. Some women leaders have also moved from local grassroots organizing experiences into positions of local authority in the municipal government.

If community organizing has not given rise to a more democratic and egalitarian social order, it has nevertheless been a way for people to gain more control over their daily lives and improve local living conditions. If governmental and nongovernmental agencies were more amenable to working with local organizations on even terms, emergency self-help initiatives and more long-term development projects would be more successful. A clear example of this occurred in 1991 when community organizations in Villa El Salvador and numerous other poor areas collaborated with NGOs and government agencies to prevent the cholera outbreak from becoming widespread. In places like Villa, where community response was strong, casualties from the disease were minimized. Community organizing in Villa El Salvador may not have measured up to the great expectations that people had of it, but its achievements have nonetheless been remarkable. Problems remain, but through community organization and the construction of a local identity, Villa's residents transformed a squatter settlement in a vast and inhospitable piece of desert into a liveable urban community.

Notes

1. The term *barriada* is taken directly from Spanish. It is not easily translatable, although it is commonly referred to in English as "shantytown." We follow Jean-Claude Driant's usage of *barriada* to suggest not only a physical space of underdeveloped housing and basic services, but also to denote a mode of access to housing based on organized land invasions and the eventual development of housing and other basic services, usually through self-help efforts of the *barriada* residents. See Jean-Claude Driant, *Las Barriadas de Lima: Historia e Interpretación* (Lima: IFEA/DESCO, 1991).

2. In 1986, Villa was nominated for the Nobel Peace Prize. It was named City Messenger of Peace by the United Nations in 1987, and it won Spain's Prince of Asturias prize the same year.

3. In 1940, Peru was 70 percent rural and 30 percent urban; by the 1980s, the figures had become inverted.

4. Gustavo Riofrio, *Se busca terreno para próxima barriada. Espacios disponibles en Lima: 1940-1978-1990* (Lima: DESCO, 1978).

5. In typical clientelistic fashion, several governments promised these squatters land titles in return for votes. Over half of the *barriadas* formed before 1971 occupied land with the express authorization of the State. See David Collier, *Squatters and Oligarchs: Authoritarian Rule and Policy Change in Peru* (Baltimore: Johns Hopkins University Press, 1976).

6. Such self-help efforts were increasingly being encouraged as a solution to growing housing demands in urban areas in developing countries worldwide, by both local governments and international agencies such as the World Bank. In Peru, private construction companies had little incentive to develop low-income housing, and government housing projects usually ended up favoring constituents. In the first Fernando Belaúnde Terry government (1965-1968), for example, several housing projects were purchased by middle-class groups, the traditional base of Belaúnde's Acción Popular (AP).

7. Velasco's reforms hinged on the existence of a "third way" between capitalism and Communism for "third world" societies to develop politically and economically. The idea of *autogestión* was based on the Yugoslav model of social property which would provide the conditions for worker participation and eventually self-management, as well as ameliorate social conflict between capital and labor.

8. There are usually twenty-three or 24 residential groups to a sector, with the exception of the fourth sector, which was developed according to a different plan by the second Belaúnde government (1980-1985), and the fifth sector, which is the Industrial Park.

9. The executive council was later expanded to seventeen members, reflecting the inclusion of new organizations in Villa that were incorporated into the CUAVES statutes after a long period of debate and discussion, among them the Popular Federation of Women of Villa El Salvador (FEPOMUVES) and the Association of Small Business Owners of Villa El Salvador (APIAVES).

10. SUTEP is the acronym for the Peruvian Educational Workers' Union.

11. The extensive literature on this stage of Villa's development does not generally acknowledge these charges of corruption, focusing instead on the withdrawal of government support for the failure of the community enterprises. My interviews in Villa, however, repeatedly attest to corruption as an equally, if not more important factor.

12. Prior to 1980, local municipal officials were appointed by the Interior Minister. The second Belaúnde government (1980-1985) implemented a broad municipal reform program, in which the members of a given district directly elected their local representatives.

13. A Convention of Unification was held the following month by the new CUAVES leadership, and was attended by 716 delegates from the residential groups. The previous CUAVES leadership refused to recognize the validity of these elections, and two competing CUAVES leaderships continued to exist for about a year. Many in the CUAVES regarded the creation of the municipality as an imposition of the State and the capitalist system. If the municipality were to exist, they maintained, it should be clearly subordinate to the CUAVES. See Fernando Tuesta, "Villa El Salvador: Izquierda, Gestión Municipal, y Organización Popular," mimeograph (Lima: CEDYS, 1989).

14. The project, formulated with the technical assistance of non-governmental development organizations, is laid out in: *Equipo Técnico de la Municipalidad Districtal de Villa El Salvador. Villa El Salvador y Su Proyecto Popular de Desarrollo Integral: Propuestas para el Debate,* 2d ed. (Lima: CIED/DESCO, 1989).

15. Michel Azcueta, Letter to the United Left, 21 June 1987, cited in Tuesta, "Villa El Salvador."

16. The Industrial Park obtained official support in 1987 under the Alan García administration (1985-90). It was to be directed by a governing body consisting of the municipal government, the central government, the CUAVES, and the APEMIVES. By 1991, 200 small enterprises were in existence, which employed some 1,200 workers. See José Tavara, Cooperando para competir: Redes de producción en la pequeña industria peruana (Lima: DESCO, 1994).

17. Not all women's organizations joined the Federation, however. Only self-supporting soup kitchens or ones with links to NGOs sympathetic to the Left were incorporated into the FEPOMUVES. Parish-supported soup kitchens, as well government-sponsored ones, remained outside the Federation.

18. The program was later expanded to include lactating mothers and children up to the age of 13.

19. Un Pueblo, Una Realidad: Villa El Salvador. Resultados del II Censo organizado por la CUAVES el 8 de abril de 1984 (Lima: CUAVES/CIDIAG, 1984). More updated data is not available, but the new invasions have continued over the past decade, despite the municipality's attempt to encourage families to build second and third stories to provide more housing, given the near-limits of Villa's horizontal growth. After 1980, expansion of the barriada was thus no longer primarily due to rural

migration, but to the doubling of families units within the barriada itself. See Driant, Las Barriadas de Lima.

20. This is one of the central factors explaining the rise of independent candidates in local and national elections. The phenomenon began in 1989 with the election of Ricardo Belmont to Lima's municipal government, and the election of Alberto Fujimori to the presidency the following year. The 1993 municipal elections saw a proliferation of independent lists and candidates, who won overwhelmingly at the district and provincial level.

25

Argentina Under Menem: The Aesthetics of Domination

Beatriz Sarlo

In Argentina, President Carlos Saúl Menem has launched a true cultural revolution, one reactionary in nature. Its consequences are visible not only in government policy, but in the very tone and temperament of public life. The country has become authoritarian through both political changes and changes in its political culture. An examination of these changes—which were brought about with remarkable ease—must take two factors into consideration. On the one hand, the specific features of the socioeconomic conjuncture were powerful enough to make a large part of Argentine society accept a much weakened parliament, a justice system and a Supreme Court ready at all times to accede to the government, and an executive branch that incorporates many of the functions of the legislature. On the other hand, more general features have affected the very conception of politics. These features can be called "postmodern" or "postpolitical," and are closely connected to the rise of television as a political medium.

The Radical Civic Union government of Raúl Alfonsín, which began in December 1983 and ended prematurely in mid-1989, was marked in its last two years by two phenomena: the increasing deterioration of relations between the military and civilian authorities, and a gigantic wave of inflation that culminated in the hyperinflation of 1989. The crisis was so acute, in fact, that Alfonsín handed over power to his successor, Carlos Menem, several months ahead of time. Between 1987 and 1989, contentious relations with the military resulted in several insurrections headed by officers who had participated in the "dirty war" and in the Malvinas/Falklands war. The Radical government confronted these insurrections with the support of the population, but without access to an obedient military power. The trial and conviction of members of the military juntas responsible for the disappearance and death of several thousand men and women during the dictatorship (1976 to 1983) left an open wound in the military establishment. Alfonsín was not able to close this wound, even when, after the conviction of the junta members, the laws of *punto final* ("full stop") and *obediencia debida* ("just following orders") were passed, halting the prosecution of those responsible for human rights violations. This episode of history was definitively closed only when Menem pardoned the military in the first year of his administration.

The trial and conviction of those responsible for unleashing the most ferocious repression that Argentina has ever known was a tremendously important moment in the restoration of an ideal of justice, and in the construction of a public memory of the events of the dictatorship. But with the abrupt interruption of the hundreds of trials and, above all, the pardon of military officers who had been convicted and imprisoned, Menem was able to put the subject of human rights violations behind him. He thus initiated a project of "forgetting" that benefited the military. This closure imposed by the government—which broke with any idea of justice—helped solve the problem of instability in military-state relations. But, at the same time, it dulled the memory of what had occurred in the preceding decade. The military pardon closed a subject that is not only juridical or political, but decisively moral and cultural in nature.

The hyperinflation, which had dramatically marked the final months of Alfonsín's presidency, raged on during the first months of the Menem government. It would only be stanched with the implementation of a new economic plan, under the direction of Domingo Cavallo, Menem's finance minister.

The recurring episodes of hyperinflation left deep imprints—not only economic but also cultural—on Argentine society. The population's state of mind can be characterized as an obsessive fear of a new surge of hyperinflation, a theme constantly repeated in public and private discourse. Thus, a large part of the population silently agreed to hand over a blank check to the government of Carlos Menem and to his finance minister on the condition that minimal stability be guaranteed.

The cultural imprints of hyperinflation can be seen with clarity today. First came the imposition of the idea that all other economic or social demands must be postponed in the face of the principal objective of achieving stable prices. Everyone—including the sectors most harmed by the new economic policy—agreed that economic stabilization was the central interest that had to be defended above all others. Society in its totality was ready to pay the price that the economic plan presented as necessary to prevent the return of the chaotic social and economic situation of the recent past. Thus the discourse of Menem and Cavallo on the virtues of the free play of market forces and the negative effects of state intervention was seen as describing the indisputable reality. The market began to be seen not as an institution reflecting changeable social relations, but as a natural phenomenon whose objective limits had to be accepted.

In the second place, the discourse of the president and the finance minister, together with the swift, drastic measures favored by Cavallo, tended to convince the population that it was impossible to respect all the institutional formalities if stabilization was to be rapidly achieved. President Menem and his cabinet presented Argentine society with a dilemma: to overcome inflation, it was necessary to concentrate power in the executive branch and not in the legislature; it was necessary to operate quickly and in unison; and it was necessary to avoid a debate in Congress. By contrast, to preserve the parliamentary forms of discussion of laws, the time required for the deliberation would be time taken away from establishing economic order. In short, the dilemma presented the institutional role of parliament in the political process as an obstacle to the common good.

In these circumstances, President Menem had recourse to two stratagems. The first was—and continues to be—that of passing over parliament for approval of his measures, and using the dubious constitutional mode of legislation by decree. Menem's "decree laws" have turned executive power into a legislating force, and weakened the parliamentary function. In the second place, both Menem and Cavallo transformed themselves into able mass-media communicators of government policy, establishing a relationship with society that is neither institutional nor based in the political forms of representation. One man came off as a charismatic savior, and the other as an infallible technocrat.

We are seeing a new *mestizaje* in which market liberalism blends with the charismatic political style that President Menem learned in the Peronist movement. In 1989 when he was elected president, people expected Menem to carry forward a populist plan with a nationalistic style. Within a few short months, however, he convinced many of his supporters of the need to take a sharp turn toward neoliberal, monetarist, antistatist policies, which Peronism had always considered to be the epitome of oligarchic and antinational politics. This ideological transformation manifested itself in all the government's actions and in its very style.

It's illustrative to compare a public appearance of Menem as a populist leader, which took place during the 1988 presidential campaign, with another event, of strong symbolic power, that occurred a short while afterwards. Between the two events, signs of a decisive cultural make-over emerged. The first event took place in a soccer stadium in October 1988, a year when the electoral campaign was in full swing. The other event, characteristic of the new style, was a military parade on July 9, 1990. These two examples reflect a change: from Menem the savior and hope of the dispossessed, to Menem the guarantor of the restoration of the powerful. In the first event, Menem displayed all the traits of a plebeian populism which is "mass-mediatized"—honed to offer the kind of images and information that mass media demand; in the second, the symbols of civilian-armed forces reconciliation exalted the military, crowning the operation that had begun with the pardon.

The cultural importance of this change of scene and of script is incalculable. The 1988 party in the soccer stadium fell back on the symbols which proliferated in the history of Peronism. Menem appeared, dressed completely in white, as the hope of righting past injustices, as the advocate for the humble, as the politician who—coming from the country's interior and rooted in the heart of the mass movement—could interpret the desires and interests of the people. He promised redistribution, full employment, and high salaries in the near future. He used words that belonged to the ideological tradition of his audience: work, respect, dignity, well-being, justice. Turning to rhetorical forms of populism, he positioned himself in a place that had been empty since the death of Perón: a charismatic head of state; a leader who has risen outside bureaucratic structures; a man from the interior among politicians from Buenos Aires; someone respectful of the historical traditions of the Peronist movement.

With this profile, Menem shaped his candidacy and strengthened an electoral campaign that was sustained by his own physical presence exhibited as a guarantee aboard the *menemóvil* ("Menem-mobile").[1] He offered to the political theater his body, to be seen and touched as a material incarnation of the message that he brought. In the event at the soccer stadium, he entered aboard the *menemóvil* followed by spotlights—like a true star of popular redemption who knows how to manage the aesthetics of pop and rock. In this event, his body became sublime. Dressed in fluorescent white and illuminated by a single ray of light, Menem moved through the stadium to take his place at the rostrum. In the processions of the presidential campaign, the body of Menem circumnavigated a scene in constant motion: people could see him arriving; they could see him passing by; they could follow him. He was there making his way through the crowd, slightly distant, but generating at the same time the illusion of proximity.

A few months later, during the military parade of July 9, 1990, the new Menem, now president, proved that this cultural citation of the Peronism of the 1950s was precisely that: a *citation*, a fragment of spectacle properly placed between quotation marks.

The scene of the military parade was remarkable: the armed forces spread out through the streets of the city; on a dais, accompanied by his full cabinet, the president, immobile, surveyed the passing column of troops. Even if the armed forces formally saluted the powers of the republic, those very powers, with their fixed gazes on the parade, legitimated Argentina's most profoundly questioned institution. Menem, who knows how to organize cultural happenings, converted this parade into a statement of the refoundation of the pact between society and the army.

Menem understood that the pardon of those who had ordered the repression of the 1970s was not enough, since it dealt with a law, not a cultural fact. Because of that, he made sure that the reclamation of the military would be captured in an urban set piece of great significance. The still-open conflict between society and the armed forces needed an allegorical resolution: the five hours of the parade, a long and tedious sequence scrolling across television screens. The visual reiteration of tanks, airplanes, and marching troops had profound ideological import, because only one endlessly repeated theme was heard: the debate over the dictatorship's past was closed. At the same time, it became apparent that any discussion about a future whose shape was already decided would no longer be welcome. Menem's reconciliation of his government with the armed forces presaged other alliances with both domestic economic powers and the United States. All of this could be read in the image of the gathering of military masses, members of the civilian government, and foreign ambassadors, during that parade of 1990.

In a country with a strong presidency like Argentina, the head of state plays a decisive role in setting the tone of public life. Menem's perfected mass-mediatized style is an important center of gravity in the present cultural-political conjuncture: he disdains ideas; he tends to shut off more complex questions; he follows recipes for a simple solution; he disdains the deliberative and discursive forms of policymaking; and he cynically rejects those values, found in the Peronist tradition, which are grounded in the ideal of a just society.

The consequences are serious because today, only deliberative policymaking, the independence of the three branches of government, and the full functioning of political institutions can counter a presidential will perfectly aligned with the interests of the powerful. By means of mass-mediatized morals, aesthetics, and culture, the base-line values of a just, equal, and cooperative society have been replaced by a market Darwinism that has left profound marks in a new individualist, anticooperative culture.

One feature of the current clash between politics and society is the weakening of public culture. As political discussion, parliamentary representation, and other forms of collective participation have become less relevant, the mass media—especially television—have come to occupy a decisive place in the construction of the public sphere. Today it is impossible to think of politics without television. This feature, common throughout the West, has distinct manifestations and consequences in Argentina where an educational crisis and a rising rate of illiteracy have converged with an audiovisual hegemony over the symbolic dimension of social life. This process is spearheaded by privately owned television channels that choose their strategies according to the laws of profit maximization.[2] A strong counterweight to private capitalism does not exist in Argentine television: the lone state channel is in the iron grip of the government, and no large public channel exists at all. Today the market completely defines the character, aesthetic, and ideology of the audiovisual sphere.

Politics and political culture is formed in a televised space that responds only to the shifts and interests of the capitalist market of symbolic goods, without counterweights or balances. The public sphere has become mass-mediatized, and the political scene is increasingly an electronic one. Mass-mediatized politics pays tribute to the image of a common culture that unites actors whose symbolic and material power are very different. This may assure a minimum of cultural cohesion, but not the type of cohesion that reflects a true sense of community.

Mass-media discourse compacts society, projecting an image of a unified cultural scene, a common place where oppositions dissolve into a polyglotism of many voices which are never necessarily speaking to one another. It's not that media are more democratic; it's simply that they need to incorporate *all* the discourses in order to present a universal sphere. Politics defers to the media aesthetic. It accepts the media as representative of the universal. And it frequently adopts the formal and rhetorical limits that the media impose: speed, variety, volubility—qualities that often call to mind the emergence of a political show or a sound bite.

Persuaded of the importance of the media in the construction of the public sphere, politicians accept the assumption that the discussion of ideas, the great debates, complicated postulates, and the presentation of sophisticated positions are "anti-television." They cultivate a media image based upon the reduction of the complexity of their message, and in the illusion of closeness and familiarity: "We are the same as you; we represent you at the same time as we mingle with television celebrities. We represent the people in that which the people have closest at hand: the television set in their living room or their kitchen." The mass-mediatized operation thus concludes in a poverty of meanings, in a thinning of the growing complexity of problems, and in a visual flow where the "now" is built on top of oblivion. To exist, politicians—classic mediators between the citizenry and institutions—need television to be the Great Universal Mediator. They are captives of the mass media.

The mass-mediatization of politics is an almost irresistible phenomenon. Policy is built by the newscasters; television news sets the order of the day. Public trust, taken away from political leaders, is now administered by the heads of the mass media. The culture of discussion has been superseded by a political simulacrum which does not thrive in political institutions, and feels more at home in the realm of television. Politics in the mass media is subordinated to the laws that regulate the audiovisual flow: high impact, large quantities of undifferentiated visual information, and arbitrary and binary syntax that is better suited to a matinee melodrama than to the public arena.

President Menem is, without doubt, an expert in audiovisual communication. His style has been perfectly adapted to the style of television. He has crafted his image not in the argumentation of ideas which permits the expression of conflicts between different values and interests, but in high-impact interventions, with perfectly unified perspectives and a simple system of oppositions in which someone is either your "friend" or your "enemy."[3]

While it is not possible to realize a dream of a nostalgic return to the forms of politics that existed prior to the mass-mediatized cultural revolution, it is difficult to accept that politics is only built within the framework that the media impose. One can imagine changes in the politics of the media. Without a doubt, not all TV news is as uniformly bad as it is in Argentina; not all television correspondents have to be sensationalist agitators. There is no destiny inscribed in television from which it is impossible to escape.

The identity of politicians is not fashioned only in the media. We can hope that politicians will remain true to their calling: expressing a will broader than their own even while working to form that will. Today politics needs to take into account the media as well as intellectual concerns. It needs ideas as well as images. The aesthetic of audiovisual media tends to expel those discourses that have an argumentative logic of an intellectual cast. This conflict is part of a relationship that has already been deeply engrained and—what is worse—has been accepted by intellectuals and politicians alike.

With few exceptions, politicians, intellectuals, and newscasters take a "descriptive" and neutral position with respect to the consequences of the mass-media hegemony of the symbolic dimension of the social world.[4] Some argue that television doesn't matter because the public recodes television messages and produces new meanings. They forget, however, that the public's freedom to construct those hypothetical new meanings is limited because people must work with the materials that television offers them. Naturally, the intellectual defenders of this position don't propose major changes in the use of the media, nor do they worry that the private interests of media owners are the true shapers of public opinion.

Opposite this position, which is characterized by its optimism with respect to the products of the capitalist marketplace, one can place perspectives of critique and reform. Intellectuals—especially left intellectuals—can play a decisive role in producing new ideas about how the media can be used in a democratic, reflexive, imaginative, and lucid manner. Certainly, these new ideas would confront an enormously concentrated power.[5] New ideological-cultural perspectives can, however, find a reasonable echo in the media precisely because the media are obliged to incorporate everything that has some public significance.

The April 1994 elections in Argentina demonstrated that it is possible to conceive of elements of a political culture that are not inevitably prisoners of audiovisual ideology and aesthetics.[6] The center-left Frente Grande emerged as an important third national force in these elections. The party's candidates used the media with the goal of introducing relatively more complex and nonbinary discussions.[7] The Frente Grande recognized social needs that were not expressed by either Peronism or Radicalism, and they knew how to take advantage of the emergence of calls for greater lucidity, honesty, and capability in politics.

The situation is particularly instructive. On the one hand, these new political actors—some of whom come from the human rights movement and others from the artistic and intellectual field—recognized the power of the audiovisual media in the construction of the public sphere. At the same time, they figured out how to work with television without surrendering to all its rituals. In fact, they proposed a new kind of political discourse in the audiovisual media.

Does this recent turn of events presage a new synthesis? It is difficult to say so today. Whatever the case, this synthesis is necessary if a new politics is to be built. This politics will have to be grounded in the recognition, first, that the audiovisual sphere is an inexcludable element in the present construction of politics; and secondly, that the unconditional acceptance of the worst features of mass-mediatized culture will not permit new ideas to emerge.

One must, then, abandon all intellectual celebrations of the media. The media must be recognized as a necessary factor, but not the only one, in the construction of democratic and progressive options. One must also reaffirm the value of intellectual practice in relation to politics: a new politics must figure out how to reapportion the places and functions of knowledge and ideas as well as those of the mass media. To achieve this, the critique of mass-mediatized aesthetics and ideology is as decisive as the critique of the traditional forms of politics. In this open-ended scenario, there is, without a doubt, a place for the participation of intellectuals.

Notes

1. The *menemóvil* was a truck crafted as a stage, on which Menem and his entourage moved about during his electoral campaign in 1988.
2. In February 1994, the Education Ministry made public the results of a national survey conducted to measure educational achievement in the last year of primary school and the last year of secondary school. The survey included a sampling of several tens of thousands of students, both from public and private schools. Of those surveyed, 70 percent could not answer questions posed after reading a simple text; 60 percent could not solve elementary mathematical problems.
3. Menem uses, with dangerous frequency, the words *inconciente* (thoughtless) and *forajido* (wicked) to describe those whom he considers to be mistaken.
4. The only exception that is worth mentioning is Mariano Grondona's current events program *Hora Clave* ("Key Hour"), which presents the debate of ideas in a form which suggests the possibility of building a true public arena in the mass media. Grondona's program was important in the victories of the opposition Frente Grande in the elections of April 1994. See also notes 6 and 7.
5. In Argentina, legislation on the ownership of communications media lacks antimonopoly clauses. For example, the largest-circulation daily newspaper, *Clarín*, owns several important radio stations as well as a television channel that is transmitted throughout the country.
6. In these elections, members were chosen for the Assembly which, in the course of the year, would be in charge of modifying the Argentine Constitution. The electoral stage was seen, for that reason, to be freer of the polarizations characteristic, up to now, of the elections for president or provincial governor.
7. The Frente Grande was formed from the convergence of groups that abandoned Peronism and Christian Democracy, of human rights activists, and of old groupings of the left. The Frente Grande was victorious in the city of Buenos Aires and in the province of Neuquén. It came in second in the decisive province of Buenos Aires. Nationally, it emerged in these elections as the third force, after Peronism and Radicalism, thereby breaking the traditional Argentine two-party system.

26

The Politics of Toxic Waste

Mary E. Kelly

The border town of Matamoros, located in northeastern Mexico across the river from Brownsville, Texas, was once a quiet ranching and agricultural community. Over the last decade, however, it has undergone a startling transformation. Under Mexico's border-industrialization program, which provides incentives to U.S.-based companies to set up manufacturing operations along Mexico's northern border, Matamoros now has over ninety *maquiladora* factories, many of which are owned by U.S. corporate giants such as General Motors, AT&T, and Zenith.

Low prevailing wage rates in Mexico, often less than one dollar per hour, combined with the Mexican border region's proximity to U.S. markets, make the area an attractive "offshore" manufacturing base for U.S. companies. Favorable customs and tariffs for border industry have strengthened the pull. There are now over 1,800 *maquiladora* plants along the border, compared with fewer than 500 in 1982. The plants employ more than 380,000 people, and have become Mexico's second largest source of foreign exchange, eclipsed only by revenues from oil exports.

Mexico's woefully underfunded and politically weak environmental regulatory program has not kept up with the rapid industrialization. *Maquiladora* plants operate without the scrutiny and environmental controls they would have faced had they stayed in the United States. Matamoros residents have experienced some of the most direct consequences of this lapse. For example, behind the Stepan Chemical plant, and just yards from the small, broken-down dwellings of Colonia Chorizo, environmental tests conducted in 1991 revealed the presence of xylene at levels more than 50,000 times the U.S. standard for safe drinking water. About half a mile away, in a canal near General Motors'

Rimir plant, investigators discovered xylene at levels more than six thousand times the U.S. standard.

In some places, the pollution is visible to the naked eye: orange and purple slime pours out of discharge pipes and flows down open canals, eventually discharging into a sensitive coastal lagoon south of Matamoros on the Gulf of Mexico. One can often see dead animals in these ditches. Children, oblivious to the contamination, play at the edge of the murky water. When the Matamoros city dump is on fire, as it often is, the billowing black smoke can be seen from the north side of the river in nearby Brownsville. A visit to the dump itself is like stepping into a nightmare of industrial society run amok. People scavenge among the acres of municipal trash and industrial waste, slogging through pools of black-grey water to find the most sought-after prize: a used industrial chemical barrel in which to collect water at their homes on the edge of the dump.

In the face of these horrendous environmental conditions, some residents of Matamoros mounted a campaign for stronger environmental protection. Working with religious, environmental, and political groups in the United States, neighborhood leaders have developed a "toxic tour" of Matamoros. "We have had visits from countless major Mexican, U.S., and foreign media organizations, environmental activists, and U.S. Congressional delegations," said María Teresa Mendez, one of the organizers. "No visitor goes away unmoved."

Efforts to call attention to the border's environmental problems had some success. In the fall of 1991, for example, then-U.S. House Majority Leader Richard Gephardt took the toxic tour of Matamoros, meeting with *colonia* and *ejido* leaders while officials of the Mexican, U.S., and Canadian governments were negotiating the North American Free Trade Agreement (NAFTA). In a major trade-policy speech to the Institute for International Economics in July 1992, Gephardt spoke about the environmental devastation he had witnessed. "In Matamoros, some of America's biggest corporations dump toxic wastes directly into the water supply—water that turns the colors of the rainbow," he said. "When I stood outside the homes of families living near Mexican factories owned by U.S. chemical corporations, the emissions made my skin burn."

Gephardt's continuing efforts, along with those of many other NAFTA critics, helped force environmental issues to the center of the public and Congressional debate over NAFTA. Critics of NAFTA in both the United States and Mexico pointed to the situation in Matamoros and other border cities as vivid examples of the results of rapid economic integration without an adequate environmental framework. They argued that in the rush to complete NAFTA, the U.S. and Mexican governments had failed to develop meaningful proposals to address the border's environmental and health problems, or to provide the necessary resources and infrastructure to handle what was predicted to be a significant increase in U.S. industrial investment in Mexico under a free trade accord.

In addition to their contribution to the overall policy debates, the "toxic tours" generated adverse publicity which eventually forced the U.S. companies operating in Matamoros to clean up their plants, something Mexico's environmental regulators had not been able or willing to do. One of the major industrial parks in Matamoros finally installed a wastewater treatment system and three of the heaviest-polluting U.S.-based plants, all of which were located in the middle of a residential neighborhood, have now closed down.

Industrialization of the border has greatly increased the amount of hazardous waste being generated in the region, but tracking is woefully inadequate. Mexico does not keep an inventory of hazardous waste and, unlike the United States, Mexico does not have a law requiring industries to publicize basic environmental data on their operations.

Many of the plants use large amounts of toxic solvents, acids, metal-plating solutions, and other chemicals that result in hazardous by-products. The U.S. General Accounting Office (GAO), using information compiled by Mexico's environmental agency, reported in February 1992 that about half of the approximately 2,000 *maquiladoras* in Mexico may generate hazardous waste. The limited environmental testing that has been done near *maquiladora* parks in the border region also shows the presence of high levels of toxic contaminants associated with hazardous waste.

Mexico's ground-breaking 1988 environmental law requires that most hazardous waste generated by U.S.-owned *maquiladoras* be returned to the United States. But Mexican and U.S. environmental officials acknowledge that they cannot account for most of the waste. According to data from the U.S. Environmental Protection Agency (EPA), many of the *maquiladoras* along the Texas-Mexico border failed to return any waste from Mexico. The GAO study concluded that, although Mexico is trying to create a stronger program to manage hazardous wastes, the Mexican government still has difficulty determining how many *maquiladoras* are generating hazardous wastes, the amount of waste generated, or the final disposition of that waste.

Hindering efforts to dispose of toxic waste legally is the lack of approved final disposal facilities in Mexico for toxic waste, which must be sealed in barrels and transported to landfills. There are currently only two authorized sites in Mexico—one in San Luis Potosí, and the other in Monterrey in the border state of Nuevo León. According to Rene Franco, an environmental consultant in Juárez, Mexico, "the geographic location of these facilities, as well as their installed capacity, are far from satisfactory for existing industry, much less the industry that will result from a free trade agreement." The Mexican border had a toxic-waste incinerator in Tijuana, but its permit was revoked in June 1992 after protests from neighboring residents.

Proposals for two large toxic-waste dumps in Texas, both of which would have been located within twenty miles of the Río Grande/Río Bravo, spurred unprecedented binational concern among governmental and nongovernmental organizations alike. Chemical Waste Management, Inc. proposed to build what would have been one of the country's largest toxic-waste landfills in Terrell County, about one hundred miles upriver from Del Rio, Texas. A newly formed company called Texcor, Inc. wanted to create a landfill for uranium mining and other radioactive wastes in Kinney County, near Eagle Pass, Texas. These sites had to first, however, receive licenses from the Texas Natural Resource Conservation Commission (TNRCC), the state's primary environmental agency, before beginning operation.

The two proposals garnered strong opposition, both in Texas and Mexico, prompting at one point a brief binational citizens' blockade of the international bridge between Eagle Pass and Piedras Negras, Coahuila. The sites sparked formal diplomatic protests by Mexico to Washington, and were a prominent issue at the U.S.-Mexico Border Governors' Conference in San Diego, California in April 1992. In an unprecedented move, the state of Coahuila, the *municipio* of Ciudad Acuña, and Mexican environmentalists intervened in the Texas state proceedings to oppose the granting of permits for either site.

At first glance, the proposed Chem Waste site looked like an ideal spot for disposal of toxic wastes, but appearances can be deceptive. Although the landfill would have been located in somewhat isolated desert territory, the area's steep side canyons, giant underground caves, sinkholes, and limestone formations contain several potential pathways by which contamination from toxic wastes could reach the ground water supply, according to Dr. Robert Kier, an expert hydrogeologist hired by the City of Del Rio to evaluate the proposed site. The aquifer below the proposed site, known as the Trinity Plateau of the Edwards aquifer, supplies several fresh water springs, among them San Felipe Springs, the City of Del Rio's sole water source. The aquifer also crosses the border into Mexico, although less is known about its exact configuration there. "If pollution escaped from the proposed landfill," said Kier, "there is little doubt that it could reach the San Felipe Springs and other important freshwater springs in the area."

Opponents of the Chem Waste site were also concerned about the company's history of environmental violations at its other facilities. "This company," said Del Rio City Attorney Jim Bayne, "has been assessed some of the largest penalties for violations of hazardous-waste laws in the United States." A Greenpeace report branded Chemical Waste Management's parent company, Waste Management, Inc., "one of the world's biggest polluters," based on its record-large payment of over $45 million in penalties and settlements in environmental cases over the last decade.

Opponents of Texcor, on the other hand, were concerned that the company did not have a track record to show it could safely operate its proposed radioactive-waste dump. According to Madge Belcher, a long-time Kinney County rancher and president of Communities Against Radioactive Environment (CARE), Texcor had never operated any waste-management site or any other type of industrial facility.

Citizen persistence paid off in the end. After lengthy and expensive proceedings at the TNRCC, the permit for the Texcor site was denied in the summer of 1993. About a year later, in August 1994, Chem Waste withdrew its application after opponents succeeded in convincing state and federal environmental regulators of the potential groundwater-contamination problems at the site.

Much of the hazardous waste generated by *maquiladoras* and other border producers is being disposed of illegally. The vast desert region of northeastern Mexico is a favorite location for clandestine dumps. In May 1992, for example, environmental officials discovered a dump of more than six hundred barrels of toxic waste located about twenty miles south of Juárez, across from El Paso, Texas. Agency investigators have begun to trace many of the barrels back to U.S.-owned *maquiladora* plants.

Exposure to illegally disposed hazardous wastes can occur in a variety of ways. In the border region, children play in open discharge canals which take waste from industrial parks, and people fish in contaminated streams or use old hazardous-chemical barrels for drinking-water storage. Exposure to such wastes can result in serious health damage, including various forms of cancer and birth defects. Recent investigations have begun to bring potential problems to light.

During 1991 and 1992, health-care workers in Brownsville, Texas documented a skyrocketing rate of birth defects, particularly the number of babies born with undeveloped brains, a condition known as anencephaly. Researchers found that anencephaly rates in Brownsville were over three times the U.S. national average. In Matamoros, across the river, they documented at least forty-two cases of anencephaly over a period of one and a half years.

"Our research indicates that environmental toxins which are emitted by many of the *maquiladoras* operating in Matamoros may indeed by one possible cause of this tragedy," said Gregoria Rodriguez, a health-care doctoral student and a volunteer at the Brownsville Community Health Clinic. After the Brownsville/Matamoros anencephaly investigation received national attention in both the United States and Mexico, health-care workers in other border cities such as Ciudad Acuña and Juárez began reviewing their limited records, and discovered similar anomalies. In 1994, strangely enough, substantially fewer cases of anencephaly were documented, and rates appear to be back to "normal" levels.

Observers say the border's toxic-waste crisis stems from two basic problems. First, Mexico lacks sufficient financial resources for a strong environmental enforcement and oversight program. Burdened by a foreign debt of over $100 billion, Mexico spent much less on environmental programs per capita in 1991 than the United States did, even though the 1991 funding levels in Mexico increased 1,000 percent over 1990. The disparity between the amount that each country budgeted for hazardous-waste management is striking. In the United States, the EPA had a 1991 hazardous-waste budget of over $300 million, supplemented by significant state spending on hazardous-waste regulation. Mexico, by contrast, had a 1991 hazardous-waste budget of only $2.3 million.

While much emphasis was placed on Mexico's increasing environmental regulatory efforts during the NAFTA debate, funding remains inadequate. According to Julia Carabias, the director of the government's National Institute of Ecology in Mexico City, her agency's total budget—which does not include enforcement—was only $20 million. She characterized this funding level as "practically nothing" in relation to the needs. While no figures are available for the enforcement budget, media reports of Mexican environmental inspectors not receiving salaries for extended periods indicate similar financial constraints.

Limited resources also impede Mexico's ability to clean up illegal disposal sites. For example, at the 600-barrel illegal dump discovered outside of Juárez, Mexican environmental investigators were severely hampered by the lack of money for testing the ground water and soil samples for contamination. Moreover, Mexico does not have an equivalent to the U.S. Superfund Law, which requires those responsible for generating the waste to pay for the clean-up of abandoned disposal sites. Therefore, "it is not clear whether the land will ever be fully cleaned up," said TNRCC Border Affairs Director Hector Villa, whose agency helped Mexico's environmental authorities transfer the barrels to an authorized disposal site.

Another basic problem is that the United States and Mexico have relied strictly on informal cooperation to deal with toxic waste in the borderlands. Under the La Paz Agreement signed by then-presidents Ronald Reagan and Miguel de la Madrid in 1983, the two countries agreed to work with each other to address a range of environmental problems in the border region. Yet neither country devoted sufficient resources to set up an adequate binational system to track the generation or disposal of toxic waste in the border.

In 1992, after the border's environmental woes were spotlighted during the early debate over NAFTA, the two countries' environmental agencies agreed to deal with pollution with a new "Integrated Plan for the Mexico-U.S. Border." Included among the plan's goals for the next few years were improved surveillance and tracking of cross-border movements of toxic wastes, and the determination of the amount of waste being generated by the *maquiladora* plants. The plan remained, however, strictly an informal agreement. A 1993 analysis of progress under the plan, prepared by the Texas Center for Policy Studies, found that the United States and Mexico had failed to implement many of the plan's proposed improvements for hazardous-waste control.

The integrated plan was the centerpiece of efforts by presidents Bush and Salinas to convince the public in both countries that they were addressing border environmental issues. The Bush administration also argued that NAFTA would improve Mexico's ability to deal with environmental problems because Mexico's revenues from foreign investment and trade with the United States would increase as a result of the agreement.

Critics in both countries argued that the Border Plan and NAFTA, by themselves, were not enough, and that the federal government should permit greater cross-border cooperation among state and local governments. "It is the border communities that are feeling the impact of this rapid industrialization on a day-to-day basis," said Dr. Helen Ingram, director of the Udall Center for Public Policy at the University of Arizona. "It is those communities that can best make concrete progress in protecting their shared environment. But they can't do that if Washington and Mexico City continue to insist on tight federal control over U.S.-Mexico environmental relations."

Calls for change were also heard in Mexico. For example, Dr. Alberto Székely, one of Mexico's leading environmental law experts who helped negotiate the 1983 La Paz agreement on behalf of Mexico, argued that although lines of communication had opened between U.S. and Mexican environmental agencies since that date, a new agreement would be needed to deal more forcefully with border environmental issues, particularly toxic waste.

As NAFTA was being debated, Roberto Sánchez, the director of urban studies at the Colegio de la Frontera Norte in Tijuana, recommended creating a new binational environmental agency. Sánchez argued that this new agency could be given oversight authority for environmental and worker-health issues in the borderlands, and could help to coordinate the efforts of various federal, state, and local authorities.

Many observers felt that without a strong new agreement or treaty on border environmental issues to accompany NAFTA, problems such as the illegal disposal of toxic waste would continue, threatening the health and welfare of the border's rapidly growing population and turning the region into North America's industrial dumping ground.

Postscript

Continued pressure by border residents and environmental groups led Bill Clinton, during his campaign for the presidency, to propose an environmental side agreement to NAFTA in October 1992. After he was elected, Clinton did negotiate such an agreement, which was eventually approved along with a labor side agreement and NAFTA itself in late 1993. In addition, the United States and Mexico agreed to set up two new binational institutions—the Border Environmental Cooperation Commission (BECC) and the North American Development Bank (NADBank)—to help fund environmental-infrastructure needs in the border region.

While it is beyond the scope of this article to discuss all aspects of the environmental side agreement, it is important to note that environmental groups in the United States were divided over whether the side agreement was strong enough to deal with the environmental problems which will accompany the increased industrialization beginning to occur under NAFTA. Many U.S. border environmental organizations, and their counterparts in Mexico, believe the side agreement does not go far enough. On the other hand, most of the border groups supported the creation of the BECC and the NADBank, believing that they offered real promise for helping to address water, wastewater, and municipal needs in the region.

There is, however, still no concrete, adequately funded program to deal swiftly and effectively with toxic-waste issues in the border. Border residents, such as those in the Brownsville/Matamoros area, will likely be left to rely upon their ability to put direct pressure on polluters. They have to hope that, even though the NAFTA spotlight has dimmed, they can still get the media, the public, and elected officials to pay attention to their concerns.

27

Why Migration?

Saskia Sassen

Years of work and arduous debate went into the writing of the 1986 Immigration Reform and Control Act, a vast revamping of the law aimed above all at stemming the flow of undocumented immigrants. Yet the flood of unauthorized entries continued to grow unabated. A new law signed in November 1990 allowed increasing numbers of immigrants with a flexible cap of about 700,000. Yet 1991 entries reached over 1 million. What is it about immigration policy that makes it so ineffective?

U.S. policymakers and the general public believe the causes of immigration are evident: poverty, unemployment, economic stagnation, and overpopulation drive people to leave their countries. Whether to accept immigrants thus becomes a humanitarian question, unrelated to U.S. economic policy or political responsibility.

These basic assumptions—shared by conservatives and liberals, the latter typically more generous than the former—have led policymakers to treat immigration as autonomous from other major international processes and as a domestic rather than an international issue.[1] They focus on regulating who may cross the border legally, and on encouraging foreign investment to alleviate the conditions which supposedly spark migration in the first place.

The central role played by the United States in the emergence of a global economy over the past thirty years lies at the core of why people migrate here in ever-increasing numbers. U.S. efforts to open its own and other countries' economies to the flow of capital, goods, services, and information created conditions that mobilized people for migration, and formed linkages between the United States and other countries which subsequently served as bridges for migration. Furthermore, the relatively open nature of the U.S. labor market, epitomized by the notion that government should stay out of the marketplace, provides a necessary condition for migration to occur.

Measures commonly thought to deter emigration—foreign investment, or the promotion of export-oriented agriculture and manufacturing in poor countries—have had precisely the opposite effect. Such investment contributes to massive displacement of small-scale agricultural and manufacturing enterprises, while simultaneously deepening the economic, cultural, and ideological ties between the recipient countries and the United States. These factors encourage migration. Proponents of the North American Free Trade Agreement between Mexico, Canada, and the United States, for example, may claim it will discourage people from leaving Mexico by providing employment opportunities there. Yet it is more likely to exacerbate the flow of people across the border.[2]

The prevailing assumptions about why immigration occurs do not explain the new immigration from certain Asian and Caribbean Basin countries. High population growth, vast poverty, and severe economic stagnation had long characterized most Asian and Caribbean Basin countries when large-scale migration flows started in the 1960s. And not all migrant-sending countries are poor: for example, South Korea and Taiwan.

In fact, emigration took off at a time when most countries of origin were experiencing accelerated economic growth according to conventional measures, considerably greater than countries that did not experience large-scale emigration. Annual gross national product (GNP) growth rate during the 1970s ranged from 5 percent to 9 percent for most of the leading migrant-sending countries. Even in Mexico, official GNP growth rates ranged between 4.2 percent and 7.5 percent in the early 1970s and then again late in the decade. South Korea is the most obvious example. With a growth rate of GNP among the highest in the world during the 1970s, it was also one of the countries with the fastest growing levels of migration to the United States.

This is not to say that overpopulation, poverty, and economic stagnation do not create pressures for migration; by their very logic, they do. But the common identification of emigration with these conditions is overly simplistic. If these factors were a constant long before emigration commenced, what accounted for the sudden upsurge in migration to the United States?

In the case of the Dominican Republic the answer seems to lie in linkages with the United States that were formed during the occupation of Santo Domingo by U.S. Marines in 1965. The occupation, to suppress a popular uprising against a pro-U.S. coup, resulted not only in greater political and economic ties, but in personal and family linkages due to the settlement of middle-class political refugees in the occupying country. U.S.-Dominican ties were further consolidated through new U.S. investment in the Dominican sugar industry to replace that which was lost as a result of the Cuban revolution.

Dominican migration to the United States began to increase soon thereafter, rising from 4,500 between 1955 and 1959 to 58,000 between 1965 and 1969. The real takeoff occurred in the early 1980s, as sugar prices fell and the United States invested heavily in tourism, offshore manufacturing, and nontraditional export agriculture on the island.

Haiti was not subjected to direct U.S. military intervention in the 1960s and 1970s. But the mass emigration which began in the early 1970s occurred parallel to a surge in new U.S. direct foreign investment in export manufacturing and the large-scale development of commercial agriculture. This created a strong U.S. presence and forced, often through violent means, independent farmers into a rural proletariat.

Despite El Salvador's longstanding poverty, only in 1981, when U.S. military involvement escalated sharply, did emigration begin on a massive scale. People left out of fear for their lives and because it became impossible to eke out a living with the war raging around them. But it was the linkages created by U.S. investment during the 1970s, and its military presence after 1980, that made emigration to the United States seem like a real possibility, even though for many the United States represented the enemy. Sarah Mahler found that many Salvadorans who emigrated to the United States had first worked as migrant laborers on export-oriented coffee plantations.[3]

Even in Mexico, where territorial continuity is routinely interpreted as a principal cause of immigration, the pattern of linkages is similar and in many ways unrelated to the existence of a shared border.[4] This is also true for East Asians. After the Korean war, the United States actively sought to promote economic development in the region in order to stabilize it politically. U.S. troops were stationed in Korea, the Philippines, and Indonesia. Massive increases in foreign investment occurred during the same period, particularly in South Korea, Taiwan, and the Philippines. Together, U.S. business and military interests created a vast array of linkages with those Asian countries that subsequently developed large migration flows to the United States.

That migrations are patterned is further reflected in the figures on the U.S. share of global immigration. Though inadequate, the available evidence compiled by the United Nations in the mid-1980s shows that the United States receives about 19 percent of global emigration.[5] The United States receives 27 percent of total Asian emigration, but 81.5 percent of all Korean emigration and almost 100 percent of emigration from the Philippines. It receives 70 percent of Caribbean emigration, but almost 100 percent of emigration from the Dominican Republic and Jamaica, and 62 percent from Haiti. And it receives 19.5 percent of all emigration from Central America, but 52 percent of emigration from El Salvador, the country with the greatest U.S. involvement in the region.

One common factor in this pattern over the last two decades is direct foreign investment in production for export, especially manufacturing and assembly of components and consumer goods such as toys, apparel, textiles, and footwear. While total U.S. investment abroad increased between 1965 and 1980 with large amounts continuing to go to Europe and Canada, investment in the third world quintupled, much of it going to a few key countries in the Caribbean Basin and Southeast Asia. A large proportion of investment in nonindustrialized countries went to industries producing for export, which tend to be labor intensive, precisely one of the rationales for locating factories in low-wage countries. The result was rapid employment growth, especially in manufacturing, during the post-1965 decade. At a lower level, this was also the case in Mexico.

According to conventional explanations of why migrations occur, this combination of economic trends should have helped to deter emigration, or at least to keep it at relatively low levels. The deterrent effect should have been particularly strong in countries with high levels of export-oriented investment, since such investment is labor-intensive and thus creates more jobs than other forms of investment. Yet it is precisely such countries, most notably the newly industrializing countries of East Asia, which have been major senders of new immigrants.

To understand why this occurs, we have to examine the impact of such investment on people's lives. Perhaps the single most important effect is the uprooting of people from traditional modes of existence. It has long been recognized that the development of commercial agriculture tends to displace subsistence farmers, creating a supply of

United States policies have consistently failed to limit or regulate immigration in the intended way.[1] The 1965 Amendment to the Immigration and Naturalization Act contained a rather elaborate system of quotas meant to open the borders in a way that would allow the government to control entries and deter illegal immigration.[2] The law's emphasis on family reunification, it was thought, would ensure that the bulk of new immigrants would come from those countries that had already sent large numbers to the United States, primarily Europe.

But the dramatic rise in immigration after 1965 consisted mostly of a new wave of migration from the Caribbean Basin, and South and Southeast Asia. Furthermore, not only did Mexican undocumented immigration increase sharply but a whole series of new undocumented flows were initiated, mostly from the same countries as legal immigration.

The furor over illegal immigration led to a series of congressional proposals that culminated in the Immigration Reform and Control Act of 1986. This law contained a limited regularization program whereby undocumented aliens who could prove their continuous residence in the United States since before January 1, 1982, and meet certain other eligibility criteria could legalize their status. It also contained sanctions against employers who knowingly hire undocumented workers, and an extended guest-worker program designed to ensure a continuing and abundant supply of low-wage workers for agriculture.

The 1986 law had mixed results. About 1.8 million undocumented immigrants applied to regularize their status, less than expected but still a significant number. In addition, 1.2 million applied under special legalization programs for agriculture. There is growing evidence of discrimination and abuse stemming from the employer sanctions program, while undocumented immigration continues to grow.

In November 1990, a new bill was signed into law that goes a step further in recognizing the demand of the U.S. labor market as a criterion for immigration. Past policy aimed at admitting one out of ten immigrants for labor market reasons: the new law raises this to one out of two.

Immigrants, while only about 7 percent of the U.S. labor force, have accounted for 22 percent of the growth in the work force since 1970, and are expected to constitute 25 percent of that growth in the 1990s. The closer immigration policy comes to recognizing the actual dynamics of immigration, the more likely it will be to succeed in its intended aim of effective regulation.

rural wage laborers and mass migrations to cities. The recent large-scale development of export-oriented manufacturing in East Asia, the Caribbean Basin, and Mexico's Border Industrialization Program has had a similar effect. In each case, the introduction of modern relations of production transforms people into migrant workers and potential emigrants.

In export manufacturing, the catalyst for the breakdown of traditional work structures is the massive recruitment of young women into jobs in the new industrial zones.[6] The mobilization of large numbers of women into wage labor disrupts village economies and rural households which traditionally depend on women's often unwaged work in food preparation, cloth-weaving, basket-making, and various other types of craftwork. Today most people in these regions have been thoroughly proletarianized.

One of the most serious and ironic consequences of the feminization of the new proletariat has been the rise in male unemployment. Not only must men compete with the new supply of female workers, but the massive departure of young women from rural areas, where women are key partners in the struggle for survival, reduces the opportunities for men to make a living there.

More generally, in some poorer, less developed regions or countries, export-led production has come to replace other more diversified forms of economic activity oriented to the internal market. The impressive employment growth figures for most of the main emigration countries do not convey the severe limitations of the type of growth involved and the frequent destruction of a more diverse economy.[7]

For men and women alike, the disruption of traditional ways makes entry into wage labor increasingly a one-way proposition. With traditional economic opportunities in rural areas shrinking, it becomes difficult, if not impossible, for workers to return home if they are laid off or unsuccessful in the job search. This is particularly serious for female workers in new industrial zones, who are often fired after a short period of employment in order to keep wages low and replace workers whose health begins to fail due to poor working conditions. Moreover, beginning in the late 1970s when tax concessions from local governments in the older zones were exhausted, many companies packed up and moved on to "new" countries where labor was even cheaper.

Due to all of these trends, people first uprooted from traditional ways of life, then left unemployed and unemployable as export firms hire younger workers or move production to other countries, may see few options but emigration—especially if export-led growth strategies have weakened the country's domestic economy.

But the role of foreign investment in encouraging large-scale emigration does not end there. In addition to eroding traditional work structures and creating a pool of wage laborers, foreign investment contributes to the development of economic, cultural, and ideological linkages with the industrialized countries.[8] Workers employed in the export sector—whether as managers, secretaries, or assemblers—are, after all, producing goods and services for people and firms in industrialized countries.

For these workers, already oriented toward Western practices and modes of thought, the distance between a job in the offshore plant or office and a comparable one in the industrialized country itself is subjectively reduced. It is not hard to see how emigration comes to be regarded as a serious option.

Beyond the direct impact on workers in the export sector, the linkages created by foreign investment also have a generalized ideological effect on a receiving country or region, making the culture of industrialized countries seem less foreign and the prospect of living there more attractive. This ideological impact turns a much larger number of people into candidates for emigration. In fact, those actually employed in foreign-owned plants, offices, and plantations (as long as they hang onto their jobs) may not be the ones most likely to emigrate.

No analysis of immigration would be complete without examining changes in labor demand. While the internationalization of the economy contributed to the initiation of labor migrations to the United States, their continuation at high and ever-increasing levels is directly related to the economic restructuring of this country.

Beginning in the late 1970s, the supply of low-wage jobs in the United States expanded rapidly, while the labor market became less regulated. Such tendencies facilitated the incorporation of undocumented migrants by opening up the hiring process, lifting restrictions on employers, and typically lowering the cost of labor.[10] The increase in low-wage jobs was in part a result of the same international economic processes that channeled investment and manufacturing jobs to low-wage countries. As industrial production moved overseas or to low-wage areas in the South, much of traditional U.S. manufacturing was replaced by a downgraded sector characterized by poorly paid, semi-skilled, or unskilled jobs.

Three trends converged: first, the growing practice of subcontracting, and the expansion of sweatshops and industrial homework (all of which have the effect of isolating workers and preventing them from joining together to defend their interests); second, the downgrading of skill levels required for jobs through the incorporation of machines and computers; and third, the rapid growth of high-technology industries that employ large numbers of low-wage production workers. These conditions make the United States an attractive location for foreign manufacturers and other types of firms, and, at the limit, make certain areas of the country competitive with third world countries as production sites.[11]

The rapid growth of the service sector also created vast numbers of low-wage jobs, in addition to the more publicized increase in highly paid investment banking, management, and professional jobs.[12] The growth industries of the 1980s—finance, insurance, real estate, retail trade, and business services—feature large numbers of low-wage jobs, weak unions if any, and a high proportion of part-time and female workers. Sales clerks, waitresses, and janitors are among the growth occupations.

The expanded service sector also creates low-wage jobs by raising the demand for workers to service the lifestyles and consumption requirements of the high-income professional and managerial class. The concentration of these high-income workers in major cities has created a need for legions of low-wage service workers—residential building attendants, restaurant workers, preparers of specialty and gourmet foods, dog-walkers, errand-runners, apartment-cleaners, childcare providers, and so on. The fact that many of these jobs are "off the books" has meant the rapid expansion of an informal economy.[13]

Immigrants are more likely than U.S. citizens to gravitate toward these jobs: they are poorly paid, offer little employment security, generally require few skills and little knowledge of English, and frequently involve undesirable evening or weekend shifts. In addition, the expansion of the informal economy facilitates the entry of undocumented immigrants into these jobs. Significantly, even immigrants who are highly educated and skilled when they arrive in the United States tend to gravitate toward the low-wage sectors of the economy.

While the transfer of manufacturing to less industrialized countries has helped promote emigration from them, the concentration of servicing and management functions in major U.S. cities has created

Annual legal entries of immigrants to the United States increased from 1965 on, reaching 373,000 in 1970, 531,000 in 1980, 602,000 in 1986, and more than 1 million in 1990. As recently as 1960, more than two-thirds of all immigrants entering the United States came from Europe. By 1985, Europe's share of annual entries had shrunk to one-ninth, with the actual numbers of European immigrants declining from almost 140,000 in 1960 to 63,000 in 1985. The top ten immigrant-sending countries today are all in Latin America, the Caribbean Basin, or Asia.

Latin Americans, including the native-born and citizens, form the single largest foreign-language population in the United States, and probably the largest population of undocumented immigrants as well. But Asians are the fastest growing group of legally admitted immigrants, with annual entries rising to 236,000 in 1980 and to 264,700 in 1985. While these figures include Southeast Asian refugees admitted in the aftermath of the Vietnam War, refugees account for only a small proportion of the overall rise in Asian immigration. The Asian countries from which the greatest number of immigrants come are the Philippines, South Korea, and Taiwan, not the refugee-sending countries of Vietnam and Cambodia. In the 1980s migration flows began from Southeast Asian nations which had not previously experienced emigration to the United States, such as Singapore, Malaysia, and Indonesia.

Total entries of South and Central Americans, excluding Mexicans, reached about 170,000 for the period 1965 to 1969, and rose to 445,000 for 1980 to 1985. Entries of Asians reached 258,000 for 1965 to 1969, and rose further to 1,612,000 for 1980 to 1985. Entries of West Indians reached 351,000 for 1965 to 1969, and rose to 445,000 for 1980 to 1985.

Between 1972 and 1979, Mexico, with more than one-half million entries annually, was by far the largest source of legally admitted immigrants, followed by the Philippines with 290,000, South Korea with 225,000, China (defined as including both Taiwan and the People's Republic) with 160,400, India with 140,000, and Jamaica with 108,400. With the single exception of Italy, all of the countries sending more than 100,000 immigrants each year were either in the Caribbean Basin or Asia. Other important sources of immigrants outside these regions were the United Kingdom, West Germany, and Canada, sending about 90,000 each during the 1970s. By 1987, 43 percent of the 600,000 entries were from Asia, 35 percent from Latin America and the Caribbean Basin, and only 10 percent from Europe.

During the 1970s and early 1980s, women made up 60 percent of all immigrants from the Philippines, 61 percent of South Korean immigrants, 53 percent of Chinese, 52 percent of Dominicans, 52 percent of Colombians, 53 percent of Haitians, and 52 percent of immigrants from Hong Kong. Even in the well-established, traditionally male-dominated migration flow from Mexico, women now make up almost half of all legal immigrants. While a majority of female immigrants still enter as dependents of various kinds, a small but growing number now enter classified as workers. This would appear to indicate that an increasing number of women are migrating independently, in some cases leaving their husbands and children behind.

In the early 1900s immigrants clustered in New York, Pennsylvania, and Illinois. Today, multiple ports of entry, improved transportation, and far-flung job distribution seem to facilitate the geographical scattering of immigrants. Yet California and New York receive almost half of all new immigrants, while another quarter go to New Jersey, Illinois, Florida, and Texas.

Moreover, new immigrants tend to cluster in the largest metropolitan areas: New York, Los Angeles, San Francisco, Chicago, Houston, and Miami. The 1980 census found that about one-fifth of all foreign-born residents lived in New York and Los Angeles. While immigrants constitute at most 10 percent of the U.S. population, in 1987 they made up 30 percent of the population of New York City and 15 percent of the populations of Los Angeles and Chicago.

---

conditions for the absorption of the immigrant influx. The same set of processes that promoted emigration from several rapidly industrializing countries has simultaneously promoted immigration into the United States. The fact that the primary generators of low-wage jobs are the major growth sectors of the U.S. economy, such as high technology and services, rather than the declining sectors, suggests that the supply of such jobs will probably continue to expand for the foreseeable future. As long as it does, the influx of immigrant workers to fill these jobs is likely to continue as well.

While individuals may experience their migration as the outcome of their personal decisions, the option to migrate is itself the product of larger social, economic, and political processes. One could ask, for example, if there are systemic linkages underlying the current East

European and Soviet migrations to Germany and Austria. Rather than simply posit the push factor of poverty, unemployment, and the general failure of socialism, we might look at the fact that before World War II both Berlin and Vienna were major receivers of large migrations from a vast eastern region. And the aggressive campaign during the Cold War years, touting the West as a place where economic well-being is the norm and well-paying jobs are easy to get, must also have had some effect in inducing people to migrate westward.[14]

Similarly, as Japan became the leading global economic power and the major foreign investor in Southeast Asia in the 1980s, a familiar combination of migration facilitating processes appears to have been set in motion: the creation of linkages that eventually come to serve as bridges for potential emigrants, and the emergence of emigration to Japan as something that would-be emigrants see as a real option.

Japan is a country that never considered itself an immigrant country, has always been proud of its homogeneity, and has kept its doors closed to foreigners. Now it is experiencing a new illegal influx of workers from several Asian countries with which it maintains strong economic ties and investments in off-shore manufacturing, but no shared border: Pakistan, Bangladesh, South Korea, Taiwan, the Philippines, and Thailand.

The free trade agreement between the United States and Mexico is perhaps the best example. At the Bush administration's insistence, immigration was kept off the negotiating table. The administration claimed, however, that an agreement would stem illegal immigration from Mexico. Yet the considerable growth of export-assembly industry in northern Mexico over the last two decades has not deterred Mexican emigration. On the contrary, it encouraged new migrations from the interior of the country to the northern border zone, which in turn served as a platform for crossing into the United States. On a broader scale, the *maquila* program has consolidated a transnational border economy within which trade, investment, and people move rather freely.

The North American Free Trade Agreement (NAFTA) will no doubt strengthen existing economic linkages and create new ones, from cross-border personnel transfers to the packaging and trucking of goods made in Mexico for the U.S. market. Such linkages would engender new patterns of communication, work, and travel between the two countries, and would further integrate Mexican workers into the U.S. economy, intensifying Mexican contact with U.S. popular and work cultures. These conditions could spawn a generalized notion that people are entitled to free movement across the border.

Perhaps we need new ways to think about the process we call immigration. The category itself, with its strong emphasis on the concept of national borders, seems inadequate. The forging of strong economic and geopolitical relations between countries of unequal development and unequal job opportunities tends to promote labor migration from poorer to wealthier countries. Until policymakers understand this basic fact, and abandon the notion that immigration control is a police matter, attempts to "stem the flood" will continue to fail.

Notes

1. This article uses materials from the author's recent books, *The Mobility of Labor and Capital: A Study in International Investment and Labor Flow* (New York: Cambridge University Press, 1988), and *The Global City: New York, London, Tokyo* (Princeton: Princeton University Press, 1991).
2. See Saskia Sassen, "Free Trade and Immigration," *Hemisphere* (Winter/Spring 1991).
3. El Salvador's tradition of internal migration for the coffee, sugar, and cotton harvests meant that peasant farmers had already been mobilized into wage labor. See also Sarah J. Mahler, "*Tres Veces Mojado*: Undocumented Central and South American Migration to Suburban Long Island" (Ph.D. diss., Columbia University, 1992).
4. The large mass migrations of the 1800s followed the same pattern. They emerged as part of the formation of a transatlantic economic system binding several nation-states through economic transactions and wars that brought massive flows of capital, goods, and workers. Before this period, labor movements across the Atlantic had been largely forced, notably slavery, and mostly from colonized African and Asian territories. Similarly, the migrations to England in the 1950s originated in what had once been British colonies. Finally, the migrations into Western Europe of the 1960s and 1970s occurred in a context of direct recruitment and of European regional dominance over the Mediterranean and part of Eastern Europe. There are, I would say, few if any innocent bystanders among countries receiving large labor migrations.
5. This figure is derived from data on permanent settlement, which excludes illegal immigration and unofficial refugee flows between countries, a growing category. This and other figures in this paragraph are from *Demographic Yearbook* (New York: United Nations, 1985) and *World Population Prospects* (New York: United Nations, 1987).
6. Most of the manufacturing in these zones is of the sort that also employs women in developed countries. Apparel, electronics, assembly, toys, tex-

tiles, and garments account for the largest share, but it is diversifying fast. For the initial phase of this process, see, for example, Norma Diamond, "Women and Industry in Taiwan," *Modern China*, vol. 5, no. 3 (July 1979); Helen I. Safa, "Runaway Shops and Female Employment: The Search for Cheap Labor," *Signs*, vol. 7, no. 2 (Winter 1981); E. Boserup, *Women's Role in Economic Development* (New York: St. Martin's Press, 1970); also E. Boulding, *Women: the Fifth World*, Foreign Policy Association Headline Series no. 248, (Washington, DC: February 1980), and June Nash and María Patricia Fernández Kelly, *Women and Men in the International Division of Labor* (Albany: SUNY Press, 1983). See also the film "The Global Assembly Line" by Lorraine Gray.

7. In a detailed examination of the employment impact of export-led industrialization, the United Nations Industrial Development Organization (UNIDO) found that, in general, this type of development eliminated more jobs than it created because of its disruptive effect on the national manufacturing sector, especially in the less industrialized countries of the Caribbean and Southeast Asia. See *World Industry Since 1960: Progress and Prospects* (Vienna: UNIDO, 1979).

8. Each country is unique and each migration flow is produced by specific conditions in time and place. Yet the general dynamic I identify for the case of the United States occurs in other countries characterized by economic dominance and the formation of transnational spaces for economic activity. This type of analysis seeks to capture the impact of the internationalization of the economy on a) the formation of migration flows, and b) the labor market in the receiving country, particularly changes that may contribute to the absorption of immigrants.

9. Comparing 1973 and 1989 income data shows that relative incomes fell for 80 percent of all families and rose for 20 percent. The truly rich, the top 1 percent, gained the most. Much of the 20 percent at the top represents an upper middle class, rather than "the wealthy." See U.S. Bureau of the Census, 1989, Series P-60, No. 168.

10. Saskia Sassen, *The Mobility of Labor and Capital.*

11. The inflation-adjusted hourly earnings of factory production workers rose by 70 percent from 1947 to 1973. From 1973 to 1987 they fell by 5.4 percent. The real value of the minimum wage fell by about 23 percent from 1981 to 1989. See Gary Burtless, ed., *A Future of Lousy Jobs* (Washington: Brookings Institution, 1990), 15.

12. These trends have sharpened over the last few years, bringing about growing inequality in the U.S. occupational and income structure. Inflation-adjusted average weekly wages peaked in 1973, stagnated over the next few years, and fell in the decade of the 1980s (see ibid.). Up to 1973 there was an increase in the degree of equality in the distribution of earnings. Since 1975, the opposite has occurred. In the decade from 1963 to 1973, nine out of ten new jobs were in the middle-earnings group whereas after 1973 only one in two new jobs was in the middle-earnings category. If one were to add the increase in the number of workers who are not employed full-time and year-round, then the inequality becomes even more

pronounced. Part-time workers increased from 15 percent in 1955 to 22 percent in 1977; by 1986 they were a third of the labor force. Approximately 80 percent of these 50 million workers earn less than $11,000 a year. Paul Blumberg, *Inequality in an Age of Decline* (New York: Oxford University Press, 1980), 67-79; Robert Z. Lawrence, "Sectoral Shifts and the Size of the Middle Class," *Brookings Review,* (Fall 1984); Bennett Harrison and Barry Bluestone, *The Great U-Turn* (New York: Basic Books, 1988). A report by the staff of the House Ways and Means Committee found that from 1979 to 1987, the bottom fifth of the population experienced a decline of 8 percent in its personal income, while the top fifth experienced an income increase of 16 percent. And the preliminary data from the 1990 Census shows that the top 20 percent of the income structure accounted for most of the increase in personal income in the decade of the 1980s while the share of the bottom 40 percent decreased.

13. A comparison of trends in New York, Los Angeles, and other major cities can be found in Saskia Sassen, *The Global City*, part 3.
14. Saskia Sassen, "Six Concepts for Analyzing Immigration: Do They Work for Germany?" (Work in progress for the Wissenschaftszentrum Berlin, Winter 1992).

Sidebar 1

1. An exception were the agreements that barred Chinese labor immigration (1882), restricted Japanese immigration (1907), and culminated in the 1924 National Origins Act. This act was the first general immigration law in that it brought together the growing number of restrictions and controls that had been established over a period of time: the creation of classes of inadmissible aliens, deportation laws, literacy requirements, etc.
2. The 1965 Act sought to eliminate several highly discriminatory clauses of earlier immigration law and to regulate the influx of immigrants by setting up a system of preference categories within the general quota. Under the preference system, the primary mechanism for immigration was family reunification and, to a lesser extent, entry in occupational categories with labor shortages, such as nurses and nannies.

Notes on Contributors

ROBIN ALEXANDER is director of international labor affairs at the United Electrical, Radio, and Machine Workers of America (UE).

THOMAS ANGOTTI is a city planner in New York and teaches in the Graduate Planning Program at the Pratt Institute. He is the author of *Metropolis 2000: Planning, Poverty, and Politics* (1993), and is a participating editor for *Latin American Perspectives*.

DAVID BARKIN is professor of economics at the Universidad Autónoma Metropolitana-Xochimilco, Mexico City. His most recent book on Mexico is *Distorted Development: Mexico in the World Economy* (1990).

BARBARA BRIGGS is a staff member of the National Labor Committee. Her and Charles Kernaghan's essay was adapted from the committee's report, *Haiti After the Coup: Sweatshop or Real Development?*

JO-MARIE BURT is a Ph.D. candidate in political science at Columbia University; she is doing her dissertation research on political violence in Peru.

MAXWELL CAMERON teaches in the School of International Affairs at Carleton University in Ottawa. He is the editor, with Ricardo Grinspun, of *The Political Economy of North American Free Trade* (1993).

HECTOR CORDERO-GUZMÁN is a researcher at the Center for Puerto Rican Studies/CUNY. "Puerto Rico: Lessons from Operation Bootstrap" was written in coordination with the research group of the Northeast Puerto Rican/Latino Roundtable on NAFTA.

MARC EDELMAN is professor of anthropology at Hunter College and a NACLA board member. He is the author of *The Logic of the Latifundio: The Large Estates of Northwestern Costa Rica Since the Late Nineteenth Century* (1993).

CÉSAR ESPEJO is a community activist in Villa El Salvador, Peru, and a student in the Department of Sociology at the Catholic University in Lima.

LINDA FARTHING, a Canadian journalist, was consultant to community-development projects in Bolivia from 1984 to 1993. She is currently regional director for the Americas for Academic Studies Abroad at the School for International Training in Brattleboro, Vermont.

JOSÉ LUIZ FIORI is a professor of political science at the University of the State of São Paulo and the Federal University of Rio de Janeiro.

MARK FRIED (translator, Foreword) is a NACLA board member and former editor of *NACLA Report on the Americas.*

HENRY FRUNDT teaches sociology at Ramapo College, and is the author of *Refreshing Pauses: Coca-Cola and Human Rights in Guatemala* (1987).

PETER GILMORE is editor of *UE News.*

DUNCAN GREEN is a researcher at the Latin America Bureau, London. He is the author of *Silent Revolution,* a forthcoming book on the neoliberal transformation of Latin America, to be published in the fall of 1995 by Latin America Bureau (and distributed in the United States by Monthly Review Press).

RICARDO GRINSPUN teaches economics at York University in Toronto. He is the editor, with Maxwell Cameron, of *The Political Economy of North American Free Trade* (1993).

DOUG HENWOOD is the editor of *Left Business Observer.* He is the author of *The State of the USA Atlas* (1994) and *Wall Street* (1995).

DANIEL HOFFMAN is a Ph.D. candidate in anthropology at the University of California, Berkeley.

MARY E. KELLY is executive director of the Texas Center for Policy Studies.

CHARLES KERNAGHAN is a staff member of the National Labor Committee. His and Barbara Briggs's essay was adapted from the committee's report, *Haiti After the Coup: Sweatshop or Real Development?*

DEBORAH LEVENSON-ESTRADA teaches history at Columbia University, and is the author of *Trade Unionists Against Terror* (1994).

DEIDRE MCFADYEN is associate editor of *NACLA Report on the Americas.*

JULIO MOGUEL is a member of the economics faculty at the National Autonomous University of Mexico (UNAM), and is the coordinator of the supplement *La Jornada del Campo* of the Mexico City newspaper *La Jornada.*

RODOLFO MONGE OVIEDO is a Costa Rican economist currently doing graduate work in community and regional planning and Latin American Studies at the University of New Mexico, Albuquerque.

MARCELO MONTENEGRO is associate editor of *Cuadernos del Tercer Mundo,* based in Rio de Janeiro.

IRAM JÁCOME RODRIGUES is a sociologist and professor in the Department of Economics at the University of São Paulo. He is the author of *Comissao de Fabrica e Trabahladores na Industria* (1990).

FRED ROSEN is editor of *NACLA Report on the Americas.*

HELEN I. SAFA is professor of anthropology and Latin American Studies at the Center for Latin American Studies of the University of Florida. Her essay was adapted from *The Myth of the Male Breadwinner: Women and Industrialization in the Caribbean* (1995).

GERMÁN SÁNCHEZ OTERO is a sociologist at the University of Havana. He presented a version of this chapter to the workshop *Integration and Alternative Development,* held in Lima in 1992. He participated in the workshop as a representative of the Cuban Communist Party.

BEATRIZ SARLO is a professor of Argentine literature at the University of Buenos Aires. Her most recent book is *Jorge Luis Borges: A Writer on the Edge* (1993).

SASKIA SASSEN is professor of urban planning at Columbia University. She is the author of *The Global City: New York, London, Tokyo* (1991).

NANCY SCHEPER-HUGHES is professor of anthropology at the University of California, Berkeley. She is the author of *Death Without Weeping: The Violence of Everyday Life in Brazil* (1992).

CATHY SCHNEIDER is assistant professor of political science at the School of International Service at American University. Her piece was adapted from her book *Shantytown Protest in Pinochet's Chile* (1995).

LORI ANN THRUPP is director of sustainable agriculture at the World Resources Institute's Center for International Development and Environment. Her essay was adapted from her book *Bittersweet Harvests for the Global Supermarket: Challenge in Latin America's Export Boom* (1995).

LAWRENCE WESCHLER is a staff writer at the *New Yorker.* He is the author of *A Miracle, A Universe: Settling Accounts with Torturers* (1991).

RUBÉN ZAMORA, a Salvadoran political scientist, was one of the leaders of the Democratic Revolutionary Front (FDR), the political wing of El Salvador's revolutionary movement during the country's civil war. In 1994, he was a candidate for the presidency of El Salvador, backed by a coalition of leftist parties.